Also by CommerceNet Press:

Opening Digital Markets: Battle Plans and Business Strategies for Internet Commerce by Walid Mougayar

The Search for Digital Excellence by James P. Ware et al.

StrikingItRich.com by Jaclyn Easton

Make Your Web Site Work for You—How to Convert Your Online Content Into Profit by Jeff Cannon

How to Invest in E-Commerce Stocks by Bill Burnham and Piper Jaffray

Understanding Digital Signatures: Establishing Trust Over the Internet and Other Networks by Gail Grant

Building Database-Driven Web Catalogs by Sherif Danish and Patrick Gannon

Buying a Car on the Internet by Jeremy Lieb

Buying a Home on the Internet by Robert Irwin

Buying Travel Services on the Internet by Durant Imboden

CommerceNet is a nonprofit industry consortium for companies promoting and building electronic commerce solutions on the Internet. Launched in April 1994 in Silicon Valley, CA, its membership has grown to more than 500 companies and organizations worldwide. They include the leading banks, telecommunications companies, VANs, ISPs, online services, software and service companies, as well as end-users, who together are transforming the Internet into a global electronic marketplace. For membership information, please contact CommerceNet at Tel: 408-446-1260; Fax: 408-446-1268; URL: htp://www.commerce.net. For information regarding CommerceNet Press contact Loël McPhee at loel@commerce.net.

THE FUTURE
OF WORK

THE FUTURE OF WORK
The Promise of the New Digital Work Society

Charles Grantham

CommerceNet Press

McGraw-Hill
New York   San Francisco   Washington, D.C.   Auckland   Bogotá
Caracas   Lisbon   London   Madrid   Mexico City   Milan
Montreal   New Delhi   San Juan   Singapore
Sydney   Tokyo   Toronto

McGraw-Hill

A Division of The McGraw·Hill Companies

1234567890 AGM/AGM 9098765432109

ISBN 0-07-134830-1

Printed and bound by Arcata/Martinsburg.

This publication is designed to provide accurate and authoritative information in regard to the subject matter covered. It is sold with the understanding that the publisher is not engaged in rendering legal, accounting, or other professional service. If legal advice or other expert assistance is required, the services of a competent professional person should be sought.
> *—From a declaration of principles jointly adopted by a committee of the American Bar Association and a committee of publishers.*

 This book is printed on recycled, acid-free paper containing a minimum of 50% recycled de-inked fiber.

McGraw-Hill books are available at special quantity discounts to use as premiums and sales promotions, or for use in corporate training programs. For more information, please write to the Director of Special Sales, McGraw-Hill, 11 West 19th Street, New York, NY 10011. Or contact your local bookstore.

To
Howard Reed Arp, a member of the Silent Generation
who never got to see the future of work

Contents

Preface

IT IS HARD TO WRITE A GOOD PREFACE. What you really want to say as an author is "please read this book." I would, however, like to offer a little perspective on how this book came about, to help you, the reader, understand where I'm coming from. There is sort of a transcendent observation that doesn't really fit specifically within the text of this book, but something that I learned in writing it.

This isn't the first book I've written. Most other books that I've written were aimed at an entirely different audience—the academic. I decided at the onset of this project that I wanted to shift my focus and reach a much wider audience, who might take some of the prescriptions I offer and turn them into beneficial actions in their own lives.

In the past I've written books about theories, research results, and speculations. All that previous work served as a foundation for this book about the future of work. What I've done here is to try to take all that I've accomplished in the past 20 years and reframe it, rephrase it in a way that is readily accessible to the business manager in today's Internet world. There may be times, as you go through this book, that it seems to lapse into a slightly different language. I hope that I and my editors have been able to correct most of that and to keep the tone consistent with that used in the everyday business world.

Another motivation that I had came from watching so many of my friends, colleagues, and clients bemoan the fact that they felt their work world was dangerous to their health, both physical and mental, and were frustrated because they didn't know what to do about it. In large part, the subtext of this book is that there is a new psychology emerging in the workplace, one that places more control in the hands of the individual worker and is much more respectful of the diversity of our communities. In that sense, it is a prescriptive book that says to you—*take these things and do something with them to make your life better.*

The other point I want to make, and to have you hold in your mind as you read this book, is that the industrial process of writing a book is changing and becoming an Internet-based process. Somewhere, perhaps halfway through this project, I began to realize that I was engaged in a creative process that I thought I had mastered, but soon discovered that the process itself was being changed by the technology that I was talking about.

That was cause for a pause in my thinking. I started asking myself, "Why does it take a full nine months from the first completion of the manuscript until it rolls off the presses?" Well, obviously there are a number of reasons for this that are all quite logical such as scheduling, market planning, and simply market timing. But that couldn't keep me from thinking about it. Then it dawned on me: the whole process of creating new literature is changing, and changing very radically.

I immediately began writing more material that continues on where this book ends. The distance between the last page of this book and the first page (or hypertext document) of my next book is measured in nanoseconds in my brain—but that brief interlude may become weeks or even months in the eyes of the audience. What I've decided to do in order to bridge this gap is to create a brand-new Web site where readers can go to find out what I'm doing now, what's happened to the people in the case studies in this book, and what new knowledge my entire community has gained about this topic since the book rolled off the press.

The Web site will be a community Web site in the sense that I talk about in this book. It will be a living experiment in which I invite all of you to participate—a real-time online creation of a new world of work. The Web site hasn't totally taken form yet, because as I write this, it is being designed by a team who shares my desire to actively create a new work world. The architecture is pretty much in place because we know we want people to have the ability to do the following:

- Upload and download files
- Have community chat rooms
- Openly communicate with one another
- Post new ideas and pose new questions
- Over time, create an ongoing dialogue on related topics

I invite you to visit the new Web page at the following address:
www.thefutureofwork.net

Let me know what you think. Also, if you have knowledge of other case studies related to the topics in this book, please use the Web site as a place to document and chronicle your thoughts, observations, and most especially your ideas.

The new world of work is going to exist as much in cyberspace as it does in a physical place. The societal transformations that took place with the invention and proliferation of the printing press in the fifteenth century have many parallels to the magnitude and scope of the changes that are occurring in our society today with the invention and proliferation of the Internet. Just as a lordly prince or bishop in Europe in the year 1500 could not have foreseen the rise of capitalism and democracy, we today have a hard time forseeing the rise of new types of economic systems, governmental structures, and ways of community life.

This book is intended to be a first step in a long journey, one we can reflect back upon from time to time to see if the course we've set is straight and true.

Acknowledgments

IT'S DIFFICULT TO REACH BACK over two years and think of all the people who have helped in writing this book. For starters, my thanks to Beth Morrow and Loel McPhee at CommerceNet for encouraging me to take on this project.

Then I must thank the crew that worked with me on the Communities of Commerce project, which was in progress as this manuscript was being written. Stacey Bressler, my boss, was most supportive and acted as a coach and editor whenever she could.

My thanks also to Kerry Radcliffe and Nancy Sovik, who prepared a lot of what you see in the case studies on communities and the information about how we developed the organizational analysis system.

A special thanks goes to Ceil Tilney, who out of admiration for my work (and some degree of insanity, I'm sure) volunteered to take on the job of editor for the entire first draft of the manuscript. My thanks for her patience and ability to see through the fluff and delusions of grandeur that authors sometimes suffer while trying to give birth to a new idea. Without Ceil, this book would never have seen the light of day.

Of course, my thanks to Susan Barry and Yedida Soloff, who helped guide me through the production process and the intricacies of progressing from a draft to finished product. Yedida went through the second draft of the manuscript word by word, line by line, helping me give it a fresh perspective and to make it comprehensible.

Finally, thanks to Ellen, my partner in life, who once again put up with an absolutely obsessed person living in her household for another year. She has been my encourager and enforcer of deadlines and my indispensable ally in the project. Also, thanks to Zak the Wonder Dog, who kept my feet warm and always agreed with whatever I had to say.

I offer an open acknowledgment to all my friends, business partners, and others whose lives have touched mine while I was writing this book. It's hard to say where some of those influences began and where they left off, but almost everyone that I've worked with in the past year and a half will see their influence coming out in this book. Certainly among them are my dear friends of old, Peter and Trudy Johnson-Lenz, and new friends like Jeff Semelchuk at VIA, who helped set me off in new directions that I had not even dreamed of when this project began.

Introduction

We are living through an extraordinary moment in human history. Historians will look back on our times, the 40-year span between 1980 and 2020, and classify it among the handful of historical moments when humans reorganized their entire civilization around a new tool, a new idea. These decades mark the transition from the Industrial Age, an era organized around the motor, to the Digital Age, an era defined by the microprocessor—the brains within today's personal computers. The mid-1990s, perhaps even 1995, may come to be viewed as the defining moment when society recognized the enormity of the changes taking place and began to reorient itself.

Peter Leyden[1]

THIS BOOK COMES FROM MY WORK with hundreds of people and dozens of organizations facing the extraordinary changes of the past several years. In the move from the industrial to the digital society, both the people and the organizations I've helped have struggled with often painful transitions to new ways of working. I've been constantly amazed at the resourcefulness of most workers, managers, and executives to come up with creative ways to help them navigate these often turbulent times. I hope this book helps them, and you, move more confidently through the workplace today. I hope it takes you beyond complaining about how confusing things are, if that's what you've found yourself doing, to a place where you're actively trying to improve your workplace, your personal life, and your community.

This book is about the future of work. It is designed for you if your work includes an increasing amount of activity that's independent of time

[1] Peter Leyden, "The Historic Moment," in On the Edge of the Digital Age, Minneapolis *Star Tribune,* 1995.

and place. The media use many terms to describe this kind of work: *tele-working,* the *virtual office,* and *alternative officing* are ones you may have heard. In 1990, I coined the term *distributed work* to describe this larger social trend when I founded the Institute for the Study of Distributed Work. This book really is a compilation, a pulling together, of all I have learned about new ways of working in the past eight years.

Many of us believe that people are searching for practical, nontechnical guidance about how to make a transition from old, centralized work practices to alternative ways of working, collaborating, and living in a global community. We've already discovered that organizational lines, political lines, and geographic separation are less-visible obstacles to productive work than they once were, but we're not sure what happens next.

You may have found yourself asking, what will my company look like a year from now? Ten years from now? What's the real meaning of this job? And perhaps from the most enlightened people comes the question, "How can I survive in a world that goes faster and faster and seems to be increasingly dominated by technologies I don't understand?"

PLAN OF THE BOOK

This book is composed of seven major sections, each a step toward our final destination: helping you understand how the changing world of work impacts you, your job, and your community. Each chapter builds on what goes before it and explains a particular topic in some detail. This is a somewhat difficult task, because all of these things interact with one another. Therefore, my separation of this material into chapters is somewhat arbitrary, but it's designed to help you follow the pathway of the transition to new ways of working.

Chapter 1 discusses the forces that are creating change in the world of work. We will spend some time talking about changes in employment patterns, looking at some historical trends in cycles of time and at how the changing values and experiences of different generations impact us in the workplace. I will also talk a bit about the impact of the globalization of work, and I'll conclude with some thoughts about technology and the increasing speed of change.

Chapter 2 focuses on the question, "What does all this change mean?" The answer speaks to the impact of change on people, work organizations, and society at large. Chapter 2 synthesizes the main idea behind this whole book—how technology is driving our personal lives to become less individual and more social. It describes how changes in technology force us to get outside of ourselves and connect more tightly with groups of people, with our work teams, and with our communities.

This chapter also looks more deeply at the organizations that surround us. These organizations define us less and less. You're less likely to think of yourself primarily as, say, an engineer who works for company X or a clerk who works for company Y than you might have been 15 or even 5 years ago. So the question you may be facing (or will be soon!) is, "If I don't get my identity from organizations, where do I get the sense of who I am in the world?"

Finally, Chapter 2 looks at technology, not from the usual standpoint of hardware, computers, and machines, but as a tool that's made up of hardware that we can feel, software that we can see, and something else I call "wetware."

> ## Wetware is your brain. Wetware is your nervous system. It is that uniquely human power of thought and emotion that adds a dimension of interactivity to hardware and software.

The first two chapters of the book set the stage. When you're done with Chapter 2, you'll have visited some of the forces shaping our new work world, and you'll have some ideas about the potential impact of these forces on you, your organizations, and your social world.

Chapter 3 looks at community. When I initially planned this book, I did not intend to talk about how technology is affecting community. But in the past year, I have found that there's a growing—even exploding—interest in community. Sort of a yearning for a return to something lost, a sense of belonging made possible by our new technologies, our new ways of working, and our personal desires. Communities of commerce, global villages, and total restructurings of our social networks are occurring as we move into the new age of working. I'll spend a little time sharing my thoughts and suggestions about how you can pull together to integrate the changes that are occurring in the workplace within the context of new community.

Chapters 4, 5, and 6 focus more specifically on people, work organizations, and technology. These chapters cover the people-work-technology triad that determines who we are and how we get on in this world.

Chapter 4 is about people. It's about you. It's about learning how to make the personal transition to the new world of work. It gives you a non-threatening, achievable road map for personal change. Chapter 4 asks you to examine my belief that, as individuals moving into the future of work, we must move our emotional centers, our affective selves, from being something we carry around only within ourselves to being something that's as visible to our work teams as are the more traditional, rational workplace skills.

Chapter 5 is about the organization of work. It's about how groups of people become teams and how teams of people come together to form companies, firms, or business enterprises. Again, I will emphasize the impacts of the forces of change on this unit of social organization. You'll see that the generational and temporal shifts that you've had a chance to consider in the initial part of this journey really have their primary impact here, in the way we group together to perform work activities.

The central focus in Chapter 5 is on those events that take place in the workplace that give us a sense of purpose and motivation. Let's face it, people don't work merely for a paycheck. There is something else we get out of engaging in activities with others that goes beyond the financial reward. It's this intangible quality of work that I will speak to in Chapter 5.

Chapter 6 talks about technology. But technology in a way I think you'll find far different than you've thought about it. Technology as a tool. Technology that moves from being something we use to get a job done to something that we use to connect and relate to others. This is a very, very important shift. At the most basic level, technology is blurring the boundaries between people, companies, and community. According to Robert Walker, former chief information officer of Hewlett-Packard, the notion of where a corporation starts and stops is going to be very different in the future. A company can get rid of a whole host of intermediaries who used to make a living coordinating and moving information. These days, HP moves its information around electronically, and there is far less need for centralized operations. The organization is more distributed—people work in an office or they work at home, and much of what they do is knowledge work. HP also uses partners a lot more now than it used to. All this was made possible by the increased ability to transfer information among people, firms, and communities.

This capacity to distribute work has the potential to reshape organizations by redefining the fundamental nature of how work gets done. Think about the telephone for a minute. When telephones were first introduced into our society only a little over 100 years ago, they were used exclusively

Organization of the book.

	Chapter 1	Chapter 2	Chapter 3	Chapter 4	Chapter 5	Chapter 6	Chapter 7
Topic	Background: an anchor	Cycles of change	Community	People	Organizations	Technology	Resources
Theme	Historic forces	Telework to the new way of working	Making connections	Personal transformation	Organizations changing	Use technology, don't be used by it	Where to go for more
Why this is important	This is the way to think about the new world: part 1	This is the way to think about the new world: part 2	This is why the new world matters	This is why it's so hard to deal with	This is what you get if you really deal with the change	This is how technology can support you	This is where to go now!
Question that the chapter answers	What's changing?	How is work evolving?	What different relationships are we forming?	How can we personally change?	Can you show me some successful changes?	Can you show me how to use technology?	OK, so what's next?

to speed up business communications. In fact, some of the early pioneers of the telephone business were quite concerned that this technology would be misused by people to socialize with one another.

As we all know, that's exactly what happened. The technology quickly moved from being something that helped us perform a task to being something that helped us stay in touch with one another. Chapter 6 will discuss how the same phenomena are occurring with computer-based technologies. I will talk about how people are now beginning to use Internet and other technology to stay connected.

Internet technology is providing a means by which people can work together without regard to where they are in time and space. Companies that can successfully assess their readiness and implement systems to manage distributed workers will have a strategic advantage over their competitors.

Chapter 7 contains some concluding thoughts. This final step in our journey is really a guide to the transition. Although I won't give you, per se, a checklist of 7 things to do or 12 things to look out for, I will offer some very specific, practical, and understandable guidelines about how you can make this transition. I will talk about what you can do in your personal life, what you can do inside your work organization, and how you can use the new technologies to improve the quality of your work and community life.

This book is a journey. It's a journey from where we stand today to where our work, art, technology, and communities are going to be tomorrow. For many people, this journey is filled with apprehension. But it doesn't need to be that way. I believe that if we have a collective understanding of where things are headed, we can prepare ourselves to arrive there in a much better state than if we simply "go with the flow." So let's get started on this journey and begin by taking a very broad look at some of the trends affecting our jobs and the workplace.

THE FUTURE OF WORK

FORCES CREATING THE CHANGE

> It really is a revolution and it really is big. There are revolutions large and small, but one this big probably hasn't come in at least a hundred years, and in the end we may look back and say this was the biggest thing since the advent of the printing press in the mid-1400s. Quite simply, digital technology is the solvent leaching the glue out of old, much-cherished social, political, and business structures. We're in a period where everything is changing, everything is up for grabs, and nothing makes any sense, and probably won't make any sense for two or three more decades.
>
> *Paul Saffo*[1]

AS THE WORDS OF **PAUL SAFFO,** a noted futurist from the Institute for the Future, remind us, change is the one constant in our world.

Consider also the musing of one of this century's most famous management gurus, Peter Drucker:

No century in recorded history has experienced so many social transformations and such radical ones as the twentieth century. [These] may turn out to be the most significant events of this, our century, and its lasting legacy.

---

[1] Paul Saffo interview, PBS *Frontline,* June 12, 1995.

Drucker goes on to say:

> In the developed free-market countries—which contain less than a fifth of
> the earth's population but are a model for the rest—work and work force,
> society and polity, are all, in the last decade of this century, qualitatively
> and quantitatively different not only from what they were in the first years
> of this century but also from what has existed at any other time in history:
> in their configurations, in their processes, in their problems, and in their
> structures.[2]

One result of the changes Drucker describes is that our work organizations, which have been built on the model of the Industrial Revolution, are
not very effective in a global, networked economy. Sheer scale no longer
offers an advantage in a rapidly changing world. Downsizing, reengineer-
ing, and mergers offer only temporary financial gain, and they certainly
don't provide the better quality of life that workers demand.

The technology which has driven so much of the change Drucker
describes continues its unstoppable advance into every corner of our lives.
Embedded chips for medical monitoring and electronic limbs and sensory
organs are moving to the marketplace. Yet there is a gap. Technology can
augment human function, but it isn't being used to augment humanity. The
work of two noted experts on the changes of the past 100 years can help us
understand the way forward to a more humanized, yet still technology-
driven, world.

HISTORICAL PATTERNS
William Strauss and Neil Howe's historical analysis of the cycles of time
that we're experiencing is called *The Fourth Turning: What the Cycles of
History Tell Us About America's Next Rendezvous With Destiny*.[3] As historians, Strauss and Howe's central thesis is that our culture goes through eras
that repeat every few decades or so. According to their model, each of us in
our normal lifetime goes through a set of four eras. Each set of four eras
equals a cycle, which lasts approximately 80 to 100 years. The sequence of
eras in a cycle roughly corresponds to a natural cycle of growth, matura-
tion, unraveling, and destruction.

Strauss and Howe call the first era in a cycle *the high*. In their model,
the high era is characterized by a strengthening of institutions and the rise
of a new civic order. The second era is *the awakening*, and it consists of

---

[2] Peter Drucker, *Atlantic Monthly*, 1994.

[3] Broadway Books, New York, 1997.

spiritual upheaval. The third era is *the unraveling,* and it covers the time when institutions become weak, individuals become strong, the civic order begins to decay, and we can see a new value system coming into existence. The fourth and last era is *the crisis.* During the crisis era we see a rapid decay of old institutions and the final birth of the new order. (See Figure 1-1 and Table 1-1.)

If we look at U.S. history in this century, we can see that the first era was the American high of the years immediately after World War II. The unbridled optimism and confidence that we found as our economy and society shifted from wartime to peace and America became the world economic leader are characteristic of the high era of a cycle.

The second era, the time of awakening, extended from the early 1960s to the early 1980s. We all know what happened during that time. Whether you personally agree with the changes the United States went through during that period, you will probably agree that the era of the 1960s and 1970s was a revolution of personal liberation and a major shift in morals.

I would argue that we're currently at the closing part of a third era, an era of unraveling. Certainly, we have seen so much change in the past decade, in the world, at work, and in our communities, that it's clear we're in some kind of transition. The unsettled feelings we have intensify as we realize the old order is crumbling and a new, as yet unknown, order is emerging.

At this point in the historical cycle, Strauss and Howe say the dominant mood is anxiety or apprehension. The uncertainty many of us feel about the changes in our work life is consistent with the apprehension that marks the cycle of unraveling. We seem to be adrift, without any firm anchors in social institutions. Our political organizations swing between the radical right and the extreme left. Our economy has undergone tremendous restructurings, from businesses downsizing to "mergermania." So, what's coming?

If history is any teacher and Strauss and Howe have gotten it right, we're about to enter the fourth era, the era of crisis. We can expect some sort of catalytic event within a few years, an event that creates a sudden

FIGURE 1-1   Cycles of change.

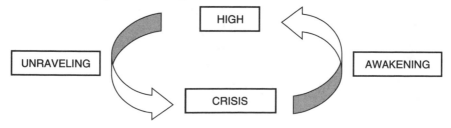

TABLE 1-1   Cycles of change defined.

Era	Key Characteristic	Recent Example
High	Strong institutions; social order	1945–1960
Awakening	Spiritual upheaval	1960–1980
Unraveling	Weak institutions; social upheaval	1980–2000
Crisis	Birth of new order	2000–2020

shift in how we look at the world and each other. This event could take the form of a natural disaster, widespread warfare, or perhaps even some startling discovery, such as finding life elsewhere in the universe. After the defining event, we can predict that society will mend some splits that developed over the past decades and that we will see a resurgence of interest in community or civic life. This newly reenergized community will then begin to shape a new social agenda.

The reshaping of the social agenda will itself create more changes in attitudes and behavior as our lives become directed in new ways. In the final part of the crisis era, we'll see a reconciliation of the opposing forces that brought about the crisis.

To get a sense of how the crisis plays out in a historical cycle, consider three crisis periods in U.S. history: the American Revolution, the Civil War, and the period covering the Great Depression and World War II. In each of these, the cataclysmic event itself was preceded by several years of growing unease and apprehension among diverse groups of Americans. I believe that the momentum toward the next great crisis in American society is driving our feelings of anxiety, uncertainty, and fear today.

Another way to understand the progression of eras in a historical cycle is by comparison to the natural development of individuals. Think about your own life. Recall your own rise from childhood through adolescence and into adulthood. I think you can see how family relationships were strong when you were a child, weakened as you entered adolescence, and strengthened again when you started your own family. Similarly, your ideals were probably stable early in your life, but became less sure as you grew up. Then you debated new ideals against those of the older generation, usually within your own family, as you struggled to create your own identity. Today, you're probably more settled in your ideas once more.

Table 1-2 summarizes Strauss and Howe's discussion of the changes people experience as they move from one era to the next in their lives. I think that the real genius in the work of Strauss and Howe is that not only

TABLE 1-2   Social and cultural characteristics of historical eras.
W. Strauss and N. Howe, The Fourth Turning, *Broadway Books, New York, 1997, p. 105.*

	First Era (High)	Second Era (Awakening)	Third Era (Unraveling)	Fourth Era (Crisis)
Families	Strong	Weakening	Weak	Strengthening
Ideals	Settled	Discovered	Debated	Championed
Institutions	Reinforced	Attacked	Eroded	Founded
Culture	Innocent	Passionate	Cynical	Practical
Social structure	Unified	Splintering	Diversified	Gravitating
Worldview	Simple	Complicating	Complex	Simplifying
Social priority	Community high	Individualism rising	Individualism high	Community rising

do these changes occur for individuals but they occur for societies at large. The changes that we go through in our lifetimes are reflected in the changes that our society goes through. And the changes in society are inevitably reflected in the way we interact at work.

A CHANGING PSYCHOLOGY OF WORK[4]

Interim Technology, in a recently completed survey of American workers, discovered a trend toward a shift in the basic social psychology, or attitudes, of workers. The major shift is in attitudes about job security, openness to workplace change, responsibility for one's career development, the definition of loyalty to one's employer, and the degree of stimulation and challenge desired at work. The following list outlines some of these basic differences in attitude between the generations.

Think of traditional employees as being older workers who have therefore usually been in the workforce longer. Typically, these workers carry with them the values of the postwar 1950s culture. Emerging employees, on the other hand, come from the group often referred to as Generation X, the post–baby boom generation that began to enter the workforce in the late 1980s.

Quite clearly, we can see that there are some basic conflicts in the attitudes of traditional versus new employees related to jobs and work. Those of you who are part of the generation between traditional and emerging

---

[4] This information regarding the changing attitudes of workers has been adapted, with permission, from a recent survey of the workforce by Interim Technology, Inc. Source data can be viewed at http://www.interim.com.

Traditional Employees	Emerging Employees
Demand long-term job security	Reject job security as a driver of commitment
Believe employers are responsible for career growth	Take personal responsibility for career growth
Are less satisfied with their jobs	Are more satisfied with their jobs
Believe changing jobs often is bad for career growth	Believe frequent job changes are part of career growth
Define loyalty as tenure	Define loyalty as accomplishment
View work as an opportunity for income	View work as a chance to grow

employees are members of the baby boom generation. You may well be feeling the tension between the traditional and emerging values that the generations before and after you bring to work.

Imagine the situation of an emerging employee who reports to a more traditional manager. It's easy to see where many significant problems in communication, motivation, and compensation will arise. Or, if you're a manager in your early 40s, consider the challenges you face if a key employee in his late 50s has a conflict with that bright young 27-year-old you just hired!

Here are key findings from Interim Technology's study:

- 44 percent of traditional *employers* believe that they cannot offer long-term job security and that there is no reason to go out of their way to help employees succeed. Only 4 percent of emerging workers hold this view. This means that a new generation of managers will emerge within 10 years who believe they have some responsibility to promote continuing education among those who work for them.
- 45 percent of traditional workers agree with the statement, "I don't like my job but it provides me with a paycheck," compared to only 2 percent of emerging workers.
- 81 percent of traditional workers believe that changing jobs every few years can be damaging to a person's career advancement, compared with only 30 percent of emerging workers.
- 87 percent of emerging workers believe employers are not responsible for an individual's career development. Only 51 percent of traditional workers agree.

- 97 percent of emerging workers believe loyalty today isn't about tenure, but about the contributions a worker makes on the job. Only 69 percent of traditional employees agree.
- 98 percent of emerging workers agree that work provides them with a chance to grow. Only 70 percent of traditional workers agree.

We can see that the social psychology of the workplace is changing dramatically. I believe that it's acutely important for us to be aware that these shifts are being driven by events far larger than ourselves and the dynamics of the particular companies we work for. They have as much to do with our period in history, the attitudes of the generations that came before us, and the emergence of new challenges that lie ahead of us as they do with the unique dynamics of individual companies.

These changes present an entirely new set of challenges to managers and workers alike. Throughout this book, we will explore specific ideas, hints, and steps you can take to manage these challenges effectively.

THE CHANGING FACE OF WORK[5]

Our values and attitudes toward work aren't the only things that are changing. Demographics are fundamentally altering how we work together. Consider that in the United States alone our workforce, which was 125 million in 1990, is expected to reach 151 million by 2005. Surprisingly, the increase of 26 million represents a slowdown in the rate of growth of the labor force. At the same time, the overall number of jobs is increasing. An increase in the number of jobs available and a simultaneous slowdown in the growth of the labor pool means we can expect an increasing need to look outside the United States for workers. As work becomes even more of a global issue, profound political and social challenges will continue to emerge. As the workforce becomes more global, its ethnic makeup is also changing. White non-Hispanic men are becoming a smaller percentage of the male workforce, with their overall participation expected to fall from 79 percent in 1990 to 73 percent by 2005. Hispanic men and women will see the greatest increase in workforce participation by 2005, rising from 8 percent to slightly over 11 percent, a 45 percent increase. During the same period, women's participation in the workforce will increase from 40 percent of the labor force to 47 percent.

The workforce will also age, with the median age increasing from about 36 years of age to slightly over 40. Older workers (over age 55) will comprise 15 percent of the labor pool by 2005, up from 12 percent now. One conclu-

[5] Source: http://www.interim.com.

sion you might reach from this is that studies of worker attitudes today tell us little about the values that will dominate the workplace of the future.

The level of education required in this new workforce will also change. The fastest-growing occupations are those that employ knowledge workers, where a college education is a minimum requirement. A picture of an older, more educated, and higher-paid workforce emerges, one that will have different attitudes and expectations about the relationship of people to their jobs. This is a theme that I will return to again and again in the following chapters.

TECHNOLOGY DEVELOPMENT: HISTORY OF TECHNOLOGY CHANGES

If social, individual, and generational changes are key to the transition we're in today, technology is no less important. Certainly technology has been affecting organizations for a long time, from the dawn of the printing press to the explosion of inventions that ushered in the Industrial Revolution in the nineteenth century. Thanks to the changes that occurred during that cycle, or series of eras, we have used telephones in business for almost 100 years. In our own series of historical eras, we've had computers for 40 years and personal computers for 15.

The basic trend that we focus on in this book is the shift during our cycle of eras from mainframe computing—and the organizational structures and systems that flow from it—to the paradigm in which network computing becomes dominant. As a framework for studying that shift, here's an overview of the changing role of computers over the past 50 years.

From a historical perspective, the role of computers in our consciousness and in our lives has gone through five distinct stages, and is about to embark on a sixth stage. Each stage has a purpose and principle, and can be thought about in terms of a distinct root metaphor.

Stage one: In the mid-1950s, we thought of computers as tools for solving scientific and engineering problems more quickly. To the computer scientists who cared for the massive arrays of vacuum tubes and steel, the principle governing their work was that the machine was preeminent. The rest of us, if we thought about computers at all, saw the application of computer power as almost mystical. The root metaphor we can use to describe the early role of computers in society is *the back room*—the place where the computer wizards practiced the mysterious art of engineering.

Stage two: From the mid-1950s to about 1967, the purpose of computer use was to centralize business data resources. What had been mystical tools reserved for scientific research began to move into the more pragmatic world of work. Computers during this period made business operations, such as payrolls and invoice processing, routine. Control became the principle as computer engineers fanned out through the business and began centralizing processing power and strengthening middle management. Where the first stage of computer evolution in this period had an almost mystical aura, the root metaphor during the 1960s was *the data processing center:* You dropped off your card deck and came back the next morning to see if your program (the batch file) had run. You didn't exactly understand what it meant for the program to run. There was still a great gulf separating the people who used computers at work from those who didn't.

Stage three: From about 1967 into the late 1970s, we saw the frontier stage of computing, characterized by an explosion of computer power. Everything, without question, was subject to automation. Computer professionals continued to be the keepers of the jealously guarded corporate database, but access to its mysteries started to open. Each business department had its own wizard who could talk to the keepers of the database, and *the warehouse* became the metaphor of the period. The department wizard would disappear into the hushed halls of the MIS department, reappearing with information and directions he or she could share with the rest of the group. That group was now connected to the corporate database, via the "dumb terminals" that sat on everyone's desk, but the information the database contained was often as difficult to make sense of as it had been in the days of the computer-as-back-room.

Stage four: As dumb terminals gave way to the local processing power of the desktop personal computer (PC), the 1980s became the decade of the neighborhood mechanic. Information resource centers sprang up all over the business with their own minicomputers and localized databases. Technical specialties grew up, as control moved from the center to the periphery. Each manager had a local guru who had responsibility for department-level data. Instead of a single, massive warehouse, the root metaphor changed again, and computing power came from *the neighborhood garage*—the local shop where even ordinary people might discover the next great thing. Conducting business without access to computers became very difficult to visualize.

Stage five: As the century draws to a close, we're in the fifth stage of the evolution of the relationship between humans and their computerized machines. In this stage, application tools let people tailor computer power to their needs. Computer professionals are seen as business team members, not wizards or arcane keepers of isolated warehouses. *Partnership* is the central image. Computer science, in the form of MIS and IS departments, often with subspecialties like finance or human resources, assists in designing core business processes to take advantage of technology's capabilities.

Stage six: I anticipate that the next stage will see the further democratization of computers, as computing power moves from under the desk to the laptop. *Hunters and farmers* will become the dominant metaphors: Some people take the tools to the field; others stay home with them. Hunters carry their tools with them. Farmers leave them at a central location that they return to on a regular basis.

What's important to take from all this is the realization of how profoundly computers have changed in our lifetimes. If you're over 40, there's a good chance you can remember a time when information stored in computers was almost impossible for ordinary workers to get. If you're over 35, you can probably remember an era in which laptop computers and cellular phones were not part of the toolbox you used at work. If you're in your 20s, the idea of taking punch cards to a mysterious basement room where a ghostly clerk runs through the computer's batch processing system at night probably sounds like something from the era of Dickens and Queen Victoria. But it was the norm less than 20 years ago.

KINDS OF TECHNOLOGIES
Just as the role of computers in the workplace and in our lives has changed, so has the concept of the "technology of work." The new technology of work is the intersection of four elements, not all of which you're probably accustomed to thinking of as technology: *education, computers, telecommunications,* and *work.* (See Figure 1-2.)

Two of these technologies, telecommunications and computer software, have been coming together for some time now. If you think about the latest cellular phones, which let you check your e-mail from the airport, send faxes on the run, receive pages—in text or voice format—and even do something as prosaic as making a telephone call, you have to agree that it's almost impossible to distinguish where computers leave off and telecommunication systems begin.

FIGURE 1-2   Technology integration: computers, telecommunications, education, and work practices.

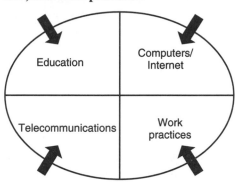

On the other hand, you probably aren't used to thinking of education and work practices as technologies. But the emergence of multimedia, virtual reality, and the World Wide Web has done more than just add new tools to the same old stuff; these technologies have transformed the nature of work and education themselves. Music TV programs now do news segments; classrooms employ videos with cartoons to illustrate points. We use technology to learn about technology, and technology gives us access to information we never would have discovered without it.

For example, when I wrote my first master's thesis, I spent about 80 percent of the year collecting information and about 20 percent of the year writing up my results. Today, with the World Wide Web, with computerized research tools, with the ability to send e-mail to fellow scholars around the world, those ratios would be reversed: I could spend 80 percent of my time writing up my results, and the overall project would probably take less than six months. But my research wouldn't just take less time. It would also be qualitatively richer, as I could draw on so many resources and ways of conceptualizing and reporting on my topic. I could use video segments on personal-computer screens, easily interchange between voice and text, and complete interactive control of my materials via virtual-reality systems. All these technologies are now coming together, enabling us to experience each other more directly by increasing the bandwidth of our communications and letting us have control over which mediums are used.

The interaction between the tools and data, in other words, is itself integral to the technological advances we're making. Think of educational data as providing the *content* of the technology. Computers and software are the *form* of the technology, its general structure. In the context of the future of work, work practices are the *style* of the communication. Telecommunications are the *channel*.

Education is not often thought of as a technology. As you'll see later in other chapters focused on technology, I hold a rather broad definition of this term. In my view, education, or the process of learning and applying knowledge to business problems, is something that is becoming a fundamental part of the workplace.

Traditionally we think of education as an activity that occurs while we're in formal learning situations such as high school or college. Education is becoming more of an ongoing day-to-day activity in the new world of work, which teaches you not only new skills (which is really training), but values, ethics, and totally new ways of thinking. Education in this context is an activity that helps shape and reshape our basic values and attitudes toward work, our workmates, and our behavior in the workplace.

The education that you bring to your job is no longer sufficient for you to remain effective in that job as the job changes during the transition to the new world of work. I believe that we need to integrate educational activities very tightly with our telecommunications channels, the style of the communication (witness what Web browser design has done to the way we view computers), work content, and also the forms of the technology. The Institute for the Study of Distributed Work completed one case study in Silicon Valley that examined over 20 high-tech firms and correlated the amount of money and time they spent on job education for their employees. We found that the most successful companies over time, in terms of increased revenue and profits, were those companies that spent, on average, 20 percent of their workers' time every week learning new things. That signifies a tremendous investment in education in the new workplace. It's my contention that people who are successful and companies that are successful in this new world of work will be those that devote a significant amount of time and energy on educating themselves and their employees.

We can change content, form, style, and channel, and depending on which one we change, we can totally alter the resulting whole that emerges from the interaction of the parts. These technologies, then, are the ones that we need to examine more closely to understand how they move from being just tools to being something that helps us stay connected. For example, take the Internet. Telecommunications (all those modems, phone lines, routers, etc.) is the roadway, or *channel,* by which you move to different locations in cyberspace. Computers and software, especially the browser, governs how we see information on the Internet—it defines the *form.* The early browsers provided a rich set of static graphics and changed the way we saw things on the Internet. It was a vast improvement over simple text. But now the form has evolved even further, and we have dynamic graphics (i.e., moving images), sound, and short video clips. Content is another matter. What we can access on the Internet is also changing rapidly. Sovereign laws of one country can't completely govern issues like censorship anymore because online data (or content) is located on a server that may be housed anywhere in the world, and unless you can read Internet Protocol (IP) addresses, you can't know *where* the information is coming from.

So we need to look at how all four of the components of communication interact. Communicating on the Web is becoming an elevated art form much like moviemaking or other creative activities. Technology has been wrested from the hands of its inventors and is being turned over to everyone to use in their own unique way to connect to others with whom they want to interact.

SUMMARY

In this chapter, we've seen that historical patterns and the evolution of our social and cultural values are interacting to change the way we approach work. We've taken a brief look at some of the different ways we're starting to think about work, and we've considered how the changes in our relationship to technology are impacting not just what we do, but how we think about our jobs. As we will see, these forces are combining to create a new technology of work, a way of being in the workplace that not only reflects the historical, social, cultural, and technology places we've been, but is shaping the changes to come.

Chapter 2 will take us more deeply into the form the new technologies of work will take.

C H A P T E R

CHANGES: HOW IS THE PRACTICE OF WORK EVOLVING?

This is a revolution that a lot of people don't see.

Ira Brodsky[1]

IN THE LAST CHAPTER, I spoke about a number of the forces that are coming together to create significant change in our work world of the future. The purpose of this chapter is to begin to link those forces to specific impacts on individuals, organizations, and technology. Before I proceed with that analysis, let me offer a few more thoughts on the significance and magnitude of the impact we will feel from the forces discussed in Chapter 1. First of all, the societal changes we're undergoing as we move from Strauss and Howe's Third ("the unraveling") to Fourth ("the crisis") Turning conform to what's called *punctuated equilibrium,* which simply means change that is sudden and significant rather than slow and incremental. When you see sudden upheavals and rapid change followed by periods of apparent calm, you're looking at a situation of punctuated equilibrium. Time speeds up. New businesses are born almost

---

[1] Ira Brodsky, quoted in G. Christian Hill, "Look! No Wires! The Cord Has Been Cut, and Communication May Never Be the Same," *Wall Street Journal,* February 11, 1994, Sec. R, p. 1.

overnight; opportunities suddenly present themselves. Witness the pace of change that has occurred in the former Soviet Union, and note how different that pace has been from the steadier pace of development during the Communist era. Think about the consequent problems the Russians have had adjusting to their new world!

Another illustration of punctuated equilibrium is the recent rapid fluctuation in the stock market. In earlier eras, the market, on average, steadily declined or increased by, say, 1 percent of its value per month, a fairly steady rate of change. Recently it has become almost commonplace for the market to increase or decrease 5 percent or more in a single day. When such a spike is followed by a period of relative calm, you're looking at a situation of punctuated equilibrium.

Organizations are also likely to undergo sudden and massive changes. A company with a steady rate of growth in market share, revenue, and employees every month is undergoing more or less linear change. However, if the company decides to lay off 20 percent of its workforce within a 30-day period, that would qualify as punctuated equilibrium. These are the kinds of changes we need to anticipate, because their impact is enormous.

The other point I'd like to make here is that the impact that we are going to feel from these changes will be magnified not so much by any one change in itself, but by the *convergence* of trends (that is, each amplifying the impact of the others). A single pebble tossed into a pond causes cascading ripples that eventually cover the whole pond, which is an apt metaphor for these changes. If you were to throw three pebbles into the pond at almost the same time but in different places, the ripples caused by those individual events will intersect with one another to create an even more complex pattern of ripples as their energies are added together. This is precisely how all of the changes we've talked about are coming together to influence who we are, how we work together, and how we live in our communities as we enter the twenty-first century.

WHAT DOES PUNCTUATED EQUILIBRIUM MEAN FOR THE INDIVIDUAL?

"You have a job, but how about a life?" was the title of a recent book review in *Business Week*.[2] The book, *The Corrosion of Character* by Richard Sennett, talks about what happens to individuals in times of historical change such as we are going through now. Many people fear that

---

[2] *Business Week,* November 16, 1998.

we are becoming newly atomized, and separated from everything we used to hold dear. The liberating effects of new technologies also lead to a sense of loss.

Sennet writes, "Character is expressed by loyalty and mutual commitment, or through the pursuit of long-term goals. . . . How do we decide what is of lasting value in ourselves in a society which is impatient, which focuses on the immediate moment?" His thesis is that we have lost our sense of time; we don't have well-demarcated beginnings, middles, and ends anymore. When do you become an adult? When does old age begin in the Internet world?

As we feel this loss, some of us move toward a nostalgic view of the past, some toward a conservatism that seeks solid moral ground for reference. Power exists in teams, but without traditional legitimate authority—Max Weber, who invented the term *bureaucracy,* is dead; and so is the organizational form he studied. We now have to adjust. We have to make the transition.

The Dance of Life[3]

It can now be said with assurance that individuals are dominated in their behavior by complex hierarchies of interlocking rhythms. Furthermore, these same interlocking rhythms are comparable to fundamental themes in a symphonic score, a keystone in the interpersonal processes between mates, coworkers, and organizations of all types on the interpersonal level within as well as across cultural boundaries. I am convinced that it will ultimately be proved that almost every facet of human behavior is involved in the rhythmic process.

Interpersonal Synchrony

It is hard to write about rhythms in English. We don't have the vocabulary, and the concepts aren't in the culture. We in the West have this notion that each of us is all by himself in this world—that behavior is something that originates inside the skin, isolated from the outside world and from other human beings. Nothing could be further from the truth.

---

[3] Edward T. Hall, *The Dance of Life,* Anchor/Double Day, Garden City, New York, 1984, pp. 155, 162.

Individuals: Time Changes

For the individual, the primary impact of change is that our lives are becoming less individualized and more socialized. The changes in technology and organizations are forcing us to get outside ourselves and connect more tightly with groups of people, to our work teams, and to our communities. More specifically, the changes impact how we communicate with one another. If you doubt that this is happening, let me ask you a few brief questions.

- How many e-mails do you get every day?
- How many messages or voice mails do you get at home every day?
- How many people do you work with who are three or more time zones away?
- How many letters have you written in the past month?

Compare your answers to what they would have been three years ago. I'll bet there's been quite a change! But if we understand and anticipate the impact of these changes, we are better prepared to deal with them.

CHANGES IN HUMAN-COMPUTER-HUMAN COMMUNICATION: SOCIAL PSYCHOLOGY AND THE FUTURE OF WORK

The very psychological nature of work will be different in the future. It is quite clear that a completely new social psychology of work is emerging as we rush toward the Internet-dominated workplace. Although the exact nature and form that this will take is still fuzzy, the basic outlines of our new ways of relating to one another at work are becoming very clear.

Social psychology is the study of how we relate to one another. Emphasis is placed on status and power relationships, on how these impact the formation of attitudes, and finally, on the relation of all these factors to our specific behavior in a given social context—in this case, work.

My basic thesis is that all the historical forces, combined with generational shifts in attitudes and the availability of more pervasive communications technology, are pulling us in the direction of more collaborative kinds of work—and away from work patterns that were based on the old industrial model, with hierarchical power structures and great disparities in status between workers.

Figure 2-1 summarizes the need to look at the emerging social psychology of the future. Perceptions of time and space will be different. Status and power relations will be different. Our social networks will change, and this will lead to different perceptions of identity. All these things come together to create a shift in attitudes and, ultimately, behavior in the workplace.

FIGURE 2-1   Composition of the new social psychology of work.

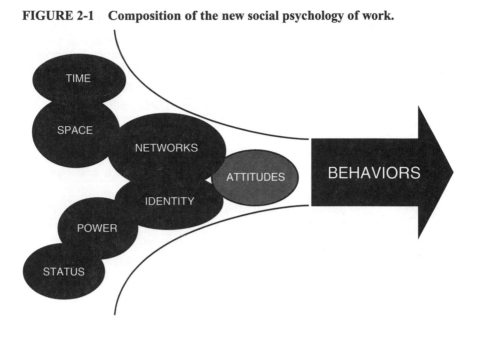

TIME

Now let's look at one very important variable in this social psychology.[4]

People perceive time in two fashions: *linear* and *cyclic*. While it's not important that you master the theory behind this statement, it's useful to see a summary of the different communication styles that arise from the different ways we perceive time. Take a look at Table 2-1.

In the linear model, people coordinate their efforts by completing serial processes. Their coordinated work is characterized by impersonal communication, largely devoid of emotional content and based on fact. Formal business letters, memos, and similar communications characterized these early stages of the use of communications technology in the workplace. I can recall a time in the not-too-distant past when I worked in a large group of people, around 30, and there was only one telephone for the entire group. There was a very formal protocol attached to phone use, which included logging your phone calls and reporting the results of the conversations directly to a supervisor.

Decisions made in coordinated work environments are usually very logical and are based on an input-output model. You are rewarded in direct

---

[4] I will examine spatial relations, power, status, community, and identity in the following chapters.

TABLE 2-1   Changes in time perception in the future world of work.

Dimension	Linear Communication Style	Cyclic Communication Style
Perception	Past-present-future	Recurrence, spiral
Scale	We have time to process things before we communicate about them.	We communicate about things at the same time that we're processing them.
Sequencing	Events (or conversations) take place in serial order. One game ends before another begins.	Events (or conversations) occur in parallel order. We're involved in numerous conversations at once.
Pace	Work goes quickly compared to changes in our community and family.	Everything goes quickly, and we develop the ability to switch contexts quickly.
Vision	Past/present. Time horizons map to business cycles, usually on a quarterly and annual basis.	Future. Time horizons extend into 5- and 20-year frames of reference.

proportion to the time you put into your work. Hourly wages and piecework are examples of this kind of decision making. Equity governs coordinated work decisions. Seniority rules: those who have invested the most amount of time get the largest rewards, regardless of anything else.

When we moved into the early 1990s, technology brought us more connectivity, linking us directly and easily to other workers. E-mail and voice mail became the norm of communication within work groups. We began to cooperate; we began to understand how each of us fit into an overall flow of work. At this time, we also began to see the emergence of an entirely new class of application software, called *groupware*. Groupware is characterized by strategies for managing information that make it easy for all members of a group to read, comment on, and change it.

The chief advantage to communication in the cooperative work environment enabled by groupware is the strong ties it can create between individuals. The social relationships among people more easily flower into friendship and often transcend the workplace. Power becomes more dispersed, and status becomes more directly connected to one's contribution to the team effort and to the ability to develop social relationships rather than solely to individual accomplishment.

Instead of the input-output model that characterizes the linear world of coordinated work, the cooperative universe that starts to arise in the cyclic perception of time emphasizes equality and nondiscrimination. This basic change in attitude predictably follows a movement from the Second Turning to the Third Turning, and thus demonstrates the impact larger societal forces can have on personal relationships in the workplace. We are now entering the Internet-dominated age of work—what I've called the *new world of work*. This is the age of collaboration. Collaboration means that knowledge workers tend increasingly to share the same value set. These common values are reflected in the sense of common purpose we bring to our work groups. Everyone in the work group knows why they are there and what needs to be done—it almost doesn't have to be communicated on an explicit level.

In other words, the new world of work is one in which people voluntarily come together and find each other as workmates based on a common personal philosophy, social attitudes, and shared behaviors. This is the collaborative workspace. This is a work space that is enabled by our new technologies and by people's desire to work with others with whom they share more commonalities than differences.

Decision making in the collaborative workplace is based on what is required for the healthy growth of the company, not on longevity of employment, level of education, or personality. But this doesn't mean that the needs of individuals are sacrificed for the good of the company. Rather, creating conditions that are good for the company is widely seen as synonymous with creating conditions that are good for you and me. The changes we've just looked at are summarized in Table 2-2.

The changes we have been discussing use technology to shift us from a "coordination" level of functioning to one of true collaboration. Time shifts for the individual; ways of organizing work change. Technology drives us toward distributed work, thus creating a situation in which we can come together in new and different ways. Our perception of time changes, and our social way of organizing ourselves changes. So, what does the workplace begin to look like when all of this happens?

TABLE 2-2   Group functioning levels over time.

Era	Dominant Work Relationship	Dominant Communication Style	Decision Rule
1980s	Coordination	Impersonal	Individual input-output
1990s	Cooperation	Strong ties	Group equality
2000+	Collaboration	Intimacy	Organization need

LIFE ON INTERNET TIME: WORK EXPANDS INTO THE TIME ALLOWED FOR IT

The degree to which we have become interconnected with one another has increased significantly in the past few years. Business moves at a faster pace than it used to. The old rules of how long it took to do something have changed. What used to take a year now happens in three months. What does all this change in time perception mean for you in the new world of work? Here are some rules of thumb to help you set a pace in today's Internet-driven world.

SOCIAL PSYCHOLOGY AT WORK

Social psychology is the study of how we relate to one another. It emphasizes status and power relationships, how these impact the formation of attitudes, and the relation of status, power, and attitude to behavior in a given social context—in this case, at work.

Charlie Grantham's Rule of Twos

Here's how much time you have	. . . to
2 minutes	. . . take action on immediate requests for your attention. *If you can't handle it that quickly, then it needs to go to someone or someplace else!*
2 hours	. . . hold face-to-face meetings. *If it takes longer than that, you're not planning!*
2 days	. . . respond to electronic requests. *If you can't get to it by then, you're wasting your time and everyone else's.*
2 weeks	. . . assemble a work team and commit to a plan. *If you can't find the right people and the right plan by then, the project will fail.*
2 months	. . . identify a business opportunity and test it with customers. *If you can't do it by then, your competition can.*
2 years	. . . do nothing at all. *If your plans reach out years into the future, the world will have passed you by long before you accomplish them.*

We've seen that technological and historical forces are pulling knowledge workers toward more collaborative kinds of work and away from work patterns based on hierarchical power structures and great disparities in status between similar white-collar workers. This evolution toward true collaboration began in the mid-1980s with the mass introduction of personal computers. It will culminate in the first years of the twenty-first century with the emergence of the truly collaborative workplace, at least for the technologically elite.

Innovation is a $24 \times 7 \times 365$ proposition in a global environment.

In practical terms, this move toward a work model of collaboration means that we're going to be finding ourselves working more in situations with small teams of 5 to 20 people and spending far less time working as "individual contributors" or as members of committees. Collaborative work teams do not have any one individual continuously in a leadership role. That doesn't mean that they are without structure and differences in power and status, but these structures change rapidly according to the nature of the task at hand.

I see the new world of work as one in which we will work together in teams, and the person who makes a critical decision for the team at any given time will be the person who is the best equipped to make that specific decision. As an example, in the context of a start-up company, often decision making is passed around like a basketball on a court. In selecting a method of financing, it's usually the CFO who takes the lead in making the decision. Conversely, when there's a design decision to be made on a technology development project, that decision falls to the chief engineering person. And so it goes. This is often difficult for people who were used to the more traditional hierarchical structure where a single individual was always in charge.

Companies such as Apple Computer, DreamWorks, and Hewlett-Packard have been practicing mastery of the structures in which the authority and decision-making process is very fluid and ever changing. Team-based work processes are nothing new. There are plenty of examples throughout history where smaller work units with flexible decision-making power have conquered in the face of less-adaptable and slower organizations. The classic example of the utility of this small-team-based approach actually comes from

America's Revolutionary War. If you think about it, the forces of George Washington, by organizing into guerrilla bands, fighting from behind trees, and then immediately disbanding and fading back into the environment, eventually conquered the large, well-structured, well-disciplined British forces.

What we're seeing with the Internet is an increased degree of uncertainty and change in the general business environment. In this situation, successful companies will be those that can organize and reorganize more quickly than their competitors, which is more easily accomplished by the new work structures comprised of small, project-oriented teams. There are a number of examples of this in the current business environment. Actually, some of the best case studies we have to offer have been taken from the entertainment industry and Hollywood, and we will discuss these in some detail in the following pages.

Organizations working in collaboration are all well and good if you are creating a new company and can structure it exactly the way you want. What happens if you live in Dilbertville? You are sitting in the cube farm, assigned to committees and task forces that are flooded with e-mail and voice mail continuously. I think that these situations present the challenge to all of us.

Ultimately, the answer comes down to one of leadership. Companies without courageous, effective leaders who can steer them into this direction of the new world of work will continue to suffer from information overload, confusion, and inaction, thus becoming less and less effective over time.

A key task for all of us, then, is to begin managing the process of change so that we can consciously make the transition to the new world of work. We need to know that the answers to our questions are going to be different from the ones we are used to getting, and it is the purpose of this book to offer you some ideas. I've seen many people in the process of making this transition try and try again with little success to have their organization change to a more humane way of working, to control over-communication, and to bring caring and respect to the work teams. In some cases, this has proved to be simply impossible. In others, success comes through persistence and construction of good solid business cases as a rationale for this kind of change.

Actually, I offer up a challenge to each of you to become the master of your own fate and begin the change process yourself. That's the only way it will work. Given the diffusion of technology, which is the backdrop of this story, I suspect that, over time, more and more of you will make the decision to leave existing large hierarchical organizations and either strike out on your own or partner with a small group of like-minded folks to begin your own exciting business venture.

However, there are steps that workers in existing organizations can take to ease that transition, starting with one of the most common problems with new technology: information overload. What I found to be very successful in my work with people in these organizations is to establish protocols of communication. That is to say, members of a work group reach an agreement about how they will communicate with one another for certain activities. Then they do that, ignoring all other communications that come outside of the proper channel or are not in the proper format. Another way to confront information overload and wasted time is to control meetings. We all hate them and often find them less than effective, especially meetings that have a standing agenda, forcing workers to devote valuable time to them, no matter what. To lessen such time wasters, many companies are starting to reconsider the value of such practices. I'm aware of at least one company that has a prohibition again standing meetings. There has to be a purpose, an agenda, and prestated expected outcomes before people may come together. This means that individuals don't attend meetings unless they are preceded by a written agenda least 72 hours beforehand. Think about what that would do your everyday work life.

ORGANIZATIONS: WORK TEAMS

If the 1980s saw the end of the era of the individual and the early 1990s saw us move toward work being focused in teams, then today's workforce is marked by the reorganization of teams into teams of teams. To see this progression more clearly, let's look at some key features of work organizations over the past 15 years.

In keeping with the spirit of Chapter 1, I've labeled these different features as components of the eras of *telework, virtuality,* and *Hollywood.* Let's discuss how we have moved from the age of telework, which started around 1989, to the age of Hollywood, where I think we find ourselves today. I would like to couch that discussion in terms of several trends I see spanning across the years: the shift in emphasis from workers as individual contributors to members of work teams; changes in communication strategies; and typical work interactions. I've included a summary chart for handy reference. As I work through my description of these changes, please refer to Table 2-3 to give you an overall picture of the transitions that we have gone through and are going through right now.

The age of coordination in business, 1989 to 1992, was also the age of *telework.* Companies adjusted to the explosion in new technologies by con-

TABLE 2-3   New forms of work organization.

Age of	Teleworkers	Virtuality	Hollywood
Time	1989–1992	1993–1997	1998–2004
Emphasis placed on	People: individual contributor	Technology: project team	Organization: teams of teams
Sports metaphor*	Baseball	Football	Basketball
Social metaphor†	Coordination	Cooperation	Collaboration
Commerce model	Manufacturing	Integrated	Networked
Exemplar firm(s)	GM	Sun, H-P	DreamWorks, VIA, Inc.
Type of interaction	Work flow	Connectivity	Community

* Role relations differ. Baseball has unique roles defined by position and action taking place in serial fashion. Football has unique roles also defined by position, but action occurs in unison. Basketball has varied roles played interchangeably and in unison.

† The underlying continuum here is one of increasing shared values. *Coordination* requires neither shared values nor understanding of purpose/vision. *Cooperation* requires shared knowledge of what comes immediately before and after a particular social act. *Collaboration* requires a shared understanding of the entire interplay of all roles/positions and a common agreement on overall systemic strategy.

cerning themselves with the productivity of telecommuters and with the cost savings that companies could realize from letting employees work at home. Company thinking emphasized people as individual contributors—individuals who could volunteer for these new kinds of work. Metaphorically, companies treated workers as members of a baseball team: they were separated in space while simultaneously working together. Problem solving and communication strategies focused on work flow: "How do I get this document from my home office back to the central office?" Such questions dominated our thinking as we adjusted to new ways of work.

Though it felt incredibly modern at the time, our model of work was really still an input-output, or manufacturing, way of thinking about the job. Managers tended to look at work in terms of how it could be broken into discrete tasks and passed from one member of the team to another. We had created a knowledge-management assembly line! Companies such as General Motors and AT&T exemplified this way of working, as they simply transferred the view of tasks as "work flow" from the physical to the information realm. Not surprisingly, companies focused on monitoring and controlling information transfer among teleworkers.

Whereas the Industrial Revolution attracted workers away from home-based community settings to central locations, the proliferation of personal computers and asynchronous telecommunication technologies began to reverse the trend. A new brand of work, termed *telework,*[5] emerged, allowing employees to utilize electronic communication for working in locations away from a central office, often from their own homes. Evidence suggests that the trend toward incorporating telework into organizational policy escalated due to the pressures of urban gridlock, lack of satisfactory nearby housing, national fuel shortages, and clean-air legislation. This has resulted in a radically different type of work community.

Distributed Work Communities

Organizations were quickly changing form in the early 1990s, driven by a variety of environmental pressures. Researchers sought to understand the influence of this change on how employees work together. These people initially worked in the same place at the same time and then moved to different-place, different-time environments.

It is this—physical colocation of organizational members—that was changing, however. Forces were causing companies to distribute their resources as they moved production capacities from expensive, high-rent locations to more cost-efficient sites. At the same time, new communication and information management technologies were evolving to facilitate the distribution of information-processing abilities. Whereas the computing facilities of 10 to 15 years ago resided in highly centralized environments, the evolution of computer technology in organizations created a structure in which computing power was shared among the nodes of local- and wide-area networks, a structure in which the network is the computer.

This distribution of computer power also facilitated the distribution of work activities among people across time and space. Electronic mail, computer bulletin boards, teleconferencing, voice mail, and facsimile machines, to name a few, were emerging technologies that dissolved the barriers imposed by geographic distance and temporal separation. Organizations were transformed from highly consolidated centers into what Rob Kling

---

[5] For a more extended discussion of the impact of telework, see Chapter 7, "Resources," which includes research details. Consult the bibliography for additional resources and pointers to relevant research.

referred to as the "web organization." The development of interest in computer-supported cooperative work was another manifestation of the trend toward the increased mediation of human communication by computer systems in web organizations.

A natural extension of these technologies allowed the residence to become a remote site for work. In this sense, the trend toward increasing spatial and temporal separation of home, community, and workplace was being reversed, as was the breakdown in community organization that was brought about by separation of home and workplace. Furthermore, as the cost-benefit ratio for relying on telework shifts due to precipitous drops in computer costs and soaring increases in energy and housing, more people are substituting electronic movement of information for physical movement of themselves.

As the work community becomes distributed across offices and into the home, the social psychology of people's relationships to the distributing technology demands better understanding. Previous research, for example, has indicated that computer mediation of interpersonal interaction can change group structure and affect the decision-making process of the group. Computer-based systems of communication are socially complex, and there are many important issues that still require basic scientific investigation. As the Internet began to impact businesses and we saw an increase of commercially available electronic communications channels, we entered the new age of work—*virtuality*. The buzz of the early 1990s about virtual reality gave way to a lot of discussion, conferences, and magazine articles regarding "the virtual organization" and "virtual teams." Technology ruled. Everyone was concerned about how to get people connected. Managers began to look at ways of working in terms of "how can I assemble a team that will not be in the same place?" To me, this began to look like a football game. Everyone on the team was trying to execute in unison.

Socially, we were beginning to operate cooperatively, to have some shared understanding of how our individual outputs might fit together. We moved from a manufacturing model to one of integration, which, not surprisingly, paralleled the introduction of client-server computing, a model that replaces the centralized, highly controlled mainframe with a more autonomous, more highly integrated technology.

Not coincidentally, the companies that pioneered the development of this technology—Sun Microsystems and Hewlett-Packard—became the case studies in its social organization. We began to move from coordination to connection, toward socially as well as physically networked organizations that would flourish in the coming years. Now we come to the current age of work, which I call *Hollywood*. The Hollywood model of work replaces coordination with teaming. I've seen this teaming evolve primarily in the small companies in the new media industry. These companies are consciously or unconsciously building organizations that parallel the structure and function of the Internet. The resulting type of organization looks like production-focused teams. They come together, blending a set of interdisciplinary skills, focusing on a particular project, completing the project, then disbanding the team as each of its members moves on to other projects.

The new media industry works like a basketball team. The blendings and regroupings of teams over time demonstrate collaboration in its true form: they're based on a sharing of values as well as agreement on the proper strategies for effective work. Similarly, work teams follow more than the integrated model represented by client-server technology. Now the business model is the totally interdependent network represented by the Internet. DreamWorks SKG stands out as an excellent exemplar of this way of organizing. At DreamWorks, community is the watchword. People organize themselves around projects in which they have a shared interest and for which their skills mesh well.

This is the age of Hollywood. How do others see it?

> Once dominated by huge vertically integrated corporations, Hollywood has become the shining model of our industrial future—a network of flexible small businesses that get things done in here-today-gone-tomorrow alliances. But the real creators of the film, responsible for everything from its special effects to payroll and security, are a host of small companies and freelance contributors who collaborate for only as long as the project requires—and who are drawn from the loose network of specialists that today holds the real power in Hollywood. Eventually, every knowledge-intensive industry will end up in the same flattened, atomized state. Hollywood has just gotten there first.[6]

THE NEW LOGIC OF THE COMPANY[7]

In the old economy, companies consolidated their functions when the cost of transacting business at arm's length was simply too high. Economic logic dictated that it was cheaper to bring functions in-house than to contract them out. With the work being done in-house, employers could command, control, and coordinate things better. The division of labor was simple: Employers ran things; employees took orders.

---

[6] Joel Kotkin and David Friedman, "Why Every Business Will Be Like Show Business," *Inc.,* March 1995, p. 64.

[7] Robert Reich, "The Company of the Future," *FastCompany*, November 1998, p. 138.

The new economy has turned that economic logic inside out and upside down, and in the process, it has irrevocably restructured the relationships between employers and employees. In the past two decades—largely because of the ease, speed, and low cost with which information technology allows people to keep track of who's doing what, where value is added, and how processes can be streamlined—coordination has become faster, cheaper, and easier. Economic logic favors outsourcing. Fewer functions need to occur in-house. Physical assets can be rented. Financial capital can be borrowed. The result: Virtual enterprises can spring up overnight, as networks of free agents come together for a single project. Costs and risks are distributed over an entire network, as is the economic value that these efforts produce. Nothing could be more flexible—ready to turn on a dime, to grab any new opportunity.

Does the rise of the virtual enterprise spell the end of the real enterprise? Hardly. Precisely because of the fluidity of these new, flexible organizations, competitive advantage now goes to those groups whose members have stayed together long enough to build on one another's strengths.

No one stays put forever, of course, and that's fine. Enterprises need fresh infusions of ideas, insights, and skills on a regular basis. The trick is to attract the best people and to get them to stay put long enough to ensure that the combination of their talents will really pay off.

Certain things can't be accomplished without bonds of trust and mutual commitment. Researchers call those bonds *social capital*. Think of them as organizational glue. The more glue there is in a group, the better that group will function. The more glue, the more willing people will be to share ideas—and to accept the risk of appearing foolish. The more glue, the less worried they will be that someone else may get recognition. The more glue, the greater the likelihood that they will learn from one another: Serendipitously, they will spark one another's imaginations. The more glue, the more they will energize one another.

3

COMMUNITY: WHAT DIFFERENT RELATIONSHIPS ARE WE FORMING?

The only limits to cyberization are our networks and our ability to interface computers with the various parts of the physical world through sensor/effectors consisting of direct connections, voice, gestures, and so on. Driven by a quest for knowledge and the economics of new industry formation and efficiency, cyberization is inevitable.

Gordon Bell[1]

O THIS POINT, we've touched on some of the coming shifts in organizations, people, and technology. In Chapter 4, you'll see how the key events that define purpose and provide basic motivations for all of us are moving from formal work organizations to individuals in control of their own destiny. In this chapter, we'll take a look at community—the social structure that links individuals, organizations, and society. We'll study how technology is affecting communities—including, but not limited to, work communities—and what new forms this enduring social structure is starting to take. Community, after all, is where we experience and live out all the changes we're talking about in this book. We need to understand the rhythms, dynamics,

[1] Gordon Bell, "The Body Electric," *Communications of the ACM*, February 1997.

constraints, and processes of communities in order to understand ourselves during this transition.

For all of human history, communities have been the "where" of learning new roles, coping with changes, and finding a place of refuge in difficult times. We are in a difficult time of transition, which requires relearning how we work, live, and learn together. It's inevitable that communities will both sustain us through the transition and be altered as a result of it. This chapter will end with a case study of communities in action. It is a case study of a year-long project aimed at consciously constructing Communities of Commerce[sm] to provide fledgling companies with survival techniques for navigating the swirling waters of the Internet and electronic commerce during their first few months of existence.

We used to live in several separate communities at the same time. What is occurring now is that there is a blurring of the boundaries between these communities. We used to have a group of people with whom we associated and shared some identity at work. At the end of the workday we would go home to our neighborhoods and enjoy a community usually composed of different people.

The separation between our work community and our living community in the recent past was exacerbated by the phenomenon of cheap transportation and urban sprawl. Over time, with the advent of the Industrial Revolution, the various communities that we lived in became separated by space and time.

The major point of this chapter is that historical forces combined with new technologies and changes in attitudes toward work have begun to make our work-based communities overlap and blend into others. For example, right now I'm dictating this book while sitting in my home office, which is obviously located in the neighborhood that I live in. It is very difficult to say where my work-based community ends and the rest of my social life begins. Is the door to my office upstairs, or is it the door to my house leading to the front yard? It's very difficult to tell these days.

Work as community—that's the concept. The whole idea is that the changes being fostered among us are creating an opportunity for us to construct new communities. Communities are important because we're social beings. I'll talk a little bit about that in this chapter to give you a better understanding of just what it is that we derive from communities.

As you read this chapter, keep in mind that humans' inherent need for community is something that is coming to be satisfied by our new work world. The extensive case study at the end of this chapter gives ample evidence that the construction of social community bears a positive business benefit. That community may become the closer connection between you and your customer, or a culture that you deliberately foster in your organization, or perhaps even a social movement that improves the quality of life you share with your workmates and your customers.

First of all, however, I would like to emphasize the point that communities as networks of people around us are the fundamental social and psychological link between our work activities and the rest of our lives. The advent of the Internet and the globalization of telecommunications have allowed all of us to be connected to each other. This new community is a powerful engine of transformation in both our work and personal lives.

COMMUNITY AS ENGINE OF TRANSFORMATION

We are going through a period of organizational, technological, and personal transformation equal in scope to that of the Industrial Revolution. Transformational times, such as we live in today, create fundamental changes with the following characteristics:

- *They are irreversible.*   We're changing in ways that go beyond mere shifts in opinion. The interaction of technological, personal, and organizational forces is giving us an education that forces us to view the world in a different way. At the end of the transformation, we won't be able to give up the new knowledge and revert to old ways of knowing.

- *They are substantive.*   Transformations create new realities that are greater than the sum of their parts. You don't move into positions of more power and authority, for example—you move into positions of substantively different, often richer, power and authority.

- *They change who you are in the world.*   Quite simply, you are called something different. New systems, made from combinations of technologies, people, and organizations that have never been combined before, mean that you're now part of things that never existed before. Identity is a most powerful force in our lives, and all transformations (if they indeed are transformations) involve a change in identity.

- *They shift your purpose.*   If everything around you is changing in substantive and irreversible ways, then who you are in the world must be changing, too. This new way of being in the world changes who you are in relation to others.

Communities are places where cultural norms are transmitted to others. At work, communities are important for two reasons: (1) they can help or hinder the implementation of a business strategy, and (2) they can promote motivation and commitment among team members. A community is the social structure where cultural values are made visible and communicated to all of the community's members. A corporation's culture both requires and helps shape and sustain a work community. We all know that businesses are far more effective if they can successfully communicate their guiding beliefs and values to all of their members. That's why so many successful businesses today spend considerable time and energy in developing a corporate culture. What is an organizational culture? Stan Davis, author of *Blur* (Addison-Wesley, 1998), gives a really good definition:

> Culture is a pattern of beliefs and expectations shared by the organization's members. These beliefs and expectations produce norms that can powerfully shape the behaviors of individuals and groups.

We can apply the ideas of organization culture to communities as well as to corporations. The community then is the structural bridge between the beliefs, vision, and core values that its business leaders have and that they transmit to other members of the business team. Ultimately, we bring these norms back into the workplace as well.

Professor Jenny Chapman, a colleague from the Haas business school at University of California, Berkeley, has looked at how these cultural values impact business. One of the things that she has found is that when people come into organizations that have strong cultural norms, they find out very quickly, usually within six months, whether they as individuals can fit into that culture. If their personal attitudes are at great variance from those of the community they are attempting to join, they usually leave. This is a good example of a constrained community shaping people's behaviors. While this chapter looks at communities outside of work, we'll return to this theme when we go back to the office in Chapter 3.

Let's talk about social norms for a minute. Social norms are expectations about acceptable and unacceptable attitudes and behaviors. In general, acceptable attitudes and behaviors seem to arise spontaneously in communities (they don't really, but the way they're transmitted to us as members of the community are so subtle that we're not even aware that it's happening). However, sometimes groups within or outside of a community will make such a concerted effort to alter the community's norms that we become conscious of the development of the new norms (or of our resistance to them). The movement to inculcate politically correct values into communities in the 1990s is only the most recent example of a conscious effort to force change in community values.

Norms are socially created standards that help us interpret and evaluate each other's behavior. So when a force like technology changes communities, we can predict that community norms may also change. Communities then become both affected by and agents of change. If community structures are the engine of transformation, then it helps to understand the role communities play in people's lives. What is it about communities that people are attracted to, that can be harnessed to help promote social and commercial development? For an answer to that, I turned to John Gardner, former secretary of education. Gardner identified 10 key characteristics of community:

1. *A forward view.*   Communities give us the norms we use to predict what will happen next. In business organizations, this sense of a forward view is what gives us a feeling of stability. When everything else is chaotic and seems to be falling apart around us, it's very important to have an anchor. In the Internet world, this is critically important. Technologies, business models, and entire enterprises are born, grow, and die almost overnight. We need community to let us know where things are going so that we feel as though we've got at least one foot on something solid.

2. *Reasonable base of shared values.*   Communities help us sift out good from bad, desirable from undesirable, admirable from contemptible. They help us evaluate the world around us in some kind of consistent way. It's hard to work around people who don't share the same values you do. Again, shared values become the source of a deep sense of community. It used to be that you went to work and, over a period of time, discovered the shared values of that company. In the Internet world, however, I find it's becoming a much more explicit process to determine what those shared values are. In the case of one start-up I worked with, called "work.com," one of the key points in any conversation with prospective members of the founding team was a statement of the core values of the group. This discussion of core values became a way to test whether people would fit well within the group. It was a "no harm, no foul" way of quickly sorting out people who shared the same values. Work.com has four key shared values:

   - Make money.
   - Have fun.
   - Continue to learn.
   - Don't deal with assholes.

3. *Wholeness incorporating diversity.*   Communities guide us to an
    acceptable range of diversity (which may differ in different commu-
    nities). Community diversity goes far beyond the racial, religious,
    and sexual differences that the word *diversity* typically means. In
    addition, it includes such things as *economic diversity* (the ratio of
    wealth to poverty we're going to be comfortable with in our com-
    munity), *diversity of political orientation* (the range of political
    views we will find acceptable in our community), and *educational
    diversity* (our willingness to accept all educational levels from
    college-educated professionals to high-school dropouts to Ph.D.'s).

Diversity of ideas, opinions, and approaches is a strong point for any healthy
organization. Again, in our new world of work these diversity issues become
a source of strength because they require creativity. The ability for a work
group and a community to reconcile differences into a unified approach to
the problem at hand is a key element in developing a process of continuous
improvement. I believe that successful businesses in the Internet age will
deliberately seek out and attract diversity as a way of building a creative
process.

4. *Caring, trust, and teamwork.*   Communities define acceptable lev-
    els of care, trust, and teamwork that we expect to show others and
    have shown to us. It's the stereotype of many suburban communities
    that its members hardly know each other at all. In contrast, the
    stereotype many of us associate with rural communities is that its
    members are far more interdependent than are people in cities or
    suburbs. These are both examples of the values a community
    teaches us to hold about the ways in which caring, trust, and team-
    work are supposed to be played out in our group.

Without caring, trust, and teamwork, no organization can last for long. As
the distinction between our work communities and our larger social communities blurs, we have to depend more and more on having trusting relationships with our workmates and know they care about our welfare. It
simply becomes intolerable to work with people who don't care about you
at a personal level and whom you cannot trust. Our old friend Dilbert and
his teammates personify this stifling work environment. Without these
most human of qualities in our work communities, our workplace becomes
injurious to our physical, mental, and spiritual health. I believe that the
destruction of caring and trusting work environments is really the root
cause of people's dissatisfaction with the "old way of doing work."

5. *Effective internal communication.*   Communities give us guidelines for how we're going to share information among other members of the community. In many urban communities in the earlier
years of this century, the front stoop was the primary location for
the sharing of information. Today, circulars and phone messages
may be the medium of choice, and someone on your front porch (if
you even have one) would be a threat more than a welcome source
of communication for your community.

Effective communication lies at the heart of any community. From the old
Indian rituals of the talking stick and the council to the modern-day work
world of open meetings and efforts of leaders to build collaboration, we see
communication lying at the heart of the development of a sense of community. We can take things we've learned about community as we've grown
up, joined organizations, and experienced that sense of belonging and
translate them back into our work environments. We need more talking over
the back fence, sitting on our front porches, and going to the barber shop on
Saturday mornings in the workplace of the future.

6. *Participation.*   Communities develop and disseminate guidelines
for the level and variety of participation expected of each of its
members. People have to participate in the social part of work life in
order for community to emerge. It's been my experience that in the
Internet world, especially with the younger generation of workers,
participation sometimes get so intense that we have to take breaks
from it to keep from being overwhelmed. But again, leaders of these
new organizations need to be very explicit about what level of participation is required to be a member of this new community.

When you see an organization in which some people refuse to go to meetings and stay in their offices or cubicles, you know you've got a problem.
Deliberate withdrawal and lack of participation in the social life of the workplace is one of the early indications of organizational dysfunction. I once
worked in organization where one of the key technical members on the work
team literally used boxes to build a barrier in his doorway so people couldn't
come in; he physically separated himself from the rest of the work group.
This person's lack of participation in the community life of the work group
eventually became a catalyst for group dysfunction. This person's behavior
was as much a result of a larger sense of alienation in the entire company as
it was a reflection of his own personal behavior. Unfortunately, the leaders
of this work group didn't have the tools or the support of management to

take a step back and examine what was really going on. They simply blamed the abnormal behavior on *him,* not on the organization.

7. *Affirmation.*   Communities help us all affirm for ourselves that we belong, and that by belonging, we demonstrate our individual as well as our social worth. Affirmation really means identity. Affirming your membership in a community gives you identity. It makes you somebody. It makes you part of something larger than yourself. And it's a very satisfying feeling. One of the trends we see here in California among high-tech companies is what I call the "hat and shirt" syndrome. You have to have a baseball cap with the company or team logo on it, and most certainly you have to have a polo shirt imprinted with the company logo and Web address. Without these items you don't have a company—that is, you don't have an identity. These quiet affirmations mean something to people, and we need to look behind the behavior and examine why it's taking place. It's taking place because people like to be affirmed in their identity. These workplace communities form core parts of our personality. How many people wear baseball caps or polo shirts that identify the physical community in which their homes are located?

8. *Links beyond the community.*   Communities typically tell us acceptable ways to interact with other communities or with people outside the community. Today's work community usually defines links outside of its boundaries first to professions, then to business partners, and finally to customers. The norms of behavior for interaction with these other interrelated communities are usually defined in terms of events. There are conferences to go to, committees to work on, and networking that needs to be done with your peers. Strategic alliances bring together people from slightly different communities to work on common problems, usually regarding sales and customer support for mutual customers. Our interaction beyond our own business community, with our customers, becomes defined in terms of customer service, marketing support, and providing (the latest buzzword) "total business solutions." The social function that these links provide often goes without recognition or discussion, although the seemingly routine activities of business are in fact providing us with the social good of helping us connect to something larger than our immediate community. It is similar in flavor to the annual summer fair of yore, where people from surrounding communities would get together to celebrate, share stories and experiences, and simply connect with one another.

9.   *Development of young people.*   Perhaps one of the strongest roles that communities have played over time is in setting the standards for both how we raise our children and how those children are expected to interact with each other and with adults as they develop. The social and technological changes impacting traditional communities today will perhaps affect the role of community in young people's development more than it will affect anything else.

I keep returning to this theme of how old learning is such a key part of the new world of work. Our formal education ends at some point in our life, and we enter the workforce. Our development doesn't stop there, or if it does, we become stifled, out of date, and out of touch. Developing our talent base in our new work organizations is a key task of executives. We call it *mentoring, career development,* or some other such phrase, but what's really going on is the development of talent. Seeing that the younger members of the work group have an opportunity for key growth experiences, rotational job assignments, and exposure to increasing levels of responsibility is all part and parcel of sustaining a healthy organization, just as it is a key part of sustaining a healthy social community. I would go so far as to say that the abdication of these developmental responsibilities by families, local communities, and schools has created a situation in which we begin to see some rather bizarre behavior by young people that shocks us beyond all comprehension. More and more young people enter the workforce lacking key developmental experiences, and consequently, their work group must take over where the rest of society has left off.

Probably many of you reading this book have found that much of what you learned early about social life in a community (perhaps during your military life or college years) had a more profound effect on the rest of your life than the skills and technical things you learned. As we enter this new world of work, more and more leaders are beginning to recognize that the developmental aspects of our new work communities can no longer be taken for granted and that this socializing ability must be built into and around everything else we do in the workplace. This means that our workplace leaders have to take on the new roles of coaches, mentors, and teachers.

10.   *Institutional arrangements for community maintenance.*   Finally, communities, like all organizations, contain guidelines and norms for self-maintenance. The activities to maintain the community in the face of change are key among these.

I used these community characteristics in a study of the attitudes of the emerging workforce to determine which community aspects were those

most valued by our new Internet-enabled workers. What I found is that people are increasingly attracted to communities where an emphasis is placed
on teamwork, recognition, communication, and conflict resolution. This
preference is particularly true for people who have come into their majority recently, that is, people whose adult experience embraces Strauss and
Howe's third era. You'll recall from Chapter 1 that the third era is called *the
unraveling,* and it covers the time when institutions become weak, individuals become strong, the civic order begins to decay, and we can see a new
value system coming into existence.

Those very qualities of social life that work against alienation and help
to form a sense of identity through civil interaction may be attracting the
children of the third era back into communities today. Interestingly, this
change seems to be reversing the decades-old migration toward the isolated, gated communities so many of us associate with suburban life. As a
result of the new attraction for belonging, the fear of urban living that drove
so much of that migration appears to be giving way to a new enthusiasm for
living in areas that permit vigorous social interaction. Although this may
sound all well and good, how does it relate to the business manager? It's
fairly obvious how the concept of community relates to effectiveness in the
workplace in the context of a start-up organization, where the culture in
community is created from scratch. But it is probably a bit more difficult to
apply for those who are in a more typical situation of working in an existing organization, perhaps with an extremely long history.

What is important to understand about community is that it exists, that
people derive a certain satisfaction from participating in its social milieu,
and that in fact it's a basic human need. So a workplace that doesn't explic-
itly promote community, as defined in the 10 dimensions that John Gardner talked about, can be expected to be a place in which people don't find
a great degree of satisfaction working. So what? Well, I think it's fairly evident both in our everyday experience and in the academic world of research
that there's a relationship between people's job satisfaction, their performance, and, ultimately, the satisfaction of the customers they serve.

I firmly believe that leaders who spend a great deal of time and attention fostering community benefit the bottom line of their organizations.
As we've seen with the shift in generational attitudes, the new, highly talented younger workforce (at least in United States and industrialized
Europe) won't work in places where they don't gather a sense of community. It's a business necessity as great as competitive compensation systems, safe and healthy work environments, and equitable treatment by
management. Community is just another element in the equation. Later

on in this chapter, and then again in more detail in the following chapters, I'll discuss a concept called *soft work*. Soft work, as you'll see, is as much a design perspective for the office as it is a social movement to build larger communities.

WHY ARE WE INTERESTED?

The theories that we have about how groups operate and how people interact with one another have been built up largely over the past 150 years by looking at the behavior of people in face-to-face settings. We need an analytic framework to learn about social behavior in the Internet age. We've only begun, within the past 20 years, to look at how computer-mediated communication creates, or maybe even causes, different sets of behaviors among people.

We don't understand a lot of what's going on in the development of our communities right now as people begin to use computers and the Internet to communicate with one another instead of using face-to-face communication or telephones. We do know from a study of history that the introduction of the telephone into industrial society radically changed a number of our behaviors, our attitudes about one another, and, ultimately, our beliefs about other communities.

As we see the Internet becoming the central communications medium that we use, not only in the business world but also in our private lives, we need to grasp a better understanding of how this medium impacts us. For if the urge toward social exchange and civil interaction I discovered in my research is going to be played out on a stage that connects us through technology rather than face-to-face, the meaning of community is obviously going to be transformed.

We are also interested in looking at communities (and their underlying social structure) because communities are where new social norms are constructed, particularly norms that support creative activity. Learning how to be creative, both as an individual and in group settings, is going to be one of the drivers of business and society in the twenty-first century.

I'm sure you have heard it said, "Innovate or die." It's not so much knowledge management that will differentiate successful businesses from those that fail; rather, the process of actually creating knowledge becomes the key area for becoming unique in a constantly changing marketplace. And this creativity will also be critical to our ability to preserve a sense of community in an increasingly computer-mediated world.

Supporting creative activities requires social norms that encourage and reinforce three central things:

- A tolerance for change
- Support for risk taking
- An attitude that mistakes are OK

In the short history of the Internet world, which is barely a decade old, there are a number of examples of companies that practice the use of central social norms, and this has contributed to their success.

In my mind, the classic example of a company practicing these new social norms has been Netscape, which was recently acquired by America Online. Netscape's entire life, when you look at it in retrospect, was characterized by a tolerance for change, support for risk taking, and an attitude that mistakes were OK. Netscape changed its business model and value-added proposition almost annually over a five-year period. To many analysts external to the company and not yet familiar with the dynamics of the Internet, this was seen as absolutely insane—it looked as if leadership had no control whatsoever. However, what was really going on with Netscape was that it had developed a hypersensitivity to the changing needs of its customer base as customers became more familiar with Internet technologies. The company had to change rapidly to remain a market leader, or else it was dead. Not only did Netscape have a culture that tolerated change, but it had a culture that encouraged change at a very basic level. When its business model changed, Netscape had to change its organization; and product development, sales, and marketing were all reorganized every time the business model shifted. But that was OK because change was the norm.

Netscape also took enormous risks. Once its market valuation began to increase, the company would use the increase in cash and stock to go on an acquisition spree. Netscape was buying whole businesses and risking literally tens of millions of dollars a time that it was making acquisitions that would add critical new functionality to its existing product platform. Some of these worked and were easily integrated into their browsers, and some didn't. Corporate decision makers supported risk in the form of acquisitions and mergers because they didn't have time to create the new technology themselves. Risky business indeed!

Obviously, members of the board of directors supported this policy. They realized that they would make some mistakes but that the overall payoff was great enough to tolerate these mistakes. One acquisition that may still appear to be a mistake was that of Collabra, which was aimed at adding functionality to Netscape's browser to help users collaborate with one another on the Web. Although the software in its functionality was embedded in the last versions of Netscape's platform, it was never really exploited to the extent that it could have been. I do believe the final chapter has not been written in this risk-taking story of Netscape. We will have to wait and see whether America Online's tolerance for change through growth in acquisition and support of risk taking will pay off as these two giants of the Internet age become one.

Without doubt, the pace of change in the new world of work being brought to us by the Internet is increasing. Not only are things going faster, but they are accelerating at a geometric rate. The only way to keep up is to increase our pace of learning—learning and being creative. Learning how to be creative allows us to improvise in situations that are unfamiliar. To me, each day in the new world of work brings unfamiliar situations and challenges. It becomes more important that I know how to learn, how to develop new skills, and how to construct novel solutions to new problems; this is more important than the absolute explicit knowledge that I have when I wake up in the morning and face the new day.

Creativity and community go hand in hand. As I've said earlier, I believe that the diversity we have in our work communities is directly related to our ability to be creative. Creativity in large part grows out of our ability to reconcile ideas—that is, to bring them together in the framework of a greater context.

Let me give you an example of how I think this operates in the everyday work world. Typically, I'm presented with situations in which clients ask me for solutions to their business problems. Usually, these questions arise after people have failed in their own internal efforts to develop creative solutions to novel situations. What they are really doing is reaching out to me and asking me to join their community, to bring my ideas and perspectives into their community in a hope that the diversity of approaches they're creating by inviting me in will lead to the development of the solution they can't see.

Often hidden in this process are the actions I take to increase the diversity of thoughts, ideas, and perspectives that I bring to the table in this creative process. Before I even enter a situation, I make a deliberate attempt to increase the depth of thinking that I can focus on that particular situation. I reach out to consult with people in my community, my friends, my colleagues, and members of my social network. I do this by asking questions, reading other people's research, and seeking different opinions. This expands the social network and, consequently, the community of people who are now directly or indirectly involved in creating a solution to the problem.

One of the measures of creative ability, in my opinion, is the extent to which any person can reach out into their own social network and gather in new, novel, and distinctly different ideas. This is where we all must display a certain degree of humility and realize that we don't always have the right answer, but that we need to engage in a community interaction process that allows us to bring together those parts and pieces that we need. Only then can we reconcile those differences in the service of finding solutions.

WHAT SOCIAL FUNCTION DO COMMUNITIES SERVE?
Communities help us answer these questions:

- Who am I?
- What am I a part of?
- What connects me to the rest of the world?
- What relationships matter to me in the world?

Four social functions describe the way communities help us answer these questions for ourselves:

1. By providing a sense of *identification,* communities help us answer the question, "Who am I?" Identification, the first source of social confidence we get from communities, is perhaps the key social value they provide.

2. By providing evidence of our *unity* with other people, values, and norms, communities help us answer the question, "What am I a part of?" You can think of this as the flip side of identity: your individual identity takes on greater meaning within the context of the group that you belong to, so in feeling unified with the group, you not only get a sense of belonging, but you also get a stronger sense of yourself.

3. By giving us avenues for *involvement,* communities answer the question, "What connects me to the rest of the world?" To what degree are you in contact with other people in your community? Are you largely isolated from them, connected to just a few, or connected to a large number of others in your community? We all know people who are intimately involved with a large number of people and communities. They are always busy going to this meeting and that function and talking to this person and that person. We also know people who are largely isolated from others and seem to gain as much from solitary activity as from participating in groups.

4.   By showing us clear signs of our *relatedness* to people like ourselves, communities help us answer the question, "What relationships matter to me in the world?" Being connected to people still isn't quite enough. There has to be some feeling of reciprocity— that is, a network of mutual understandings, obligations, and expectations of behavior on the part of others. You achieve a sense of wholeness by being part of a community. Being related to members of your community says that you recognize mutual commitments and obligations to each other. You know you can rely on your community for support, guidance, and help. You feel good that you, as a member of that community, have a corresponding set of obligations to support, guide, and help others in your community, too.

The point here is that the communities we build around ourselves, beginning in the workplace and extending into the other parts of our social lives, answer these four basic questions that all humans have. The breakdown of more-traditional communities and the fragmentation of society in general makes it more important every day that we have a place to gain a sense of community. And that places more and more emphasis on our work life as our work life blurs into the rest of our world.

This may sound like basic social science and something better left to a college course, but I believe it to be a central issue that the business leaders of the future will have to solve. Business leaders will have to solve this because it's not being addressed elsewhere. Every day, with the increased ability of the Internet to connect us to a much larger world, our communities give us identity and become a way for us to relate to one another.

Let me give you a very practical example of how I think all this community behavior is going to work itself out in our new world of work in regard to identification, unity, involvement, and relatedness. By some estimates, the Internet job market will reach a level of $30 billion in total salaries by the year 2005. The Internet job market identifies you as somebody who is looking for work, what profession you belong to, what level of activity and experience you have, and your personal references to other people in that same job market. Now simply take out the words *job* and *market* and substitute the words *identity* and *community,* and I think you can see why it's important to understand the underlying social process involved in using the Internet to advertise yourself, to seek employment, and, ultimately, to conduct work with your workmates over the Internet.

While many firms are beginning to move into this large emerging market, I think the ones that will be successful, ultimately, will be the ones that consciously and deliberately build their systems and processes around fostering community among the clients that they serve. As we go to press, there's one company that bears watching, and I would encourage you to follow its progress. That company is Gig2Gig.com.

ISSUES THAT COMMUNITIES RESOLVE

Communities are not static. They have a rhythm, a pace, and a dynamic in the interaction among their members. In this sense, communities, as social structures, deal with a number of issues that arise out of the interaction of their members. These issues include the following:

1.   Conflict among members
2.   Maintenance of boundaries between groups
3.   Creation of new communities
4.   Definition of status and roles

Let's look at each of these dynamic aspects of community in turn.

Conflict is a fact of social life. It arises from differences in beliefs and attitudes. Any community that continues to exist over time must develop mechanisms to resolve conflict among its members. In the social and political world, these conflicts are usually resolved through debate and argument at an individual level and through the judicial system at the societal level. Communities provide us with norms for resolving conflict.

As we move into an increasingly computer-mediated age, we need to decide how conflicts get resolved in electronic communities, or communities that have a lot of interaction which is mediated by computer technology—this is a central issue we must look at as we integrate these technologies more and more into our community and work lives.

What we need is an explicit agreement among community members regarding what process will be used to resolve conflict. Then communities must develop the community "mediator" as an approved social role, much as community ombudsmen act as approved political liaisons in some communities today.

In the Internet world, this mediation task usually falls to the person who establishes the bulletin board or sets up the chat room or generally functions as the cybercommunity organizer. Whether the system administrator is the best choice for complex electronic community mediation work is open to question.

Maintaining and delineating the boundaries between communities is another important dynamic function. Most of us are members of a number of communities at the same time. There's the community of family, the community of workmates, the community of those who share our spiritual beliefs, and probably a community of some special interest that we share with people outside of these other groups.

How do we know who's in and who's out in these different communities? How do we move smoothly from one community to another, while respecting the boundaries of each? The answers to these questions have to arise out of the interaction of community members. We have a number of social rituals that we use to establish boundaries in traditional communities. In college, there's the hazing ritual; in the armed forces, there's basic training; in most religions, there's a ceremony of commitment. Social clubs hold meetings that demonstrate visibly who's in (the members), and who's out (everyone else). Art galleries maintain their boundaries by selecting whose work they buy (*in*) and whose they don't (*out*). And so forth.

In the cyberworld, boundaries are easily maintained by denying access to people through the use of passwords and accounts. Such boundaries are easily maintained because the technology allows us to exclude people as an administrative function. But this is boundary maintenance at only the grossest level, analogous to the admission procedures that determine who gets accepted at a university and who doesn't. As we all know, groups with powerful boundaries quickly form among the accepted. How do we manage the boundaries between similar groups online?

Again, the control of this boundary-maintenance function usually falls to a person who monitors the interaction of the community members and takes on the responsibility for maintaining these boundaries. I find it interesting to note that in some cases, passing information back and forth across the boundaries deliberately weakens these boundaries. I believe that the most particular, and interesting, aspect of community boundary maintenance in our Internet world is that most preexisting political boundaries (which usually define communities at large) are becoming very permeable, transparent, and in some cases, disappearing altogether. As we scale up the workplace from small, geographically based physical locations to a global economy, I believe that there are very important implications in the political arena arising out of the disappearance of historical community boundaries throughout the world.

Creating new communities is another way we redefine the idea of boundaries in cyberspace. Let me return to the business world for a minute to explain. Think about what the creation of a new business enterprise really is: the creation of the new social structure, a new community. And with it comes the creation of the rules, norms, and culture that surround development of any community. Here in Silicon Valley, we are used to this experience. The formation of start-ups, often new communities spun off from existing ones, is a fact of life. As these new companies are created, or spawned, there's a community development process that comes into play during even the earliest stages. A couple of examples quickly come to mind. These start-ups usually begin in a basement, a garage, or in someone's home. By starting a community in this way, you immediately pass on to new members the home environment and the set of symbols, rituals, and ways of doing things that are taken directly from the experience of the founding members.

In one case, I'll call it Excitable Software Inc., the founders began the business in a house that was undergoing renovation. This gave the entire enterprise a flavor of confusing, simultaneous activities conducted in the middle of a very incomplete and difficult environment. The confusion of trying to build a business in the middle of a physical space that was itself under construction finally began to show itself in the team's inability to focus on one product, one market, and one unified approach to business development. A point came when the board of directors (who met on a regular basis with the founders in this home) finally demanded that the business be moved to a "regular office" to establish some sort of order to the venture.

The community of Excitable Software Inc. never gelled. Underlying disagreements about the core values of the work group were submerged every time they started to surface. Although it's not unusual for start-ups to be maniacally focused on getting their first product to market, the fact that no time was spent on developing personal friendships and openly discussing differences in business perspective eventually proved disastrous to this fledgling company. If you reflect on the basic functions that communities serve and the issues that they can resolve, you've got a pretty good checklist of what went wrong with Excitable Software Inc.

When I later returned to interview members of the start-up team after the company's demise, they all reported feeling that they "never belonged" and "never really felt connected" with the leadership and the investors of the effort. Clearly, this was a case of failed community. The chaos in which the community was launched simply didn't go away when it moved to a different physical space. The new space remained cluttered and disorganized, which I believe was a direct reflection of the norms and rituals that the community began with. Unfortunately, in this case the leader proved not to be strong enough to break the pattern and form a successful business venture.

The bottom line is that the initial investors, to the tune of over $300,000, lost their investment because of their inability to form a community around firmly held beliefs and focus on the goals of the group.

In another case, which I will call MellowWare Inc., the venture also began in the home of the founder. In this case, the physical space and atmosphere that surrounded the venture was a combination living room and den. All of the pictures, knickknacks, and furniture reflected the personality and lifestyle of the founder. Things were orderly, neat, subdued in color, and very comfortable. This venture has been successful. It has moved out of the home and into a regular office environment, and it has grown. MellowWare Inc. has raised significant venture capital and is well on its way to being a very successful start-up business.

In contrasting these examples, I find it interesting that the quality of the leadership was directly reflected in how the community development process occurred. In the case of MellowWare, potential candidates for membership were invited to the home environment for interviews and conversations. It was quite clear that a number of these people found themselves uncomfortable in this relaxed environment and really needed something that was much more structured and formal. These people simply didn't fit the community that was being built. The core values of the leader and his new company were more familial, open, relaxed, and respecting of informal interaction. People looking for more structured and traditional work environments found themselves uncomfortable in this atmosphere and either left very quickly or were not asked to join the new venture.

The founders usually bring their own central cultural values to the group. The company itself (this new community) becomes a reflection of the core values and beliefs of the people who created it. As new members are recruited into the start-up, one of the first tests that they face is a matchup of their values with those of the founding team. Implicit rules of "how we do things around here" become explicit very quickly, and people who have been invited into the new group and who find they don't agree with these norms of behavior are quickly excluded from the group.

Good leaders of start-ups have an uncanny knack of knowing who's going to fit and who's not going to fit. In many cases, the failure of the start-up can be traced directly to the lack of solid community formation during its early stages. In the case of MellowWare, several people who joined during the first six months were gone within 90 days. Key engineering and marketing talent came in, went through a quick socialization process, and then parted when they realized that they didn't fit. What I found interesting in the situation was a very open and explicit tolerance of this process among the executives and other members of the team. It was quite simply OK: no blaming of individuals for perceived shortfalls on their part, no criticism of different perspectives or regrets for having asked these people to join the team in the first place. The attitude was, "We tried it and it didn't quite work out for them and we all have to get on with our lives." These open, accepting attitudes were healthy for everyone. That kind of community spirit became a defining characteristic of MellowWare.

One reason that people who don't "fit" are so quickly excluded is that communities maintain and define people's status and social roles. Even in a world of shared values, status and roles are often changing, and this is especially true in start-ups. As teams come together for specific project focus, new roles emerge and the status that we had with another team does not necessarily carry over to the new community. So it's imperative for the community's ability to survive in a changing world that its members share some core values.

If you are a member of several different communities, you are going to have a number of social roles. Your status in each may differ. These kinds of role conflicts and status differences can create personal issues for many people, especially if they're not consciously aware of the different roles that people play in different circles. You can simultaneously be the leader of one group and a follower in another group. In the new world of work we are entering, we will occupy numerous roles at the same time and, in fact, may even be forced to switch roles on an hourly basis. This requires a deeper understanding and appreciation of what social role and status means in the context of interacting with our fellow community members.

In short, we need to always be conscious of which community we are interacting with at a given moment in time and what our specific social role and status are within that group. Being clear about these issues lets us operate in a more fluid fashion within our communities. As a result, we experience less negative stress and confusion as individuals, too.

SOCIAL NETWORKS

Our social networks are our communities. The tactical description of our social networks gives us a measure of community. Looking at the structure our social networks makes it possible to take the somewhat obtuse and fuzzy concept of community and turn it in the something we can analyze, quantify, and measure. Our social networks are expanding every day with the use of the Internet. Increasingly, we become more connected to people with whom we never would have had an opportunity to connect before the advent of this technology. Our community expands.

Therefore, it's important for us to look at what we know about computer-supported social networks. There's a rich tradition in the research world of looking at social networks. I first began my study of this topic over 20 years ago with a simple curiosity about the impact of an individual's friendships upon his or her interactions with a spouse. In those early research projects, I found that there was a direct relation between our friends and how we interact with them and the quality of the relationship we experience with those closest to us.

Translating that into a business context, I would say that the people who belong to our social network have a direct impact on the way that we relate to our superiors or peers or those who work under our direction. That's a pretty powerful statement. It means that if we can understand what impact these social networks (our community) have on how we interact with one another in the workplace, we give ourselves another tool to increase our creativity, effectiveness, and satisfaction with our jobs and our work life.

There's a very simple equation that explains this relationship: community = social network = work effectiveness. I talked earlier about the relationship of our community to our creative ability, and this is reflected in our social network structure. Creative people have the ability to reach out and bring novel ideas together in ways that nobody else can. The size and relatedness of our social network is directly related to our creative ability in the Internet world of work. The pace of changes is so quick that we do not have the time to individually create solutions to rapidly changing problems. We need to learn to reach out and rely on others to help us in that process. Some would call this teamwork; others would call it networking; but I prefer to see it is a process of conscious community development.

If we want to get better at being creative in the workplace, and if we want to get better at effectively managing the relationships among members of our work team, then we need to consciously understand how the structure and function of our social networks impacts those things. Further, we need to develop a very good understanding of how computer-mediated communication overlies this entire community development process. For a deeper understanding of that, we can turn to the research work on social networks. As Barry Wellman suggests,

> When computer networks link people as well as machines, they become social networks. . . . The nature of the medium both constrains and facilitates social control. Computer Supported Social Networks have strong societal implications, fostering situations that combine global connectivity, the fragmentation of solidarities, the de-emphasis of local organiza-

tions (in the neighborhood and workplace), and the increased importance
of home bases.[2]

Wellman's thinking is what prompted me to seriously look at the concept of
the social network as a *metaphor* for community—and more specifically,
for the communities we are creating in our new workplaces. Social networks are relatively persistent patterns of interaction among members of
unique communities in space. However, in the world of cyberspace, concepts of time in space seem to change and take on different qualities. So we
are faced with a challenge if we are to use social networks (conceptually)
as a way to study community and as a vehicle to develop some design
implications for computer-mediated communication patterns.

Social networks have been used as a field of study for decades to look at
the impact of communications patterns on a number of variables such as the
psychology of people involved, the spread of innovations among groups, and
the impact on health issues of having a solid social support group around you.
Therefore, I think that the concept of social networks can certainly help us
examine the impact of all kinds of things on how people communicate with
one another in new environments like the communities we're creating online.
We've seen that online communities don't look like traditional communities.
We've seen that online communities have to use different processes than traditional communities to achieve community goals. And we've seen that these
goals don't just include the stated goals of a community. They also include
the goals of fulfilling people's need for identity, relatedness, and stability.

Two questions we have to answer if we're to achieve these goals in
online communities are as follows:

1.   How do we provide *structure* across time and space?
2.   Which tools facilitate key social interaction *processes?*

There are certainly other subsidiary issues: How is socialization conducted? How do we agree on the meaning of symbols that can be shared?
How do we expel members of the community when required? The answers
to many of these questions are beyond the scope of this book, but you need
to be aware of them and keep seeking answers.

For our purposes here, I would like to confine my analysis to looking at
just interaction and identity as functions of social networks. Within that
bounded space, we can look at several structural aspects of social networks

---

[2] Barry Wellman, J. Sataff, D. Dimitmva, L. Garton, M. Gulla, C. Haythornthwaite, "Computer Networks as Social Networks: Collaborative Work, Telework, and Virtual Community," *Annual Review of Sociology,* vol. 22, 1996, pp. 213–238.

and see how these qualities, or dimensions, are directly related to maintenance of interaction and forming of identity, keys to the success of communities online.

Table 3-1 shows the most common dimensions of social networks, or community, the implication of how difficult it will be to sustain community for that dimension, and the online capability that will let that dimension be realized in new community forms.

TABLE 3-1   Community on the Internet.

Dimension	Implication	Online Capability
Size	*Interaction:* The more members in a community, the greater the possible interactions, but also the greater the difficulty for any individual member to find the interactions he or she wants.	Bulletin boards, chat rooms
Frequency	*Interaction:* The more the community norm is for frequent interaction, the greater the chance for satisfaction, but also the more important it becomes for each member to find the other members who are most compatible with him or her.	Bulletin boards, chat rooms, instant messages (IMs)
Intersection of nets	*Interaction, identity, boundary maintenance:* The more the community interacts with other communities, the greater the chance for a richer individual experience, but also the greater the chance that one or more of the communities will not be compatible for a given member.	Links to URLs, IMs, personal Web pages
Density	*Identity:* The deeper and more reciprocal your relations with other members in your community, the greater the sense of identity, but also the more difficult it might be to expand beyond the community to form new bonds.	Chat rooms, IMs, pictures, quick-time movies

Density refers to how tightly connected to the other members of a network you are. There are different types of density in networks, but in all cases, the more dense a network, the greater the impact it will have on you. If you are tightly connected to all members and there are a majority of reciprocal relations, the power of the network to influence your behavior is greater.

The density of your social network is the prime influence on the development of your identity within the network. Increasing the density of your social network gives you a greater sense of uniqueness and identity and leads to greater satisfaction in your interactions with others in your group. In terms of its application to work, this suggests that a dense social network at work will increase the quality of your work life and your job satisfaction. I use this principle in the everyday management in my own company. I strive consistently to promote the inner connections and reciprocity among all of my team members. I do this in an effort to promote their sense of identity as individuals by stressing the unique contribution each makes to the group. I also focus on enhancing their sense of being a part of something larger than themselves to give them a feeling of belonging. We have individual Web pages, pictures of team members with biographies they provide, chat rooms (we're rarely together physically), and all kinds of informal activities that occur on our Web site and elsewhere on the Internet. This means that as we are working in the distributed workplace, we have to make sure that we allot sufficient time to interact with one another in a face-to-face fashion. It's through this face-to-face interaction that we develop the bedrock quality of our community—*trust*.

I believe the challenge of all of this is to take the metaphor of social networks and use it to model new structures that reach across time and space for the community. The idea of the social network also gives us strategies for promoting positive patterns of interaction. I don't believe that the technology to do this effectively exists today, although we're getting there. So this discussion of community and social network may be taken in part as a challenge to the technology community to create the tools that we all need to work together in the future.

CASE STUDY: COMMUNITIES OF COMMERCE^{sm}

INTRODUCTION

In February of 1998, CommerceNet proposed and initiated an economic development project targeted at increasing electronic commerce activity among small and medium-size enterprises (SMEs) in Southern California. The year-long project was funded in part by the California State Trade and

Commerce Administration, Office of Strategic Technology, and by CommerceNet, an international consortium providing research, advocacy, collaboration, and business development opportunities to members interested in keeping abreast of and directly influencing the growth of global electronic commerce. CommerceNet managed the project in association with the Institute for the Study of Distributed Work (ISDW). This case study documents the project from its inception and represents the scope, objectives, processes, methods, key findings, and lessons learned from this pilot initiative.

PROJECT CONCEPT: LEVERAGE E-COMMERCE TECHNOLOGIES TO GROW SMALL BUSINESSES

The Communities of Commerce initiative was designed by CommerceNet as a pilot economic development project focused on small and medium-size enterprises in the greater Los Angeles area. Southern California was the target for the area's rich resources and projected job growth because of an apparent lag in electronic business activity compared to other regions in California. The purpose of the project was to help small businesses grow their operations by leveraging the Internet and electronic commerce technologies. The project plan was built around a business network model and the creation of a "community" of small to medium-size enterprises with similar or complementary e-commerce business needs.

THE GOALS: CREATE E-COMMERCE BUSINESS DEVELOPMENT METHODOLOGIES FOR SMES

A key objective of the Communities of Commerce project was to create e-commerce business development methods and to observe, test, and learn as the evolving methodology was applied to a series of small and medium-size enterprises working in complementary markets. Ultimately, the goal was to expand the use of Internet-based electronic commerce for business-to-business and business-to-consumer relationships among those small to medium-size Southern California organizations. Specifically, the Communities of Commerce project was designed to do the following:

• Help participating small businesses learn about and leverage e-commerce technologies to grow their operations (specifically, to improve business processes, increase revenue, create new jobs, etc.)

• Develop and document e-commerce business development processes and methods tailored to small and medium-size enterprises that are transferable and can be replicated in other geographic areas

- Facilitate the creation and growth of an electronic small-business network that will continue to thrive beyond the life of the project and allow community members to share resources, develop strategic alliances, enter joint marketing relationships, and leverage themselves for increased business, both foreign and domestic
- Learn from and improve upon project experiences so that lessons learned and best practices may be applied to future e-commerce development initiatives

EARLY FRAMEWORK: INTERNET COMMUNITIES

In the early planning stages, the Communities of Commerce project members worked to define a conceptual model that would guide the direction of the year-long initiative. The initial framework used for discussion purposes during these first phases was based on the creation of common communities of businesses that share a variety of similar objectives and needs. These communities would use the Internet as the basic medium for conducting a wide range of business activities. This model brings together members of vertically aligned industry segments that have a number of common and complementary business processes. Even though these processes will often be independent, the assumption is that many of the processes can be provided in common, and even integrated to offer a greater degree of value and synergy, thereby creating new service levels and business opportunities. (See Figure 3-1.)

FIGURE 3-1   Early conceptual model for the Communities of Commerce project.

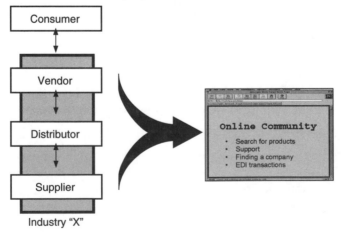

In this vertically aligned e-commerce model, the complementary processes and services from partnering companies within an industry are streamlined and connected via Internet-based transactions (the sharing of inventory status information, electronic bidding and procurement processes, etc.). The original Communities of Commerce project plan was to identify select vertical markets, target and recruit companies within a chosen industry group, identify and integrate the common/complementary processes within the target group, and finally, connect these common processes via Internet technology to support electronic business transactions among the partnering companies.

This e-commerce model was the foundation that drove the industry research and company recruitment/selection processes in the early phases of the project. However, for reasons highlighted here and later in this case study, this framework was revised even further. The identification and successful recruitment of small businesses within the same vertical market, which also met a series of other predetermined selection criteria, proved to be challenging. In sum, the key findings from the industry research and selection process created a conscious shift in the conceptual framework of the project.

THE COMMUNITIES OF COMMERCE MODEL: E-COMMERCE INCUBATORS

Today the Communities of Commerce project model is concentrated on the process of nurturing, developing, and guiding small businesses in preparation to engage in strategic partnerships that will ultimately allow them to conduct all or a portion of their business on the World Wide Web. The Communities of Commerce project model has moved away from a primary focus of integrating and electronically linking vertically aligned businesses. (See Figure 3-2.)

FIGURE 3-2   Current framework for the Communities of Commerce project.

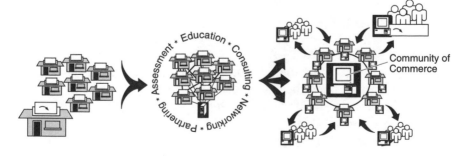

   In this model, what the recruited small to medium-size enterprises (SMEs) have in common are geographic location, organizational readiness, and feasible e-commerce business needs, as well as a commitment and enthusiasm to bring their objectives to fruition. Agreeing to participate in the project means that these companies join a community network of similarly focused businesses. In this business community, alliances are formed with fellow participating companies as well as with CommerceNet consortium members. The project facilitators who provide the means and forum for the participants to engage with one another oversee the community. Integral to guiding these small business to meet their e-commerce and business development needs are programs designed to educate, train, and coach the business representatives to a state of readiness. This developmental process can be likened to a small business "incubator," which prepares the participating companies with knowledge, resources, and guidance to take the preliminary steps necessary to grow their business via the Internet.

PROJECT PLAN AND STRATEGY
The Communities of Commerce project was structured as a multiphase effort (see Figure 3-3). The key elements of the plan include the following:

1. General administrative planning and start-up
2. Industry research/company selection and recruitment
3. Community building/e-commerce education and business consultation for the member companies
4. Connections, alliance building, and partnering within the community network as well as with CommerceNet consortium members interested in participating and contributing time and/or resources
5. Concluding activities, such as formal project evaluations and focus groups to solicit feedback from participants and discuss the future of the community once the project has concluded
6. Wrap-up phase, including any internal administrative activities such as writing summary documents, government reporting, and compiling lessons learned.

PHASE 1: PROJECT START-UP
Planning for the Communities of Commerce project began in February of 1998. This start-up phase began to define the "who, what, when, why, and how" of the project. During February and March, overall project business planning occurred. By April, steps were being taken to determine a general process and a project timeline to follow, as well as to secure the additional people and resources to manage and implement those plans.

FIGURE 3-3   Communities of Commerce project activities and timeline.

Phase	0–1	2	3	4
Month	Feb/March/April	May/June/July/Aug/Sept	Oct/Nov/Dec	Jan/Feb/March
Goals	Project start-up	Research and selection	Education and community building	Connections and wrap-up
Key members	CommerceNet and consultants	Consultants	Consultants and community members	Consultants, community members, CN consortium
Activities	□ Develop business plan □ Hire lead consultant □ Internal design/planning □ Allocate resources □ Goal setting □ Start-up administration	□ Conduct industry research □ Determine selection criteria and measurement □ Target and contact organizations □ Conduct organizational assessments □ Determine final cut □ Host kickoff reception	□ Address training needs (starter kits, business planning sessions, other) □ Conduct individual work-planning sessions □ Recruit CommerceNet consortium participation □ Begin communication program (newsletter, Web site, other) □ Begin informal feedback gathering □ Host community building events	□ Rollout of individual consultation plans □ Facilitate connections with CommerceNet consortium members and other community members □ Formal project evaluation □ Wrap-up event □ Identify lessons learned and next steps

Which Companies Should Participate, and How Do We Find Them?

The key challenge of the project start-up phase was to create a plan to identify and target appropriate industries, markets, and small businesses to participate in the project. At this point, the project planners were following a conceptual framework based on vertically aligned industry segments. Therefore, the most significant accomplishment during this phase was the development and testing of a market and business research process that would be used as the foundation for identifying appropriate vertical markets and, ultimately, potential company participants within those markets. (See Figure 3-4.)

PHASE 2: RESEARCH AND SELECTION

Phase 2 of the project began in May of 1998. A large portion of this phase included the implementation of the research, analysis, and assessment processes designed in Phase 1 in order to identify the industry segments and small businesses suitable for the project. The team initiated recruitment campaigns not only to attract company participants, but also to attract partner participation among CommerceNet consortium members. Phase 2 activities concluded with the project's first community organizing event, a reception for all participating companies to meet and get to know each other.

Industry and Company Selection Methodology

The industry and company selection methodology developed during the start-up phase laid out a framework for collecting data and determining the selection criteria to pick out the most viable market segments from which to recruit small businesses. The research approach incorporated a weighted scoring process to rank and analyze the collected industry data. The process included checkpoints to review findings with industry experts and validate them against other published industry data.

FIGURE 3-4   Research and selection methodology for the Communities of Commerce project.

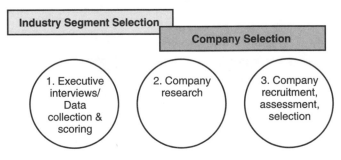

Part One of the industry segment selection methodology consisted of a series of approximately 40 executive interviews with electronic commerce service providers and various industry leaders. The interviewees were identified in part from previous projects. These interviews were used to identify industry segments in Southern California that were beginning to exhibit an interest in and need for e-commerce services. The executive interview participants identified *multimedia, manufacturing, financial services, professional services, transportation,* and *construction* as the leading industry candidates for e-commerce.

The interviewees were asked to discuss the key drivers of electronic commerce in California, the issues impeding the growth of e-commerce, and possible solutions for reconciling those inhibitors. The project team also asked the industry experts to comment on a series of factors that had been identified in prior ISDW research as critical to the success of distributed work programs. The interviewees confirmed that several of those same factors are relevant determinants of viable electronic commerce programs. The list of key e-commerce factors reviewed and validated by the interview participants is as follows:

Size: Absolute size. Annual revenues and number of employees.

Density: Degree of vertical integration. Number of firms in the value chain.

Information content: Degree to which information content is a product or service delivered in the value chain.

Speed of transactions: Need for immediacy in business transactions across organizational boundaries.

Organizing group: Is there a responsible industry organizing group or professional network?

Growth rate: Absolute growth in dollar revenue terms.

Technical sophistication: Prevalence of computer and networking technology.

Time in business: Years in business.

Competitive forces: Degree of competition within sector.

Further, the interview participants were asked to assess the extent to which each of the e-commerce factors impacted the business effectiveness of their particular industry or expertise. Based on this information, the project team rated, by industry, the relative impact of each factor using a 3-point scale (high = 3, medium = 2, low = 1). The results reflect the industries' suitability for incorporating e-commerce methods and tools into existing business models. Figure 3-5 summarizes the results of the interview and scoring process.

FIGURE 3-5 Industry selection matrix: results of industry segment research.

Factor	Weight	Multimedia		Manufacturing		Financial services		Professional services		Transportation		Construction	
		Raw	Final	Raw	Final	Raw	Final	Raw	Final	Raw	Final	Raw	Final
Size	2	2	4	2	4	1	2	3	6	1	2	1	2
Density	2	3	6	2	4	2	4	3	6	3	6	2	4
Information content	3	3	9	1	3	3	9	2	6	2	6	1	3
Speed of transactions	1	2	2	1	1	2	2	2	2	1	1	1	1
Organizing group	3	2	6	3	9	3	9	2	6	3	9	3	9
Growth rate	1	3	3	1	1	2	2	3	3	1	1	1	1
Technical sophistication	2	2	4	1	2	2	4	2	4	1	2	1	2
Financial strength	2	1	2	2	4	3	6	2	4	2	4	2	4
Competitive forces	1	2	2	2	2	2	2	2	2	1	1	1	1
Total	17	20	38	15	30	20	40	21	39	15	32	13	27

The analysis revealed that the most likely targets for effective electronic commerce business models in Southern California were financial and professional services and the multimedia industry. Additionally, these findings were compared against employment projections through the year 2001. The project team researched statistics via the Internet from the State of California, Employment Development Department, Labor Market Information Division. Analysis of the industry employment projections for each county in the metropolitan Los Angeles area validated that the groups targeted in the Communities of Commerce initiative were indeed healthy, growing industry segments worthy of consideration for the project.

In Part Two of the selection process, the target industry groups identified from the executive interviews were researched and analyzed further. Concurrently, the project team began to identify potential company participants within the most promising industry segments. The project team conducted this research using a licensed business research database. The databases include general company information and articles on all organizations registered with the federal government. Companies are categorized in the databases by Standard Industrial Classification (SIC) code.

The team did a series of iterative searches using Southern California postal zip codes and the government SIC codes that most closely corresponded to the leading industry targets (Multimedia, manufacturing, financial services, professional services, transportation, and construction). The search criteria were based as closely as possible on the e-commerce success factors, but the process was somewhat limited by the parameters of the database. The specific inputs were as follows:

- Small companies (defined as having fewer than 500 employees)
- Revenue and assets of less than $10 million
- Located in Southern California (Los Angeles area)
- Founded after 1988

The early database search results were evaluated and ranked by the number of database hits (potential business leads) they yielded. Initially, the database search criteria included any metropolitan areas south of San Jose. The results were vast and produced hits in all but a few SICs. When the criteria were narrowed to a concentrated area around Los Angeles, only five SIC categories generated results.

Later, regionally focused industry searches showed that businesses falling under the general "professional services" description seemed to produce the most attractive and plentiful small-business leads. After several iterations, the project consultants focused the research primarily on businesses falling in this category, which includes "business, motion pictures, communications, amusement and recreation, and printing and publishing." Although the finance, insurance, and real estate (financial services) segment ranked a distant second in the number of hits, organizations in this group/industry segment tended to be either too large or too organizationally mature or complex to suit the project. So were the findings from the manufacturing, transportation, and construction industries. Initial company searches within "professional services" produced as many as 200 hits. Centralizing the target region in the metropolitan Los Angeles area helped to reduce the company lead list. Eliminating the very large companies and the very small companies as well as the franchise operations brought the potential "recruit" list to approximately 140 small businesses.

As previously mentioned, the targeted industries reflected in the industry selection matrix were derived from recommendations during the executive interview process. It is worth noting that in many cases the database industry name, description, or categorization was different from the industry "titles" provided by the interviewees. For instance, whereas multimedia (or new media) was recommended as an industry target by interview participants, it is not a recognized industry segment in the database. Companies that might generally be considered multimedia are found in the database as a subcategory of professional services. Given this, it took a considerable amount of creative, iterative searching as well as some good investigative follow-up by phone to find viable target companies within a given industry segment. For example, one of the more successful techniques for coming up with high-yielding searches of the vast database involved scanning the phone book Yellow Pages and using the directory classifications as guides for key word inputs.

Part Three, *recruitment* (the process of contacting targeted companies and recruiting them to the project), proved to be a more difficult process than anticipated. The project consultants contacted businesses via phone or fax, and followed up this interaction by sending project information.

The information mailed to the companies was a two-page marketing piece developed by the consultants. The first page was titled "Communities of Commerce^sm—Why Get Involved?" and included a "Quick Check—Is My Business Ready?" self-administered quiz regarding Internet/e-commerce readiness to generate the reader's interest. Page 2 of the informational piece, titled "Southern California Communities of Commerce^sm Project," was a brief fact sheet describing the goals of the project, the types of small businesses that should participate, and what participating would mean to organizations that join the community. This mailing was followed up with another phone call to answer questions and, hopefully, close the deal.

Lessons Learned from the Research and Recruiting Processes

One discovery made during the research and recruiting process was that accessing the most up-to-date company information is difficult. The consultants discovered that government-assigned SIC codes are typically not updated unless a business reregisters with the government, as in the case of a business name change. This meant that in some cases, the nature of the business had evolved or changed completely, but the SIC classification had not been updated to reflect that. How best to find and target small and medium-size enterprises in a particular geographic area or industry segment is a very important value-added process worth refining. Further exploration of useful tools and alliances to complement or improve this process might be beneficial (e.g., area small business associations, professional organizations' member lists).

What the consultants found during this recruiting effort was that reaching the appropriate person within the organization to discuss the project was challenging in small and medium-size enterprises where roles and job titles vary. Through trial and error, the best contact people seemed to be high-level managers or officers in the company (CEO, CFO, COO, if these functions existed). The consultants were often referred to the marketing professionals within the organization, presumably since the Internet and e-commerce are perceived as a sales and promotion channel falling under the marketing scope of responsibility.

The consultants also had a difficult time establishing credibility and trust with potential company participants. Without case histories of similar efforts, it is difficult to entice companies to devote time to learning more about a difficult and rapidly evolving technology base. Should the Communities of Commerce project be replicated, the new effort would undoubtedly benefit from a track record of present project experiences as well as community member testimonials. Hindsight wisdom tells us that the big roadblocks in the recruiting process were skepticism about project goals and concerns regarding financial and time commitments. In the future, clarification of project sponsors and funding, time commitment estimates, and success stories will help allay some of these concerns and make the recruiting process easier.

A suggestion for future "community" projects would be to include a marketing phase in the project plan. Targeted advertising to select industry segments via the Web, print, or various business associations (chambers of commerce, etc.) might be an effective way of promoting the project and establishing some degree of credibility up front. Doing business on the Internet and being associated with an organization like CommerceNet were clearly major draws for those companies who expressed interest early on, even if they did not fully understand at that point what their participation would mean. In the future, creating a marketing campaign that incorporates those key incentives that attracted current members to the project would be effective.

Recruiting Summary

In sum, the recruiting process produced 17 companies interested in participating. Approximately 50 percent of the recruited companies were found as a result of database research. The other 50 percent were referred to the project via word of mouth by friends and business associates who were already participating. The final group selected falls under the broadly defined "new media" industry.

The list of selected members would change slightly over the next few months as a result of the organizational assessment process described in the next section or by natural attrition (change of heart, change of business plans, change of company direction, etc.). However, the overall demographics of the community remained fairly consistent. The demand was such that a waiting list of interested companies had been created, and as some participants dropped out, new companies were invited to participate. By the end of June, the project team prepared a market-segmentation analysis to reflect the demographics of the participating companies. The analysis (see Figure 3-6) reflects a good spread of companies across the business/professional services sector, with varying levels of sophistication in technology use and business maturity. This mix was designed to allow the team to draw significant conclusions from the impact of the program on small and medium-size businesses and on economic development.

Organizational Assessment and Selection

Assessing the operational readiness of each company was the next part in the selection process. The team conducted a series of interviews using the Organizational Analysis System (OAS), which is a diagnostic instrument measuring organizational effectiveness. The assessment methodology is based on a five-factor model that looks at information systems, human resource management practices, customer relations, strategic planning, and operational performance (see Figure 3-7). Survey participants were asked to respond to questions in each of the five areas. Each category is measured

FIGURE 3-6   Market segmentation analysis.

Segment			E-Commerce Sector		
Facilities management	1	6%	B-B		
Manufacturing	2	12%	Business-to-business	11	65%
Business services	6	35%			
Video	5	29%	B-C		
Community group	1	6%	Business-to-consumer	6	35%
Technology	2	12%			
Total 17			Total 17		

Level of Sophistication			Level of Maturity		
No Internet experience	1	6%	Start-up business	3	18%
Computerized options	6	35%	Formation business	7	41%
E-mail/no Web site	6	35%	Mature business	7	41%
Initial Web site up	4	24%			
Total 17			Total 17		

by a set of indicators (questions). Participant responses are ranked by the interviewer on a 5-point scale and weighted to reflect the relative importance of each indicator. The OAS methodology has been tested extensively for statistical reliability. (See Figure 3-8.)

A tabulation of the OAS results shows the differences between the Communities of Commerce sample and national norms (see Table 3-2).[3]

[3] National norms are compiled by ISDW as part of an ongoing research program in organizational development.

FIGURE 3-7   Model of the Organizational Analysis System (OAS).

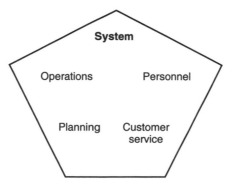

FIGURE 3-8   OAS assessment factors
OAS scores were rated on the following scale:

5   Highest rating, very descriptive
4   Above average for industry
3   Average for industry
2   Marginal, organization experiencing difficulty in this area
1   Significant operational problems experienced

- The group scored below the national norm for planning. This may, however, reflect the large number of start-up businesses in the community.
- The group scored high for customer service, indicating a very close relationship between the organizations and their customers. This may suggest that organizations seeking to use electronic commerce models may be more in tune with their customer base and desire even more intimate connections through the Internet.

Lessons Learned from the Organizational Assessment Process

A major discovery from the organizational assessment process was that small and medium-size enterprises (SMEs) require significant assistance in developing their business plans as a precursor to moving their operations to the Internet. This assistance can be provided most effectively in a tailored consultative mode geared to the specifics of each business. Further, these discrete needs can form the basis for the development of "affinity relationships" among businesses to construct our Communities of Commerce.

The findings of this phase of the project are significant in two respects:

1.   They demonstrate the relative *importance of business analysis.*
2.   They indicate the robustness and *utility of the methodology.*

TABLE 3-2   Communities of Commerce OAS results.

	Planning	Personnel	Systems	Customer Service	Operations
Communities of Commerce	3.41	3.45	3.14	4.14	3.64
National sample	3.85	3.14	2.94	3.5	3.11

Importance of Business Analysis

The OAS methodology proved to be adaptable to highlighting both strengths and weaknesses of business operations across a wide variety of sizes and types of firms. It is a useful technique for helping owners and managers isolate areas for improvement in companies.

In fact, four firms (23 percent of those interviewed) were dropped from the program as a direct result of the OAS. During the process of collecting data, it became apparent to the researchers and the executives of these four firms that they probably wouldn't be successful in implementing e-commerce programs because of deficiencies in their operations. In each case, the business plan was found to be insufficient for identifying key markets, establishing market communications, and outlining their value-added proposition.

A major conclusion that can be drawn from this analysis is that businesses *must* have in place a good, complete business plan before they should contemplate using the Internet as an adjunct to their operations. Without clear direction and market identification, e-commerce will probably only speed the demise of marginal firms.

Business first; Internet second!

Utility of Methodology

The methods employed to find out where the most leverage could be gained may be applied in other venues. The project team applied a diagnostic method usually employed in cases of proactive business problem analysis. The assessment methodology was found to be equally effective in designing business operations and processes prior to their implementation. As such, the process could also be used in the following ways:

- Performing due diligence investment analysis for Internet-based businesses
- Selecting key business partners
- Allocating internal resources for business development

There is no reason why this process of analyzing a business could not become an adjunct to other consultative and educational marketing programs. For example, it is feasible that an Internet systems provider (ISP) or a Web site builder could use this method, or an equivalent organizational development technique, as a precursor to constructing an elaborate and expensive Internet business operation. This type of analysis could be bundled with a more traditional technical requirements analysis from the ISP as a way of adding even more value to routine services.

In addition, other business service providers targeting SMEs for their other product lines could use an organizational analysis, keyed to the uniqueness of e-commerce models, in the same way it has been used here. For example, automobile buying services offer product reviews and ratings as a way of helping people decide which car to purchase. Money is made through brokering the sale, with the advice as a loss leader. This idea fits with our observation of a new trend: that companies are providing a number of free services on the Internet as part of a larger value-added proposition.

CommerceNet Partnering

During the process of industry and company research and selection, a recruitment campaign began, with the project and CommerceNet leaders encouraging needed participation of CommerceNet consortium members. The ongoing campaign started in the early months of the project via conversations with CommerceNet members. In June of 1998, the first of several introductory presentations, titled "Building Electronic Communities of Commerce: An Invitation to Participate," was delivered at the CommerceNet quarterly membership meeting. The discussions and presentations provided audience groups with an overview of the project objectives and structure, the types of small businesses participating in the project, and the general ways in which the consortium members could benefit from participating. Specifically, the following incentives were shared with consortium members:

- *Opportunity to directly influence research:* Companies are invited to use the community as a resource to explore how it can best address small-business needs.

- *Early-requirements analysis:* CommerceNet companies can use the community for early-requirements gathering and analysis for new product development.

- *Safe exposure to new markets:* CommerceNet companies can gain new visibility for existing products among small and medium-size enterprises.

- *Test bed for new products:* CommerceNet companies are invited to use the small-business community as a testing ground for beta versions of new products.

The presentations were well received and resulted in many follow-up conversations. Some consortium members expressed interest in in-kind participation. However, as the project progressed, it became clear that consortium members needed more specific information regarding the project and the individual company needs before they could be comfortable committing time, resources, or services. The one-to-one business planning sessions conducted by project leads during the education and community-building phase of the project were designed to identify the specific needs and action plans of the small and medium-size businesses participating in the project. This information was important to establish worthwhile connections with CommerceNet consortium members. "Invitation to participate" presentations will continue to be delivered, with more up-to-date information regarding the project, accomplishments to date, and the areas in which consortium members could be involved.

Additionally, promotional information and status updates regarding the Communities of Commerce project were made available to consortium members via CommerceNet's own online newsletter publication. Ideally, the project team would have liked to provide the community members and CommerceNet consortium members with direct electronic access to each other, perhaps through the CommerceNet Web site. This way, consortium members could rely less on newsletters or progress reports to inform them of what is happening on the project and more on seeing and participating in the current discussions and commenting on new plans and ideas as they develop.

PHASE 3: EDUCATION AND COMMUNITY BUILDING

A significant conclusion of Phase 2 was that electronic community building must start with structured face-to-face interaction. The organizational assessments were complete, the "final cut" was made, and companies were chosen to participate in the project. It was now time to bring everyone together and begin to develop the community. On September 25, 16 of the 17 Communities of Commerce companies gathered at the Los Angeles Children's Museum (one of the network members) for a meeting and reception. The gathering of participating companies, project leaders, and sponsors was intended to generate excitement, allow everyone to get to know one another, and help clarify the goals of the project.

Team members individually addressed the group to provide some background details that led to the group gathering that day and to set some expectations for going forward. Aside from the speakers' comments and introductions, the afternoon focused on networking and relationship building. To facilitate this process, the project team devised some activities based on an "affinity mapping" exercise completed prior to the gathering. In preparation for the event, the team had brainstormed the likely connections that existed within the group, such as similar business needs or complementary services or offerings. Each member received an envelope with the names and details of a fellow Communities of Commerce project participant whom they should seek out during the reception. This activity proved to be a successful way for community members to introduce themselves and get to know one another. At the conclusion of the social hour, the project team had the group complete their own "affinity mapping" exercise based on all that they had learned about fellow community members during their discussions. Participants drew lines on poster paper linking bubbles that represented the individual companies in the group. The lines reflected the connections and potential partnering opportunities that were already apparent to the community members after only brief discussions. The group recognized many links, and thus the poster was filled with lines to and from nearly every company.

Also significant about the kickoff reception was that community members left with a pack of printed materials and resources compiled by the project team as part of the e-commerce education program. These "starter kits" included various books, articles, training materials, and Internet Web references related to a range of topics that included Internet basics, e-commerce business strategy, and online marketing. Recognizing that the Communities of Commerce participants included start-up companies as well as more mature organizations, the starter kit materials were intended to have some relevant information for all groups. An indexed guide helped the readers select the right starting point to review the materials based on their own level of Internet experience and technical expertise.

The education and community building phase of the project began in October and continued through December 1998. The project consultants conducted several individual meetings with each company to identify specific needs and goals as well as to establish feasible action plans. During this time, the team created and implemented a communication plan and a community building program.

Individual Planning Sessions
A valuable yet time-consuming component of Phase 3 included individual business planning sessions. The project consultants determined that in order to move forward effectively, each business in the organization should establish an individual growth plan for the project. The participants were

asked to dedicate two to three hours of face-to-face time with the project consultants to determine goals, next steps, and implementation processes for going forward. The goal of the planning sessions was to establish a common language of issues and needs for each organization so that resources and efforts would be targeted in the right area. In addition, the consultants used this time to develop their relationships with each organization by providing coaching and design suggestions.

Prior to meeting the individual organizations, the project team completed an overall assessment matrix of business needs for each participant. This matrix was used to begin each discussion and to keep it focused on the company's needs. In addition, the matrix helped the consultants gauge if they were correct in their assessments of the organizations thus far in the project.

Communication Program

The consultants recognized a need for an organized and formal communications vehicle. Those in need of the most detailed information on a regular basis were the participating companies. A communication plan was designed to provide this group with regular project information, updates, and education. It was determined that regular contact with the group and clear, useful information were essential to establish credibility and buy-in. Included in the plan are reports on project goals, status, progress, successes, and lessons learned among participants and other interested parties. Secondary goals included generating enthusiasm and active participation.

Community-Building Events

A key goal of the Communities of Commerce project was to facilitate the connections within the community, with the sponsors, and with CommerceNet consortium members. In addition, members asked for even more education in common areas of interest. To meet both needs, the project developed community-building events. These events included monthly receptions and monthly business seminars.

The receptions occurred once a month from June to December and were informal, unstructured gatherings allowing members to network and develop business-to-business relationships.

PHASE 4: CONNECTIONS AND WRAP-UP

The connections and wrap-up phase of the project began in January and ended March 1999. The project consultants assisted each company in the project with the rollout of their individual plans. In addition, they served as liaisons to facilitate the connections for possible partnerships with other organizations. Finally, the project ended with a formal project evaluation and wrap-up event.

Rollout of Individual Consultation Plans

The focus of this phase was largely the development and rollout of individual company plans integrating business operations with e-commerce capabilities. The responsibility of day-to-day implementation of each strategy fell on the shoulders of the individual organizations. The consultants focused on one or two core needs of each company. A matrix of company needs and key community issues was created to help the consultants focus on the most important information for each organization. In addition to the specific needs for each company, two major community needs were identified:

- Organizational development consulting on how to structure internal Internet management functions (four companies)
- Formation of strategic business partnerships for Web branding (five companies)

Facilitate Connections with Community Members and CommerceNet Consortium Members

Upon facilitating connections within the community, the consultants found that the initial assumption that SMEs need to form partnerships for aggregation of supplier demand was not realistic in today's Internet commerce world. Many members of the project explained that they (SMEs) could obtain most goods and services themselves without being explicit members of consortia.

However, further findings illustrate that SMEs' needs for higher-level business services could be met through clustering. Therefore, the project team developed a recruitment plan to bring together these various resources from the existing CommerceNet membership base. Three distinct clusters of common business interests emerged from the group:

1. *Video on the Internet*
2. *Production facilities management*
3. *E-commerce infrastructure*

Other Significant Findings During This Period

During this phase, two of the participants were presented to new media investment interests in Los Angeles as exemplars of our location, selection, and evaluation processes for the SME market. These conversations led to the refinement of the project business model for future use in developing successful community business models for this narrow sector. Key findings include the following:

- A mere Web presence is no longer a competitive advantage for e-commerce applications.

- Business propositions must be aimed at market segments of $1 billion, at a minimum, to be viable over time. This means a combined community market of $1 billion is the only avenue for small companies, which provides the business incentive for aggregating markets.

- A competitive advantage may be shared across several SMEs by coinvesting in unique technologies, majority market share leadership, and negotiation of exclusive distribution channel agreements. All of these advantages are not available to small, discrete entities, thus providing even more leverage for electronic communities.

In addition, the project consultants learned of the critical continuing and expanding need for small and medium-size enterprises to obtain "state of the practice" education on Internet-based business processes. In response, they located a potential resource—Santa Monica College—to provide this type of ongoing support.

Postmortem of Unsuccessful Efforts
Of the 17 original firms that were selected and recruited into the project, 7 failed to complete the program. In retrospect, the original organizational assessment system indicated significant weaknesses in these enterprises. Early on, the consultants were hopeful that the project resources devoted to the business development of these seven companies would have overcome these issues. Following is a synopsis of the events that surrounded the failure of these businesses to move to an e-commerce model.

Uniware
This company's chief proponent of e-commerce, the vice president for marketing, left the firm one month after the project began. His departure left a business development leadership gap. The business planning process stopped, and the company failed to secure second-round funding. Within three months, the business collapsed.

Analysis: Failure of execution

Weakness on OAS: Planning, personnel, and leadership

Marketing Forum
The founding partners dissolved the firm 10 months into the project. They failed to capture sufficient market interest to generate adequate revenues. We believe their initial business plan was not focused enough on nonmedia sectors to support their intended educational efforts. Their value proposition was not distinct enough. This, coupled with a late-developing Web presence and rise of competing interest in the market area, created a climate that led to their failure.

Analysis: Failure of execution

Weakness on OAS: None

Hard Products
The internal champion of e-commerce, the CFO, left the firm after only two months on the project. His replacement, the vice president of marketing, departed two months after that due to declining sales. The company's catalog sales operation failed to move quickly enough, and senior management shifted its emphasis to existing sales channels under competitive pressure.

Analysis: Lack of commitment

Weakness on OAS: Leadership, information systems, personnel

Networking Systems
This company found it impossible to attend our community-building events after an initial commitment. This behavior was evidence of a lack of commitment to the project by senior management. The external consultation and competitive analysis we performed for this firm was not incorporated into its systems development plan. The company's use of Web-based technology is lagging others in the facilities management field.

Analysis: Lack of commitment

Weakness on OAS: Information systems and personnel

WagerWare
This company failed to make any investment in information technology. It attempted to launch its business operations using conventional telephony technology (e.g., 1-800 dial back). Their business plan never incorporated direct input from customers. WagerWare dropped out of the process when it became clear they could not incorporate value-added feedback into their planning process.

Analysis: Lack of commitment

Weakness on OAS: Customer service and information systems

Networking Services

This company maintained a very narrow view of technological capability even in the face of intense educational efforts. The shift from radio-spectrum information distribution to Internet-based systems proved impossible to complete. While the leadership appeared visionary at the outset, when time came to actually shift the business model, personnel in the firm could not execute.

Analysis: Lack of understanding of technology potential

Weakness on OAS: Information systems

Acme Start-Up

It was a start-up under considerable time pressure to develop its business model. A death in the founder's family caused a three-month hiatus that pushed the company off the critical path. Absence from the community-building process during this critical time removed company decision makers from the necessary social interaction.

Analysis: Insufficient time frame

Weakness on OAS: Information Systems

Lessons Learned

Our analysis indicates that the OAS was a very effective instrument in predicting potential success of firms moving to e-commerce. Our false-positive rate (firms that the OAS rated high but were unsuccessful) was 5.8 percent, well within normal limits of statistical reliability.

As with most pilot projects, our initial operational plan changed somewhat as we moved through the project. Our major findings for developing e-commerce in the small and medium-size business sector are as follows:

1. Recruitment of small and medium-size firms is more difficult than anticipated. Without case histories of similar efforts, it is difficult to entice companies to devote time to learning about a difficult and rapidly evolving technology base.

Going forward, this doesn't appear to be a significant issue. However, the resistance we experienced initially can be expected to arise in other sectors that are new to e-commerce, such as construction and manufacturing.

2. The major lesson learned is that there is a wide variety of learning needs, even within this restricted sample.

Even within these 16 companies, we found three distinct levels of educational needs, ranging from those of novices to those of the very knowledgeable. The design of our "educational starter kit" reflects this diversity. The implication is that some type of assessment is required to slot businesses into the most appropriate track for e-commerce education.

3. Some companies that initially qualified had insufficient internal business planning processes to support making decisions to move specific functions to e-commerce models. We experienced a 23 percent attrition rate as a result.

Electronic commerce highlights inefficiencies and disconnects among internal business processes. Paper-based processes that are highly redundant (copies of everything everywhere) break down when information flows are automated. This learning implies that a comprehensive work-flow process engineering project should precede migration of operations to the Internet.

4. Electronic community building must start with a structured face-to-face interaction.

This finding is of little surprise to those familiar with the literature of electronic collaboration. Our process of building affinity groups incorporated this learning. What we experienced in terms of client feedback was a high level of demand for routine and for structured events that would allow community members to interact personally. This in turn gave rise to our monthly community learning events, which at the conclusion of the project had evolved into educational presentations and business case analyses of community members

5. There is a need for an organized and formal communications plan among all project participants.

Networking cannot be left to chance. Unfortunately, we had not anticipated the budgetary requirements needed for a unique, stand-alone, Web-based communications service. This was one of the major criticisms of the project from the community members. Electronic communities need an easy, accessible, private, and supportive Web-based communications medium. During the course of the project, the technology has developed to the point where this can be accomplished with approximately $2000 in server costs and monthly access fees of $80.

6. A mere Web presence is no longer enough to build significant competitive advantage in e-commerce applications.

When the project began, having a Web presence and e-mail was enough to embark on e-commerce with your customers. Developing standards such as XML, portal sites, and now the growth of e-commerce "market makers" have taken us into a new era. At its lowest level, Web presence can be a calling card and "brochureware," but customer demand quickly pulls you toward secure electronic interaction with customers. Moving businesses in this direction requires the development of back-office infrastructure before establishing a Web presence.

7. There is an expanding need for small and medium-size enterprises to obtain "state of the practice" education on Internet-based business processes.

The pace of change in e-commerce technology, regulation, and business models requires continuous education of business leaders. A combination of professional organizations such as CommerceNet, public education such as Santa Monica College, and industry leaders need to come together to provide ongoing leadership for this.

Other e-commerce firms, such as insurance companies and banks, that want to serve this SME market can leverage this need for continuous education as a marketing tool to build relationships with firms that may at some point have need of their core business services.

8. Successful movement to e-commerce requires the unique role of the "Internet business development specialist" or "producer" in addition to the normal complement of business acumen. Traditional business models exclude this role, and a "project management" skill set is adequate.

Participants need an internal champion who is willing to commit focused time and energy on e-commerce/Internet initiatives.

The role that the consultant team played in this project has begun to solidify around a key set of value-added service functions. Ironically, these functions have been developed in the new media sector in response to increased competition, development of technology, and globalization. We have termed this new role "the producer" and detailed how it can be used in the future, especially in the new business development arena.

9. Our most significant learning has been the need for an institutionalized mechanism for leadership development of e-commerce businesses.

Leaders of successful e-commerce businesses need to develop a new set of skills that were not emphasized in the industrial era. Visioning, community building, and managing at a distance are new skill sets for these leaders. E-commerce is the future of work. It will require shifts in people capabilities, organizational structures, and methodologies for designing technology infrastructure.

Many of those who dropped out of the project either did not have a champion within the company or were unwilling to give sufficient time and energy to the program. The project results indicate that SMEs that are leery of committing to e-commerce and the Internet as a new business component risk getting left behind in a fast-moving "eat or be eaten" market.

THE PATH FORWARD

The Communities of Commerce project has demonstrated the distinct and unique value of adding a new type of manager to help SMEs compete— specifically, a manager who is focused on business development for small and medium-sized enterprises practicing electronic commerce. This new role is analogous to that of a "producer" in the media market. Producers bring together all the elements (human, financial, and physical resources) needed for a new, growing enterprise to be successful. In addition, they perform the role of facilitator as these resources work together and become a high-performance team. Traditionally, a project manager assigns roles, sets targets, reviews performance, and manages a schedule of tasks. In this case, a producer's role also integrates the technical requirements, organizational structures, and the personalities of the people involved in the endeavor.

The Communities of Commerce project team has been serving in this new role of "producer" for emerging new media businesses in Los Angeles. In the later stages of the project, the project team realized that providing a connection point between these growing enterprises and members of the CommerceNet consortium offers tangible business benefits to these larger companies that are seeking to enter the SME market space with their established products and services. The overall driver for continuance of this project is the increased growth rate of Internet-based businesses. One of the major inhibitors for rapid growth in the SME market is lack of business infrastructure (e.g., marketing, financial management, and product design services).

Overall, this case study demonstrates that the process of helping companies form Communities of Commerce is not easy and is fraught with many pitfalls. However, in the context of business, this case study amply demonstrates the added value of business communities, especially in the Internet age. New business opportunities were created, the quality of investments improved, many new jobs were created, and businesses grew profitably—in part as a result of participating in this community-building process.

C H A P T E R

PEOPLE: WHY IS THIS SO HARD?

The more you know the less you understand.

Tao Te Ching

BEING A PART OF THE CHANGE

This chapter is about being. It is about how to become more aware, how to transform the person of the old reality into the whole person of the new reality. Curiously, I think that technology, which today so constrains and overwhelms our lives, will be a powerful tool in our awakening process. This chapter is designed to help people make a transition when emotional life becomes more social and less individual. As you move closer and closer to the true digital workplace, your capacity to live and work without interacting with others decreases. Many of you have already begun to experience this. Constant e-mail messages, faxes, and phone calls have placed you in touch with others so much that sometimes it becomes painful. Your ability to maintain your emotional life as a private, personal thing is rapidly disappearing. Even when you don't want people to intrude into your personal space, they seem to do it. As a result, your emotional life is becoming more social and less individual.

Some of us deal with the increasing pressure to share emotions as an intrusion. People who have these feelings are those who tend to be introverted, and they probably prefer a lot of private time. (This is ironic when you consider that many of the computer scientists who created the technology that's causing this increased sharing are likely to have been introverts themselves.) Others take this increase in amount of connections with others as a pleasant thing. However, even those people, who tend to be extroverted, sometimes feel overwhelmed by too much interaction and too many questions about how they feel. Even extroverts can reach a saturation point with e-mail, faxes, and voice mail.

Because our emotional lives are becoming more social and less individual with the coming of the digital age, we could say that we're becoming "more feminine" and "less masculine." Today's management theorists maintain that the collaborative model of organizations that's replacing the old command-and-control approach represents a move away from the male and toward more female models of work; so, too, we find that technology is enabling, sometimes imposing, greater female-style interactivity in our emotional lives as well.

The traditional model of how we interact with one another, particularly at work, was based on a premise that our emotional lives are something we carry around inside and don't let out into the public eye. This was in part the outgrowth of a mechanical, Western ideology that grew out of the Industrial Revolution. We see the ideology of privacy everywhere—from the emphasis on a personal rather than a collective relationship with God in some Western religions to our insistence on silence in movie theaters (as though we need to believe we're experiencing something in private even when we're surrounded by hundreds of our fellow human beings).

Most of us find it easy to deal with our emotional lives in the context of our family, our immediate friends, and our community. They're part of the circle of privacy as that traditional ideology defines it. But somehow, we leave behind this way of relating and dealing with our problems when we enter the workplace.

At many of the organizations I've been exposed to, the only accepted forms of emotion are the placid good nature we all show to people we don't know very well and the aggressive anger that still passes for leadership in too many executive suites. One of the jobs I had several years ago put me into an organization that may have been extreme in its dysfunction, but I think all of us can recognize elements of our own experience in it.

Of the ten people with whom I interacted on a daily basis, four were undergoing significant turmoil in their marriages, two others abused alcohol, and I later learned that one had resorted to physical violence in her family. As you might expect, it was obvious whenever we got together that people were distracted, unhappy, and not always ready to give their all to the work at hand. Yet with all of those signs of trouble, management's response was clear: "You leave your personal problems at the office door." Supposedly, by pretending that the stresses and strains we brought to the table weren't there, we could go on as a productive, fully functioning organization.

Rather than risk letting their emotions out, people kept silent in meetings, depriving the company of their ideas. To maintain the illusion that they'd left the emotional turmoil from home at the door, they came up with work-related problems on which to vent the anger they were really feeling about their lives outside of work. The woman whose husband's drinking was making a hell of her life was known in the office for her ruthless criticism of the slightest infraction by those who worked for her. The woman who was abusing her own children was so accommodating and conflict-averse at the office that her teams rarely ever got anything done. It seems to me now that management's desire to solve emotional problems by pretending they didn't exist—this denial of the truth that we're all human, even in the workplace—made it more, not less, difficult for us to get anything done.

The frequency of violence in the workplace, armed violence in the schoolyard, road rage, and other events that permeate our nightly news has certainly increased in the past few years. Why? These increases of emotional outbursts and inability to control anger really are the final steps in a pathway of industrialization. The pathway has tended to dehumanize everyone in the workplace, so the increased pace of change that technology makes possible has lit the fuse to the powder keg we built when we denied emotions at work.

The increased pace of change has also increased our need for the stability that strong relationships bring. When everything's up in the air, strong emotional bonds give us the strength we need. It's ironic that the technology that increases our need for strong social systems to sustain us emotionally through times of great change also isolates us physically from each other. For example, telecommuters may be electronically plugged in to their colleagues, but they're usually working alone. Office workers may be surrounded by hundreds of cubicle dwellers like themselves, but most people spend much of their time interacting with others via computer, phone, and fax. And often that interaction is message-to-message (e-mail instead of conversations, voice mail instead of live chats) rather than real-time social exchange.

As technology allows us to work together from separate places and at separate times, we become socially isolated. If our ability to overcome the social isolation is a key factor in our being successful in the digital workplace, you can begin to see how important it is that we figure out how we can stay connected to one another while we're physically apart.

Many of us are already feeling an increased need to build community, to connect with each other emotionally. However, even as we recognize the human need for this type of connection, we also have to acknowledge that it flies in the face of conventional wisdom and rules of etiquette in the traditional workplace.

These old models of workplace behavior make us feel that we constantly have to censor ourselves at work and that we're controlled at work by forces outside our power to influence. When you feel this way, you get anxious and confused. When you are anxious and confused, you are distracted, you're not productive, and you probably are not pleasant to live with. Is this the way that you really planned to live your life? I doubt it. However, as many of you know, this traditional reality is the *reality of today.*

THE COMING TRANSITION

We're at the beginning of a transition away from the old reality and toward a new reality in which our emotional lives can flower at work as well as in our homes and communities. As the transition evolves, we're starting to become more aware, more purposeful, and more in control of our total lives. We're waking up! Why do I think this transformation is already under way, when so many of us are still stuck in traditional jobs? Because technology has permeated even those jobs, and it offers the key. Let me give you one example of the small signs I've seen, signs which, taken together, point to a transformation in the way we're using technology.

In doing research for this book, I interviewed many people who are going through this transition. These people were using commercial services such as America Online and CompuServe to connect with one another and share stories, concerns, questions, and at last their feelings. They weren't just buying books and trading stocks on the Internet. They were using it as a vehicle to connect emotionally with like-minded souls.

For example, Bobo had always been a shy person. Meeting people and developing friendships was always difficult. For a long time he avoided getting into situations where he had to interact with others. School was especially painful because you had to participate in class, which included asking questions in front of other people. Bobo had to come out of his shell when he started college—somewhat late in life because of his introverted nature. But college in the Internet age is radically different than it was as late as the 1970s—especially for older students who aren't there primarily to find a mate.

Bobo started using a computer to write papers, and he found it was much faster than using a typewriter. Within the first month after he began using the computer, he discovered e-mail, the Internet, and chat rooms. A whole new world opened up: a place to connect, to collaborate, and to learn—easily navigated because he could control how much of himself he exposed to others. Friendships formed, colleagues were found, and his intellectual discussions, which started in the classroom, all of a sudden became global in scope. Bobo was making a transition that he perhaps might not have made in his entire life without the power of technology to help him connect in a way he was comfortable with.

Another example is that of Clarice, a very sociable person who is generally the life of the party and has a very sharp political instinct. She had labored long to finish her professional education, and she worked in a typical office setting with traditional doors, secretaries, and the proverbial evil boss. But that changed. Clarice was riding the wave of change and, due to her outgoing personality, finally got noticed by a prominent professional services company. They offered her the job of a lifetime—twice the pay, stock options, and the whole New World of the professional knowledge worker. But there's a catch. Most of the senior people in the firm worked out of their homes using the Internet to connect with one another and with clients. Clarice had to move away from a social workplace to one where she felt isolated, cut off, and away from the interaction she craved. It always amazes me how fast people adapt to these situations. Within two months, Clarice had built a new network of professional friends through e-mail and buddy lists. It wasn't a complete substitute for her old face-to-face interactions—but it was enough to make her less anxious in a new setting. Now she had time to concentrate and work at home. Her new cyber–social network supplemented more focused face-to-face interactions with family, friends, and workmates. She relaxed, knowing she could reach out and connect whenever she wanted (or needed) to.

You could say that the activities of the people I studied were merely the outgrowth of what we used to derive from newspaper personal ads, pen pals, and long hours on the telephone. We've moved from writing letters and making phone calls to using e-mail, chat rooms, and bulletin boards. Yet there's a depth of connection people seem to be finding in their online relationships that is absent from the personals, from letter writing, and even from many phone calls. In fact, some of the people I interviewed admitted that this new way of interacting in cyberspace was becoming almost an addiction, in part because online interaction lets them connect with huge numbers of people at once. I find it most curious that people would feel "addicted" to a new medium that allows them to interact in a more intense, personal way with larger groups of people than they ever experienced.

But *addiction* may be the right term, insofar as one role of an addictive substance or behavior is to alleviate built-up tension. In this case, however, the satisfaction comes not from ingesting a drug or engaging in some other kind of harmful behavior, but from satisfying an inherent human and social need that has been unsatisfied in the workplace for so long.

If technology forces us into a world where we can't help but interact with more people, more frequently, and perhaps more intensely (if less physically), how do we use it responsibly to enhance the quality of our social lives? Well, this chapter is about how to take the first tentative steps in that process. You need tools to see the new reality and to know it when you get there. You need to know who you really are before you can transform yourself at work. Let's take a brief look at some of the behaviors that have gotten us in the rut of anxiety and unhappiness at work. Armed with this new understanding, we'll be able to see ways to use technology to enhance our well-being on the job.

OVERCOMING FUD (FEAR, UNCERTAINTY, AND DOUBT)

We often acquiesce to unhappy situations because, on some level, we prefer them to any alternative we can see. When you accept a situation you don't really like, such as being unhappy at work, there's a good chance that FUD has played a role. FUD stands for *f*ear *u*ncertainty, and *d*oubt, and it is a powerful motivator. (See Table 4-1.) Where you feel fear, uncertainty, or doubt about change, you stay in the world you know even when you don't much like it.

If you agree that the traditional, impersonal workplace isn't something we like, then it's possible that some combination of fear, uncertainty, and doubt have perpetuated that dysfunctional model of work. Let's see how that might have happened. Let's look at how this old way of working reinforced people's fears, uncertainties, and doubts.

First of all, I believe that the most basic fear any of us have is a fear of not having an identity, of not knowing who we are or where we fit in the larger social structure. This basic fear comes out of the struggle we all face

TABLE 4-1   FUD in your life.

Fear	Uncertainty	Doubt
Basic fears that create absolute panic	What we don't know about the future	In our abilities, in our leaders, in our deeply held beliefs

in adolescence when we're trying to establish ourselves as separate and unique beings from our parents, but still within the bounds of the community that we've been born into.

The traditional workplace deals with this basic fear by giving us an identity and giving us a community. The classic example of this is the company town of yore. We haven't had company towns for decades now, but corporations have continued to provide a similar sense of identity for their workers. As so many of our other sources of identity have been fragmenting—church membership declining, time for volunteer work disappearing, neighborhoods lacking any sense of community—our corporate identity has become an even more powerful source of security. Regardless of the uncertainties and dislocations you face outside the office, at work you have a job title (your identity) and a sense of belonging to a company (your community). By providing us with an identity, however limited, the traditional workplace helps us hold the line against a basic human fear.

In exchange for the company protecting you from your fear of losing your identity, you had to agree to its rules. Primary among these was the rule to leave your emotions at the door, to pretend with everyone else that the workplace is a purely rational environment, free from the emotional outbursts and irrational urges that drive us in other areas of our lives. Even though the denial of feelings created problems, you were willing to pretend it didn't if that meant you could escape the fear of not knowing your place in the world.

The way the traditional company capitalizes on our uncertainties is also easy to understand. Uncertainty refers to feelings of anxiety about what the future holds. I'm sure all of you have experienced this once or twice in your life. Where will we get the money to pay the rent? How can we afford to send the kids to private school? Or perhaps even more basic for a lot of us, where's the money going to come from to buy food? We dealt with these uncertainties in the traditional way by getting steady employment.

Employment not only provides a concrete way of getting rid of basic uncertainties (like how we're going to pay the rent), it also helps us handle uncertainty about what kind of people we want to be in the world. Corporate cultures, those invisible pressures to be and act a certain way, to conform to the overall values of the organization, help us answer everyday questions: "How do I feel about this policy?" "How should I vote in the next election?" "What role should volunteer work play in my life?" "Am I the kind of person who regularly goes to church?"

Whether we're conscious of it or not, corporate cultures include strong messages about the "right" way to act in our communities and at work.

These messages go a long way toward helping us reduce psychological and emotional uncertainty in addition to physical uncertainty.

In exchange for helping us avoid uncertainty, the traditional company expected us to behave in a certain way. The expected behavior included leaving our feelings at the door and following company rules.

Doubt is the twin sister of uncertainty. We can feel doubt in our own abilities, doubt in our leaders, and in some cases, doubt in our own deeply held beliefs. The need to avoid feelings of doubt is a powerful motivator. How does the traditional way of working help us deal with doubt?

The corporation helps us overcome doubt in our abilities by providing us with positions of influence or power. Did you ever wonder why there are so many meetings, why, as Andy Warhol said, everyone gets his or her 15 minutes of fame? By providing a forum for people to display their competence, to influence others, or to wield power, meetings are a great way companies make it possible for us to overcome self-doubt. It's hard to doubt your own abilities when people are taking down every word you say!

Similarly, doubt in our leaders is often difficult to admit. One of the reasons we find Dilbert and his pointy-headed manager so funny is that the cartoon directly acknowledges doubt in leadership, a doubt that corporate cultures typically make it difficult for us to face. Implicit in the endless stupidities of Dilbert's boss is the truth that in our real jobs we all pretend that our leaders would never act so dumb. And one of the reasons we're all willing to play along with the game at work (refusing to believe that the emperor has no clothes) is that it helps us avoid feelings of doubt in our leaders.

But perhaps the most insidious doubt is that of doubting our deeply held beliefs. What's fair? What's right? This form of doubt addresses our basic issues of integrity, sincerity, and how we treat our fellow human beings. For example, if we believe that people should be rewarded based on the time they spend in companies and that people who are senior to us deserve respect, then seeing behaviors that make us doubt that belief is going to make us very uncomfortable.

The traditional corporate structure makes it easier for us to avoid seeing unfair situations, thus helping us avoid the tension of doubt. As long as companies rewarded loyalty, we could escape having to question whether that's the right thing to reward. As long as seniority commanded respect, we could be secure in the knowledge that we'd gain respect the longer we stayed in the same job.

Traditionally, then, companies offered us security: financial and social protection from the vicissitudes of the larger world. In exchange, we agreed to stay put. When the 1980s ended the mutual loyalty that made it possible for workers to stay with one company for their entire careers (and for companies to use layoffs as the last resort rather than the first), the traditional workplace could no longer protect us from FUD. As a result, we've been newly confronted with thoughts about our place in the world, our values, our beliefs, and our dreams.

GETTING A GRIP ON REALITY: WHO ARE WE?

There are many, many different ways of looking at oneself, and they run the gamut from astrology to deep psychotherapy. I'll provide you with a way to combine three resources to answer basic questions about your own reality.

As I've said before, the transition to the new world of work is going to require personal change as well as organizational change. I'm sure most of you have been exposed to some sort of personal development training or assessment, perhaps during a team-building exercise, at an organizational development program, or in your own personal quest for better understanding of who you are. What I'm suggesting to you is that any program of self-development needs to begin with some assessment of who you are and how you interact with others.

The next section of this chapter may be a little confusing for some of you who haven't dealt with the arena of self-development before. I would ask that you suspend judgment by simply going through the material and then reflecting on what it may mean for you in your particular situation. Chapter 7 of this book, "Resources," has even more detailed information on a number of the assessment approaches I will speak about briefly. This chapter is certainly not meant to be a complete and comprehensive guide in this field; it is simply a pathway that you can choose to follow at some later time.

I think that there are four critical questions we must ask ourselves and our coworkers when we embark upon a program of change. In the new world of work, where we find ourselves thrown into situations with new coworkers and new bosses almost on a weekly basis, it becomes much more important to understand how we interact with others and how they interact with us. Just as the Internet has pushed us into a position where "business as usual" no longer applies, the Internet is also pushing us as individuals to better understand who we are and how we relate to others so we can more quickly integrate ourselves into the new work teams with a minimum amount of interpersonal friction.

Table 4-2 outlines the four basic questions that I believe are important, along with brief descriptions of how I think these things are going to change in our new world. The discussion that follows briefly outlines just why I think this is important and how I think it's going to impact you, at the

TABLE 4-2   The four critical elements.

What's important	How it's going to change
How you process information	There will be more of it, and it will come more quickly
How you interact with others	These interactions will be separated in time and space
How you deal with conflict	There will be more diversity in your social worlds
Where your motivation comes	You will need to know where to go to get it from

personal level, in the new world of work. I will also outline some assessment approaches that I have found to be very helpful in answering these questions. I hope it will give you a flavor, at least a glance, of how powerful these techniques can be in leading you toward the personal change that is becoming necessary.

HOW YOU PROCESS INFORMATION
We all process information differently. Information processing is one of the key tasks that all of us, especially knowledge workers, perform in the workplace. As our work changes from manual labor to intellectual labor, processing information becomes increasingly important in the workplace. Understanding how we, and those around us, process information is critical simply because this activity is increasing exponentially in the newly emerging workplace. The necessity to read faster, manipulate numbers, and use graphics to express ideas is coming at us at a blistering pace. I'm sure you know people who have the ability to concentrate intensely on a specific problem and shut out everything else around them. That's one style of processing information, and there are several others.

Issues arise when different members of a work team have different styles of processing information and don't appreciate the value that the other styles bring to the team. When a person who can concentrate intensely works with a person who likes to scan the horizon, they probably will irritate each other at times. Just as understanding how individuals process information differently is important, it is also useful to understand how different work groups perform the same task.

For example, if you ever sat in on a meeting that involved people from engineering and people from marketing, you know what I'm talking about.

The marketing people tend to see a broader picture, have longer time horizons, and talk in images. People from engineering like to crunch numbers, deal with details, and be very explicit. Getting the individuals in these two groups to understand how they process information differently would go a long way toward improving their effectiveness. I've had great success with people in these situations by having them profile how they process information and then sharing with each other the nature of these profiles.

Sometimes this process is uncomfortable, because we're beginning to open ourselves to others, starting to discuss our differences, and trying to appreciate those differences. The workplace of old implicitly prohibited this kind of open, intimate discussion. The workplace of the future will not only permit such activity but encourage it.

In another case I dealt with, the conflict between the marketing and the engineering groups was so great that projects were coming to a halt, budgets were being overrun, and new products were not being delivered to market on time. The executive in charge of the company approached me and asked for help, saying, "We have to solve this problem." When we began the assessment process, there was a great degree of apprehension among a number of folks about sharing their profiles with others in the work group with whom they were having some conflict. Quite amazingly, as we entered into the process, a number of people began to understand why they were having conflict with others.

In many cases, it came down to differences in how people processed information. They really didn't know how to talk to each other in a mutually understandable way. Newly armed with a deeper understanding of themselves and their coworkers, they began to develop new means of communicating with one another that took into account each other's preferences. I'm happy to report in this case that after about six months of working on this process, most of the conflict issues disappeared and the company was able to get itself back on track. Case studies like this make me a great believer in the assessment processes discussed in this chapter.

In the case of how we process information and also how we interact with each other, the assessment approach that I prefer is called The Attentional and Interpersonal Style (TAIS) Inventory. Let's look at this inventory in a little more detail.

The Attentional and Interpersonal Style (TAIS) Inventory

I like TAIS as an assessment system. However, I am quite biased because I use it in some of my research. So I'll let others say it better. Here are some excerpts from a *Fast Company* article.

Measuring the Building Blocks of Performance[1]

Once an individual has developed the knowledge base and technical skills required to be successful in a highly competitive job or sport, what is it that determines success or failure? The answer is simple: it's the ability to stay focused, to concentrate on task-relevant cues. Nothing is more basic to performance or more critical to success than the ability to concentrate. The Attentional and Interpersonal Style (TAIS) inventory is a tool that measures basic concentration skills.

To be successful, people need to be able to shift their focus of concentration along two intersecting dimensions: width and direction. When they can make those shifts in response to the changing demands of performance situations, they can "do it all."

[There are] four basic concentration styles people need to be able to shift between. [See Figure 4-1.]

1.   *A broad external focus of concentration* is the style used for awareness and sensitivity to surroundings. A master of the martial arts needs this focus to be ready to respond to an attack from any direction. A good salesperson uses this focus to be sensitive to customers' reactions.

2.   *A broad internal focus of concentration* is used to strategize and to creatively problem-solve. A coach uses it to make adjustments in a game; a manager uses it to develop strategic goals and objectives for his division or for the company.

---

[1] This excerpt is reprinted with permission from "Can You Perform Under Pressure?" by Kate Kane in *Fast Company,* Dec. 1997, p. 54.

FIGURE 4-1   Four factors of TAIS.

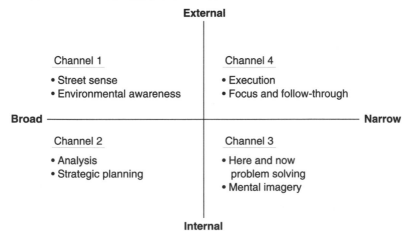

3.   *A narrow internal focus of concentration* is used to create a logical set of systems and/or procedures. A diver uses this style of concentration to mentally rehearse his performance. Managers use it to create a set of rules or steps that lead to the accomplishment of a production goal or corporate objective.

4.   *A narrow external focus of concentration* is used to execute, to get the job done. This is the type of concentration used to catch or hit a ball in sport. It's the kind of concentration a production line worker uses to drill a hole, or a writer uses to type a letter.

In other words, there are certain concentration skills and interpersonal characteristics that are important contributors to performance in almost every situation. A convenient way to think of these characteristics is as the "building blocks of performance." The Attentional and Interpersonal Style (TAIS) inventory measures these building blocks of performance. As a result of biological factors, genetics, and learning experiences, some of the building blocks measured by TAIS become more highly developed or traitlike than others. Each of us develops a slightly different pattern of scores. Those characteristics in us, that are more highly developed, become more traitlike when our emotional arousal level gets outside the optimal range. With increasing arousal, we lose our ability to adapt and change style. We become controlled by our dominant characteristics.

There is no perfect or ideal pattern of scores on TAIS. Whatever the pattern of scores, that pattern will contribute to success in some situations and lead to failure in others. The challenges we all face are to select performance arenas that play to our strengths or dominant patterns and enhance performance by gaining greater control over emotions and our focus of concentration to keep our more dominant building blocks from controlling us. That is what Attention Control Training (ACT) is all about. Teams build by establishing relationships with people we trust, people who have characteristics that are complementary to our own.

TAIS, more than any other inventory available today, provides the information needed for selection, performance enhancement, and for team building in situations where people must perform at extremely high levels and/or when individuals are under a great deal of pressure to perform. However, TAIS tells us less about our individual qualities—the predispositions we bring to our interactions with others—and we need to understand those if we're to adapt successfully to the digital world.

HOW WE INTERACT WITH OTHERS
Interacting with others in the new world of work is going to be more difficult than it has been. These interactions will be spread out in time and space and we will no longer be able to depend upon sensing the "nonverbals" and

other not-so-obvious signals that we use in our everyday life when we are face-to-face with people. Our interactions are going to become much more ambiguous and difficult to interpret.

In the traditional world of work, we were hired and assigned to a department or work team without much regard to our personality or our style of interaction. We'd been taught from early childhood that we needed to learn how to get along with people, but we could not be too "personal." Well I believe those days are rapidly disappearing. As the Internet opens new worlds to us and we find we can pick and choose the projects and the people we want to work with, we need to understand much better how we interact with each other.

The assessment instrument that I introduced, TAIS, is one good way of developing a better appreciation of our interaction style. This is not to say that there's anything good or bad about the different styles, simply that they're different. I believe there is a core value inherent in these different styles of interaction that leads to creativity.

How we interact with others is closely tied to how we process information. But it's more than that. Some people are more aggressive and others are more passive. Some folks are more outgoing and others are more reserved. There's a whole host of these different dimensions, and we all fall someplace within each one. What creates the frustration in work teams is interpreting these different styles of interacting as meaning something more than they really do. For example, people who are more contemplative may want to listen to information and take some time before they react to it. This may seem like a simple thing, but how does taking time to mull something over appear to a person who is used to quick and rapid interaction? I think he or she would become frustrated. The quick person may misinterpret the contemplative person's behavior as signaling lack of respect, lack of importance, or lack of concern, thinking, "Why didn't she respond?" On the other hand, the contemplative person is probably thinking, "Why is he always in such hurry?"—and feeling frustrated by the pressure to react quicker.

In a face-to-face environment this can be bad enough, but when you extend it to interaction over the Internet it can become critical. Say I send an e-mail to a colleague in Europe, and I'm the kind of person who expects and appreciates rapid interaction. The person in Europe, being more contemplative in nature, receives my message and decides to go out for a long lunch to think about the message before responding—or perhaps even takes a day or two to the ponder it before formulating an answer. I'm sitting in the United States, anxiously checking my e-mail several times a day, waiting for a response, and getting more frustrated as the hours drag on without a response. Now I start sending e-mail asking, "What's the problem? Why haven't you answered?" My colleague reads these e-mails and starts thinking, "Those crazy Americans." Now we've got a situation that can escalate into dysfunctional conflict because there's a lack of understanding and appreciation of our different patterns of interaction. If we have an understanding of this before we even enter into these work arrangements, I think that the quality of the collaboration of these Internet-based work teams would improve.

These patterns of interaction go very deep. Just as there is an overlap between how we process information and how we interact with one another, there's an overlap between how we interact with one another and how we deal with conflict, which is our next topic of discussion. One way of looking at how we interact with one another and how we deal with conflict is called the *Enneagram,* which is gaining a great degree of popularity in the workplace recently. Again, it's just a model, and there are many others, but here I will present the Enneagram to you as a way of getting a better handle on the answer to two key questions:

1.   "How do I interact with others?"
2.   "How do I deal with conflict?"

The Enneagram

The Enneagram (*ennea* means "nine" in Greek) is an increasingly popular tool for interpreting how personality affects relationships, the workplace, and one's inner life of thoughts and feelings because it answers the question, "Why do people do what they do?" For me, however, the real strength of the Enneagram is that it also identifies the behaviors we exhibit when we're under stress.

The Enneagram is easier for many people to work with than other personality systems, which can easily overwhelm you with the details of people's many characteristics and preferences. The Enneagram presents nine personality types, structured in terms of our unconscious motivations as human beings, as shown in Figure 4-2.[2]

The nine personality types are as follows:

1. The Achiever	An intense, hardworking, focused perfectionist
2. The Helper	An empathetic, service-oriented, flattering rescuer

---

[2] Go to http://www.hurley-dobson.com, a website with more information on the enneagram.

FIGURE 4-2   The Enneagram.

Copyright © 1990 Theodore E. Dobson and Kathleen V. Hurley

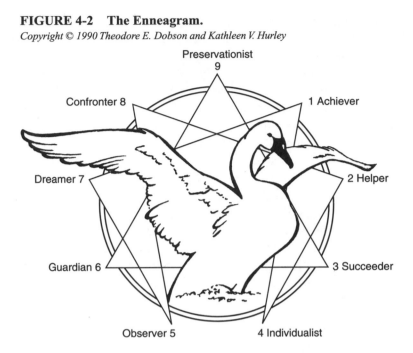

3. The Succeeder	An image-oriented, accomplished, efficient performer
4. The Individualist	A self-absorbed, sensitive, creative over-analyzer
5. The Observer	A noncommittal, deliberate, reflective loner
6. The Guardian	A responsible, opinionated, community-oriented moralist
7. The Dreamer	An analytical, entertaining, self-indulgent fantasizer
8. The Confronter	A competitive, blunt, passionate maneuverer
9. The Preservationist	A secretive, unemotional, affable problem solver for others

I encourage you to study all of the Enneagram types. Space doesn't allow us to examine each of these nine types in detail. I'd encourage you to follow up on the resources in Chapter 7 of this book and select one of the many other tests for a more detailed study of the Enneagram. To give you a preview as a point of reference, let me pick one of these types and talk about it just a little bit so you'll have a basic understanding of how insightful this assessment methodology can be. I'll discuss number 5, *the Observer,* because I'm "an observer." When you read this description, you'll begin to get some insight into me, how I interact with others, and how I deal with conflict.

The Observer[3]

Observers are factually oriented people who focus their thinking and calculating on the world outside themselves. Their goal is objectivity; their method is to live in the world of ideas as if it were the outer world. Peering out from their sacred ivory towers, Observers sit back and watch the world in a cool, dispassionate manner. They think distance creates an objectivity that allows them to discover the real meaning of any issue, person, or situation. This separation from the world disconnects them from their true inner strengths of communication, sensitivity, and versatility. After gathering data they withdraw to an interior cloister to consider, calculate, and finally reconstruct all they have observed according to a pattern that is logical to them.

Observers feel caught in, and so they want to avoid, a feeling of personal emptiness. Their dysfunctional motivation results in a striving to feel full of knowledge. Their basic life issue is knowing, and their prime psychological addiction is greed.

Observers will tend to avoid decisions in the realm of relationship, leaving those to people they deem more qualified. Their approach is impersonal, and they can tend to overlook others' feelings as they examine the pertinent facts. Facts will override feelings in the decision-making process when an Observer is in charge.

They research the facts thoroughly, methodically categorize the information, and reach logical conclusions. Because they complete this process quickly, they are generally impatient with the process of group decision making. In committees, for example, they think that others have not done their homework and so are wasting valuable time by rehashing old material and focusing on inconsequential details. One of the most difficult things for Observers is to learn to be open to examining and valuing alternative points of view.

When they are responsible for decisions, they plan ahead for any possible obstacle that might arise. Thus many people think they spend far too much time in the planning phase. Yet, once the project begins, it moves quickly, and there are seldom cleanup or corrective measures that need to be addressed later. All the details are taken care of with a precision that is amazing to others.

---

[3] This is excerpted with permission from K. V. Hurley and T. E. Dobson, *What's My Type? The Nine Prime Addictions,* HarperCollins, 1992.

HOW DO I DEAL WITH CONFLICT?

Conflict is a fact of life. We all deal with it every day at different levels and with different people. In the workplace of the future, dealing with conflict becomes more of an issue because the degree of diversity of the people around us increases. Different value systems, different realities, different beliefs, and different worldviews all get brought into the new workplace and present us with new situations to deal with.

Not all conflict is bad. The word *conflict* seems to have a negative connotation in our everyday use. But if we reframe it and look at these differences in perspectives, different ways of processing information, and different ways of interacting with one another, it takes on a more positive light. So understanding how we tend to deal with conflict becomes important.

The tools and assessment techniques that I just talked about can go a long way toward understanding how we tend to deal with conflict, and this can help smooth over some of the normal bumps in everyday work situations. Not all conflict stems from simple differences in style and preferences, but understanding how people tend to deal with conflict can help in the middle of critical negotiations or strategic decision making.

One way of dealing with conflict for many people is to simply avoid it. Avoiding conflict in cyberspace is much easier than in face-to-face situations because you get to choose whom you talk to and when. How many of you screen calls on your answering machines? How many times do you simply delete messages from your voice mail when you hear who they are from? All of the ways in which we seek to control the flow of information that comes at us can also be used to avoid dealing with situations that we find unpleasant and conflict-laden.

This is perhaps the most uncomfortable aspect of interpersonal behavior that we all have to deal with. The first step in dealing with conflict is to realize that it exists. I suggest in many cases that people use the third-party facilitator to help them deal with serious conflict in work groups. The reason for this is that it is very difficult once we are engaged in a conflict situation to realize the part each of us has played in creating the situation and to significantly change our own behavior to resolve the issue.

The strength that facilitators bring to this situation is their ability not to be emotionally engaged in the situation and to objectively assess the differences in styles, opinions, and approaches that may be contributing to the situation at hand. In the Internet world, this is difficult to do, because you're already separated in time and space. However, we're beginning to see the emergence of a new social role in these work situations—a role that deserves close attention.

A good example is the use of a moderator, or host, for chat rooms and bulletin boards. The major function of moderators is to monitor conflict situations and quickly help resolve them before they destroy the entire quality of the conversation. This moderator, or facilitator, role is one that I believe is becoming increasingly important in our new world of work. It's a skill set and talent that needs to be developed and probably will come to us from the more traditional form of an organizational development specialist or psychologist.

WHERE DO I GET MY MOTIVATION?

Motivation is a tough issue. We all are motivated by different things: some by money, some by fame, and yet others by glory. Politicians relish power and businesspeople think about making profits and creating wealth. And some of us are motivated by nobler ideas that come from deeply held beliefs. Nonetheless, we're all motivated by something, and a lack of motivation leads to dissatisfaction with our work life and, eventually, burnout.

People's motivation and compensation systems need to be tied closely together or they won't work. Putting a person who is motivated by security into a high-risk situation is asking for disaster. The new work teams that we are forming are complex pictures of different motivations. Being able to understand and sort out these different motivations is key to the success of these new work teams. It often falls to the leader to determine what these motivations are and to make sure that they're all satisfied as best they can be.

Our motivations, I believe, form our basic approaches to life. They speak to our passions. What do you love to do? Answering that kind of question can get to the heart of what our motivations really are. What do you live for? That's another excellent question to ask. Motivations draw us into situations because we can somehow sense that by doing that, being there, or working with that group we will be very satisfied at some deeper level.

In the workplace of the future, there is a significant distinction between a "job" and the work that we like to do. A job is a set of tasks that we perform in order to receive a paycheck. Work is something that we do because we find it intrinsically satisfying and because it serves as a self-motivator. Not that we would work for no pay, but we certainly find that other characteristics of work can be more satisfying. In the first chapters of this book I talked about the changing face of the new worker and the factors that motivate people more than the traditional pay-and-benefits formula.

I think we have to go even deeper than that and understand the basic factors that motivate us. At some level, this gets down to understanding our true purpose—why we were put in this world. This book is not the place for that level of philosophical discussion, but it may be a topic that you wish to pursue. If so, some of the references in Chapter 7 can help you begin that journey.

Well, back to understanding the workplace of the future. The approach that I like to use to develop a deeper understanding of a person's motivations is called the Life Colors perspective. As with the other assessment instruments that I've talked about, let me give you a little flavor of what this approach can do in terms of helping to understand what motivates us and what motivates the people on our new "cyber–work teams."

Life Colors[4]

The Life Colors approach is far richer than we can go into here, but take a minute to study the key qualities of each color type. Think about which most closely describes you. Then think about which most closely describes someone you work with, perhaps someone you don't get along with very well. Could you learn to accept some of the qualities that drive you crazy today?

Blue

Blues are some of the most loving, nurturing, and supportive personalities of the aura colors. They live from their hearts and emotions. Their purpose for being on the planet is to give love, to teach love, and to learn that they are loved.

Blues are constantly mothering and taking care of everyone. They want to make sure that everyone feels loved and accepted. Consequently, they remember everyone's birthday, take care of him or her when they're sick, and consistently provide a shoulder for everyone to cry on. People are always turning to Blues for comfort and counsel because Blues will always be there for them. They are the natural counselors, teachers, and nurses.

Yellow

Yellows are the most childlike personalities in the aura spectrum. These playful characters have a great sense of humor. They love to laugh and to make others laugh. Their life purpose is to bring joy to the planet and to help heal it.

Yellows believe life is meant to be enjoyed. They do not like to take life seriously, nor do they like to work. Their work must be "play" for

---

[4] This excerpt is reprinted with permission from Pamala Oslie's *Life Colors,* New World Library, Novato, CA, 1991.

them. Yellows advocate relaxing, keeping life light and having fun. They like to keep life spontaneous.

Violet

Violets are here to "save the planet" and change it for the better. Violets have an inner sense that they are here to do something important, that their destiny is greater than that of the average person. Because this is a "Violet Age," any Violets who are not accomplishing what they came here to do are, at this time, experiencing an inner "push"—even an inner "earthquake." Some inner force seems to be shaking them up and pushing them to move into action, to fulfill their purpose for being here.

Violets have very charismatic and magnetic energy, so people are drawn to them. Violets also love to be the center of attention. They are natural performers. Violets are developing their skills and taking on their roles as leaders on the planet. While some are showing up as leaders, others are joining together in groups to work for common causes, such as Greenpeace, Comic Relief for the Homeless, Farm-Aid, International Wildlife Coalition, and "We Are the World" 's Band-Aid.

Green

Greens are extremely bright and intelligent. They process quickly, jumping from one to ten. They do not like dealing with all the steps and details in between. A project which is too detailed is slow, tedious, and boring for Greens. Instead, they prefer to deal with ideas and concepts. They prefer to develop the idea, organize the plan to accomplish the end product and then delegate or hire someone else to take care of the details.

These quick-thinkers are very organized and efficient. They write lists and efficiently check off the items on the list as they are completed. Greens recognize patterns and discover solutions very quickly. These ambitious personalities are driven to accomplish, becoming very intense and serious when working toward their goals. They push themselves, always appearing to be in a hurry. A Green is the prime example of a workaholic and a perfectionist.

KNOWING WHO WE ARE IN THE WORKPLACE

Well, how do you put all these parts together? What does it mean on the job? Let's examine two examples to see how these people would interact with one another in the workplace.

Our first example is Ted. Ted's TAIS profile is characterized by a broad external focus of concentration. On the Enneagram, he is a number seven, the Dreamer. His predominant life color is violet. Ted is the kind of person who is very aware and sensitive to the things going on around him; he tends to be analytical, outgoing, and very entertaining to be around; he also is very charismatic, and people find themselves drawn to him.

Ted is the kind of person who usually excels in team roles that require him to be the grand synthesizer and interact with a lot of people outside the team environment. Ted is very good at this and probably is also excellent in marketing roles requiring him to focus on the big picture and to bridge the gap between his own work group and other work groups. Ted is also absolutely lousy at keeping track of details, focusing on one thing at a time, or being concerned about things like the cost of the project.

Now let's look at an example of someone with a completely different profile. Betsy's TAIS profile reveals a narrow internal focus of concentration; she is an Observer from the Enneagram perspective; and her major life color is blue.

Betsy gravitates toward roles that place a premium on concentration and matter-of-fact ways of looking at the world. But, given her life color, Betsy is also a person that people turn to when they need help. Betsy is the "keeper of the flame" on most teams. She stays focused on the task at hand.

How are Ted and Betsy going to get along within a team? Probably, they're not going to get along very well, at least at first. Ted's tendency to go off in seven directions at once will absolutely infuriate Betsy, who can't understand this bundle of energy who seems to be bouncing off the walls all the time. On the other hand, when Ted looks at Betsy he is totally baffled by the fact that she can focus on one thing continuously for a long time and never miss a beat. There are two things to be learned here:

1.   It takes a great variety of different types of people to make a team function effectively.

2.   We all need to learn to respect each other's differences and value what other people can do that we don't do very well.

In the case of Ted and Betsy, I would say that it is very important for each of them to share their profiles with each other. This way they can, in a nonjudgmental way, learn what the other person is really like. When a project runs into tough times, when the pressure is on and the deadlines are tight, a mutual understanding would preclude a lot of surprises, angry feelings, and misunderstandings that might take weeks or even months to overcome. Learning how to respect each other's differences also leads us in the direction of thinking about assembling teams of people who deliberately are selected *because* they have different profiles, tendencies, and likes and dislikes. In my own company, for example, all the members of a work team voluntarily participate in this process, so each of us has a very complete and detailed picture of the others. We do this to give teams balance and ensure that we have the right mix of people pulled together to meet client needs.

Back to Ted and Betsy. If I were assembling a work team, I would put Ted in the position of client management. He would be the person primarily responsible for interacting with the client, translating the client's needs into ideas for the project, and presenting the work product to the client. Betsy, on the other hand, probably would be an excellent project manager, the person who would keep track of all the deadlines and budget figures and organize the team's output into something that would be understandable and comprehensive.

These different ways of looking at yourself and others can be extremely useful. In most work settings, if you're really lucky, you may sometimes use a single method or instrument to gain a deeper understanding of yourself and your team members. But I maintain that in the new world of work, where a premium is placed on teamwork and we are members of several teams or social networks at the same time, we absolutely, positively need to have a way to quickly understand each other without long periods of interacting. We may find ourselves on a team with a tremendous amount of work to do a short time, and we won't have the luxury of being able to spend two weeks just getting to know one another. The approach outlined here is one way to come up to "social speed" very quickly in these new work environments.

THE SEVENFOLD WORK: THE PATH FORWARD[5]

We started this chapter by talking about the necessity to make personal transitions. We discussed some current realities of work and some emerging new realities. We spent some time looking at why some of us may be stuck in the "old reality of being" and considered some key questions about who we really are. Then we spent some time examining three different ways of looking at ourselves.

At this point in our journey, we need to explore just how we're supposed to be able to make this transition. Considering that we have a fairly good understanding of who we are, how we interact with others, and how we take in information, we must now decide on a process that can move us forward and help us become more comfortable and effective in the new world of work.

Let's begin. There's a seven-step process that you can use to guide yourself through this transition. Table 4-3 outlines these steps in the order you'll take them. For each step you'll see the name of the *state* associated

---

[5] The Sevenfold Work comes from the ideas of John Bennett, *The Sevenfold Work,* Coombe Springs Press, Coombe Springs, WV, 1979, and is part of a larger metaphysical work.

TABLE 4-3   Seven-step guide for transition.

Step	State	Quality	Activity
1	Initiation	*Assimilation:* Active taking from outside to inside. Your focus is on your *world.*	Awareness that something is lacking and time is passing. You move to get something you need. You begin seeking answers to nagging questions: "Why am I so anxious all the time?"
2	Involvement	*Struggle:* Active inside ourselves to inside ourselves. Your focus is on *myself.*	Looking at the internal states we don't want to look at. Introspection: "Is it me, or is everyone around here nuts?"
3	Separation	*Service:* Active from inside to outside. Your focus is on *community.*	Duty, intentional suffering. Sharing what we know to build future capability in others. Giving of oneself to others, usually seen as community service actions. It gives us emotional room to separate from old patterns and to focus on something outside ourselves.
4	Harmonization	*Manifestation*	Tao. We are a vehicle through which creativity is expressed. The "flow state." You begin to act in new ways, building off the old, and feel rejuventated.
5	Insight	*Receptivity:* Opening up to take in from the outside. Your focus is on *community.*	Being open to help from others. Trust the universe to bring you what you need. Relaxation and openness from knowing that you are firmly committed to a pathway of change.
6	Renunciation	*Submission:* Receptive inside to inside. Your focus is on *myself.*	Letting go of ego. Emptying the vessel within of baggage. Moving from selfishness to improving your state of being.

TABLE 4-3   (*Continued*)

Step	State	Quality	Activity
7	Completion	*Purity:* Receptive to what is beyond us. Your focus is on your *world*.	Waking up! Consciousness comes to us. Realization of your part in the universe, a spiritual awakening.

with that step, the *quality* you should be feeling during that particular stage of transition, and the *activity* you'll associate with that step.

Initiation

Step 1 is the state of initiation, a beginning. This is where you are right now. You have begun the journey toward transformation; you have initiated some action. The quality that I believe you should be experiencing at this stage is one of *assimilation*. You are taking things from outside yourself and bringing them inside—mentally, emotionally, and spiritually. The recent popularity of self-help books, tapes, and seminars is a good example of the prevalence of this initiation step in our society. People are finding something wanting in their lives and are beginning the journey. The very act of reading this book and, in particular, this chapter is a good example of assimilation—of taking in. The activity that began with this stage of the transition is your basic awareness that something needs to be done. I would suggest that a large part of your motivation in buying this book and beginning to read through it comes from some deeper sense that something is lacking, that something needs to be done for you to feel more comfortable with the future of work.

The new world of work could be characterized as one in which initiation is a continuous process. Involvement in numerous projects at the same time means we are constantly engaging with new people, new ideas, and new situations. Realizing that each of these situations initiates for us a different process of change is important. The new technology connects and relates us to even more situations. We need to realize that we're placing ourselves on several pathways of change at the same time. Knowing that we are going in several directions at once can help bring some understanding to the confusion we sense around us in this fast-paced ever changing workplace. So I would ask you to look at each of these situations as parallel efforts at initiating a process of change for you.

Involvement

As you move deeper into this process, you begin to become more involved in the process of discovery and of thinking your way through the transition you want to make. This is step 2 in the process of change. This is the *struggle*. This is the point at which many people fall off the path because they begin to see the difficulty, the struggle, the day-to-day challenge they have to engage in to make a transition. This is a very internal part of the process; the struggle is going on inside us: the struggling with the new, habits giving way to new behaviors, different attitudes and viewpoints emerging, the leaving behind of the familiar friends and/or ideas that once made us very comfortable. We are looking at the internal states that we prefer not to look at. As with the Enneagram, we're forced to look at our addictions as they intensify. Oftentimes, we don't want to deal with these things. Some of us go into denial and go back to our old ways of behaving. But if we have persevered this far, and if we realize that this is a natural part of the transition process, we are able to tolerate the struggle with grace.

The Internet forces involvement. Engagement with people in dispersed work teams creates a situation where you must make an effort to become involved with them. Your communication is something that needs to be better planned and more conscious. You can't leave things to chance. In a strange way, a number of choices that you would normally have about whether to engage with people or not engage with them are taken away in this workplace dominated by communication technology. And then the struggle begins. It usually begins with an effort to better understand those people around us and to spend more time working on the "softer side" of our interactions with our workmates.

On one hand, the technology promotes a workplace in which communication seems to be more difficult, and on the other hand, this communication becomes more intense and more intimate as we seek to develop a clearer appreciation of what it really means to work with people. In essence, your involvement with your workmates is a journey in which each of you and all of you are on a pathway toward change. You affect each other much more and, as a result, stand to gain much more from these interactions than you would have in a more traditional workplace. The Internet workplace—the workplace of the future—is one in which we will all become more involved with one another.

Separation

As we enter step 3 of the process we begin to see ourselves separating from comfortable things. We begin to open up to the possibility of new jobs, new friends, new careers, and perhaps even new communities. Many people today, as I spoke about in earlier chapters, are separating themselves from more traditional ways of working and are physically moving to new locations to begin completely new career patterns that are better suited to them and the times in which we are living. The quality of this stage is one of *service;* it's giving of ourselves to something larger. We become very engaged with our work, and it begins to seem like it isn't really "work." We begin to feel that in our new work, we are *serving* in the true sense of the word. At this stage of transition, we begin to feel that we are learning something important that we need to share with others. At this stage in my own transition, I decided that I needed to take everything I had learned about the future of work and put it in a form where it would be accessible to others. I felt it was my duty.

The workplace of the future, as I've said many times before, is one in which we move from having a *job* to one in which we *work.* It allows us to separate ourselves from old situations that were uncomfortable and dysfunctional. It provides us with an opportunity to move away from the old and toward the new.

Separation from old habits, old viewpoints, and old networks is easier in this Internet world. No longer do we have to physically pick up and move to a different town to get a different job and have different neighbors. We can do this electronically while remaining physically in the same place. Separation becomes easier and so does the process of change. We have more options now because we're connected with a much wider and more conscious world. Working in this new world facilitates your own process of personal change because it provides you with an easier way to let go of old things and find the new things that we all need to be connected to.

Harmonization

Step 4 in the process is what I call *harmonization.* It's a blending together of old qualities with some of the new. It's the recognition that no matter what type of individual we are, our old predispositions and patterns of behavior need to blend with new dispositions and new behaviors. We harmonize the old and the new. What we're doing is beginning to manifest, or bring into being, those new qualities that will help us fit better into the new world of work. This step is the one that I find absolutely the most interesting. It's not predictable, and it doesn't appear to happen at any particular time—it is a sudden realization that we are vehicles through which creativity is expressed. This is the point at which artists get their inspiration; this is the point at which scientists have breakthroughs; this is the point at which students say to themselves, "Ah ha!"

Some of you may think that this would be the end of it. We've sought out information and new knowledge, bringing it to ourselves and combining it with elements of the old, beginning to separate from the old, and finally putting all the pieces together. But it's not that simple. Once we've gotten to this point, it's doubtful that the transition will be permanent if more work isn't done. We need to move beyond a simple realization that we are making a change, and we have to bring into ourselves more information and knowledge. It's at this point that we begin to *learn how to learn*. The Internet is about harmony. One of the major contentions of this book is that the technology is no longer simply a task-based tool like a word processor, but an extension of us into an entirely new world of relationships and connections and resources we never even dreamed about. The Internet, and all of its associated technology, is the lifeblood of how we learn; it's how we connect and how we relate to others. This new world of work is helping us to be more in harmony with our workmates, our customers, and the larger world around us.

Insight

Step 5 is where we gain insight. This is where we have to be even more open to taking in new knowledge and ideas from our community. The first four steps of the transition process lifted us out of our old rut and into a new community. Now that we are there, we have to pay even more attention; we have to be even more self-observant and continuously try to integrate what we've learned into our everyday work. We need to be open to others, and we need to trust that the community (our new friends, our new jobs, and our new ideas) will bring us what we need when we need it. That's a pretty metaphysical statement, and it takes a lot of trust—but it will happen. Our normal inclination in the old world of work was to go out and find what we needed, not to relax and trust that it would come to us. Step 5 of the transition is a stage of joy and easing of tensions. I've watched a number of people make the transition to the new world of work. One of the things that very predictably happens after about one year of engaging in these new work practices is that people begin to change the very way in which they work. This is the moment of insight. This is when people realize that they don't have to write memos the same way that they used to, and they don't have to attend the dozens of standing meetings, and that they don't have to work with just the tools given them but can reach out and get the tools they need.

I often tell my clients that they need to prepare themselves, because after a year or so of helping their employees move to alternative styles of work, their very organizations will be changed fundamentally. As workers begin to gain the insight that they needn't be locked into the old ways of doing things, as they begin to see that they can create new businesses and relationships with customers, they begin to take control of the situation and use these insights to reconstruct the workplace.

I'm not to sure if this is anything that has to do specifically with the characteristics of electronic communication and the Internet, but it is probably reflective of what happens when technology in general impacts us. Gaining these insights of shifts in structure and organization has occurred before in history and undoubtedly will occur again in the future. What is unique to this time is that, perhaps for the first time in human history, we are collectively more conscious of the insights that we are gaining because the power of technology allows us to more freely communicate these insights with one another.

Renunciation

Step 6 takes us one level deeper in the process. Once we've learned to relax, to trust our community, and to be open to others who can help us in our continuing transition, we need to do something of a similar fashion internally. We have to learn to trust our own instincts. We need to learn to open up and follow our intuitions and not second-guess ourselves. We need to learn how to be receptive to our own insights. I have a little sign over my desk that says "trust your instincts." This is a very difficult thing for me to do—even though I tend to be a very intuitive person. Oftentimes in business I tend to overanalyze the situation instead of going with my gut instincts. I'm struggling with this, struggling with the old ways and struggling to let go of the ego, or as we say here in California, "Go with the flow, dude." Our new world of work is characterized by the existence of new communities. In some ways we need to renounce our membership in our old communities in order to fully engage in and be involved with our new ones. One of the things I like about using the Internet as a medium for my work is that I can instantaneously follow up on making connections with other people in new communities. This is a process that in more traditional workplaces would have taken days, if not weeks.

Let me give you one personal example of this. During a recent move from Silicon Valley to the wine country of Sonoma County, I discovered I no longer needed a luxury automobile that was comfortable on the freeways and was sort of my capsule of privacy during my many hours commuting in congested traffic. So I renounced that old way of working which was related to my transportation patterns. Given the remoteness of my new physical workplace, up on a mountain over a dirt and gravel road, I decided that I needed a four-wheel drive vehicle. So I bought a Jeep—not a new one but an old restored one. That met my transportation needs perfectly.

In purchasing the Jeep, I discovered that I had become a member of the new community of people who restore old vehicles and take quite a sense of pride in belonging to this "club." The point of the story is that I could have gone through this transition in many other contexts, but having access to the Internet and its technology allowed me to find the other people in this Jeep community and connect with them literally in a matter of minutes. On the Internet I was able to find all of the people in my neighborhood, in this case Northern California, who owned similar vehicles and shared a passion for them.

Completion

Finally, we get to the end of the process of transformation. Step 7 is the *completion*. This is a point at which we become openly receptive to what is beyond us and realize that we're only a small part of the larger world. In the context of the future of work, it's at this point that we really wake up and realize that we only have purpose or value as part of the larger social group (our work team or community). Consciousness comes to us! We wake up! However, the transition process really does not have an end, and step 7 is merely a prelude to step 1 of the *next* cycle of change, and the process begins over again.

One of the ways that you can use the Internet to help you in a process of personal transformation is to seek out others who are going through the process, enjoying their little groups, and staying in communication. I have a network of people with whom I interact on a regular basis on the Internet. They are spread out all over the planet, and they are all interested in ideas about personal change, growth, and development.

What I get from these people are helpful hints, references to things they think I should read or know about, and an expansive set of connections to like-minded folks. The process of transition itself has changed with the advent of the Internet and our new world of work. The two things that come together for me are that the new world of work is ever changing and that I have to be ever changing in order to continuously adapt to it. I know that I have to learn how to use the new communications technologies, including the Internet, in a way that allows me to connect to that larger world, and I have to be continuously going through this change process.

There is no one correct way to go through a process of personal transition. What I have presented here is one view of that process with some examples taken from real-life, my own and those around me who are going through significant personal change processes. *One thing I have learned about this transition process is that it is very difficult to travel the journey by yourself with no road map, no compass, no guide.* I will return to this point in a little bit with some very practical suggestions about how you can embark upon your own transition process.

People often ask me, "Just how long does this take?" I don't have an answer to that. It takes different times for different people, and I don't think it's a process that can be forced or "engineered." Another little story: At one time in my professional life I had a job in a large bureaucracy whose mission is one of research and discovery. However, the organizational context was such that everyone's behavior was very rigid and structured. On one occasion, I had a supervisor inform me that I was supposed to be at my desk every morning at 8:30. And further, that he expected me to be, in his words, "creative from minute one." You can't tell somebody when to be creative. You can't tell somebody when to leave stage three of this transition process and enter stage four. It happens differently for all of us. In my own reflections on my personal transition process, I've noticed that the steps don't necessarily go 1, 2, 3, 4, and so on; sometimes they go 1, 3, 2, 4.

The point in presenting you with The Sevenfold Work is to give you a map. And in the words of some old scholar, "The map is not the territory." So be patient with yourself and keep this as a guide. If you find that some of the steps are missing, look back and see what hasn't happened that needs to happen to allow you to move forward. One little interesting exercise you may want to try is to lay out a chart that looks like a table and then add one blank column on the right-hand side. Then sit back and reflect on a major transition that has taken place in your life before, perhaps going to college and graduating or perhaps some other significant shift in yourself, your understanding of yourself, or the way you were living your life. Given that frame of reference, begin to walk your way through the process, being sensitive at each step to the events, feelings, internal mental states, and any other thing that jumps to mind that occurred at that step in your former transition. Once you've gone through the exercise, sit back and look at the complete picture to determine if anything is missing or if there are any additional parts or pieces that are uncovered by this map.

This exercise will give you a personal picture of how you yourself go through transitions. When you remember the times of struggle and the times of insight, you can begin to develop some faith in the process. You've been down this road before; you are going down it again; and chances are you will have to travel it several times more in your life.

BUILD YOUR OWN BRIDGES, BE YOUR OWN PILOT: CONTINUOUS TRANSFORMATION

Now let me return to the basic question of this entire chapter: How do I make this transition? I presented several different ways of looking at yourself to give you an idea of how you tend to answer the four basic questions of transition, about how you process information, interact with others, deal with conflict, and derive your motivation. Although this is well and good as a general guideline, it still doesn't give you concrete and specific things to do to embark upon your own transition process.

Making the transition to the new world of work is not going to be easy, as I've said repeatedly. This section of the chapter on personal change is devoted to some very specific things you can do to help make this transition. But why should you? What is it about the new world of work that requires you to make these transitions?

The future of work is, at its core, a process of continuous change: change at the individual level, change at the organizational level, and change at the community level. You need a plan. You need a map. You need some guidelines about how to go through this transition process not once, not twice, but quite probably six to ten times during your professional work life.

I would like to offer some specific suggestions about how to engage this process of change the first time, the second time, and so on for as long as we find that the coevolution of technology and the workplace continues. I will close this chapter with two very specific recommendations for concrete activities you can begin almost immediately to carry yourself through the transition process you need to engage in to be successful in these new worlds of work. The first of these recommendations has to do with establishing your own internal guidance system, and the second has to do with how you establish something external to you—a governance system. After you have gone through the process of identifying why you are stuck in the old way of working and have a clear understanding of who you are and how you operate in the world, you will be able to embark upon a process of change. But it's not a one-time event, as I have said before.

There are two basic, concrete things that you can do to ensure that the transformation process is ongoing and effective. After all, as we saw in the first couple of chapters of this book, this process of change is not something that's going to stop tomorrow. So you need to build the basic functioning capability to continuously change and stay in sync with your business environment, yourself, and your community. The two things you can do are as follows:

1.   Become your own gyroscope.
2.   Establish your own personal board of directors.

Become Your Own Gyroscope

Becoming your own gyroscope means that you are going to start taking your "sense of correction" internally instead of externally. The shift here is in how you view where your purpose comes from: Your purpose, your orientation, your gyroscope should really come from inside you now, not from an external organization or group. You need to learn how to follow your own advice. That is not to say that you won't seek out new knowledge, opinions, and guidance from others, but you'll do it in a way that *forms only part of your motivation—it doesn't become your motivation.*

I have some very specific ideas about how you can seek and find this external guidance and use it as part of your transformation process, especially during steps 1 and 5. I call it a *personal board of directors.* In a company, the board of directors functions as a governance council. It's a place where long-term strategic and change-oriented decisions are made. It stays above the everyday fray of operations. It's a place were executives can go and seek counsel concerning serious and long-lasting actions that they're contemplating. It is ultimately the place where the long-term health of the organization is maintained.

Establish Your Personal Board of Directors
Who: Criteria

I think all of us need our own personal board of directors—a place where we can go to seek counsel or new knowledge to help guide us in our own transitions. You may ask yourself, "What's the difference between this and just my friends?" Well, the basic difference is that this is a small group of people, usually five to seven whom you have deliberately sought out and brought together to help guide you in periods of transition. It's not necessarily based on family, physical community, the workplace, or historical accident.

What are the criteria for selecting members of your own personal board of directors? I think you need to look at the factors that can help you realize your full potential. Find people who have some expertise, who are compatible with you from a personality perspective, and finally who can offer you some critical balance in the areas that are not your strong suit. For example, if you're a person who pays attention to the world in a broad, external fashion (as determined by TAIS), seek out someone for your board of directors who has as their natural focus a narrow, internal perspective. This will help balance your decisions.

I think you need someone who can advise you on personal decisions, crises of consciousness, and ethical matters. You also need someone who is very sensitive to the larger issues of the business community and personal finance. Third, you need someone who can help you continuously improve, such as an educational adviser or someone who specializes in transitions. Then I think you need an older, wiser person. A mentor. Someone who's been there, done that, and can keep you from making mistakes along your pathway. I think there should be yet another person on your board of directors who really is what I call "the Challenger." You need to have one very strong person who ultimately has your best interests at heart but will always challenge you on any anticipated decision and won't simply go along with you.

Your ideal personal board of directors would include the following:

- Ethical adviser
- Financial matters expert
- Educational adviser
- Mentor
- Challenger

How to Select the Board

It looks like you'll need about five people, all playing different roles, but how do you go about finding these folks? Go through your address book in conjunction with your role list, writing names in the appropriate category. By doing this, you'll develop a list of candidates. The next step is to interview them. Sit down with each of these people and explain to them what your transition process is like and what you're doing. In short, recruit them; explain to them what role you would like them to play and what you expect from them.

As strange as this may sound, it is not difficult to do. My own experience has been that you will find people very receptive to this idea, quite thrilled by the concept, and actually honored that you asked them to play this new role in your life. You may find yourself actually entering into a reciprocal relationship with some of your board members. You may be able to perform a like role for them.

Selection of the final group of people for your board should be done only after you share with them the results of your own assessment, clarify your own direction of change, and get them to agree to play the role. Finally, I think it comes down to your own courage about how strong you want this group of advisers to be. This will be the group that perhaps tells you not to enter into a business venture, to break off a relationship, or some other significant advice that you'd prefer to avoid. You are placing yourself in a position of deliberately seeking external feedback and guidance—and sometimes you won't want to hear what your advisers have to say. So select them carefully. Make sure that you are putting together a group that offers you considerable diversity in approach and opinions and that at the end of the day they are motivated to help you improve and continuously be effective in a new world of work.

Frequency of Interaction

How frequently should you seek them out and ask questions and review with them actions that you are contemplating? I think you need to meet on a regular basis, as you would with any other counselor. How often do you see your accountant? How often do you sit down with your attorney? Or perhaps, how often do you seek the counsel of a minister, pastor, or other spiritual leader? You have your own rhythm to your decision-making process, and you should use your board of directors at a similar pace.

I seek out my own personal board of directors usually on a quarterly basis, or more frequently if there are significant events such as opportunities for major new projects. Also, my board and I meet on an annual basis for a review of my own personal development plan and my business plan, looking for places that need to be adjusted or changed. And, of course, they are available for individual conversations should matters pop up.

Removal and Upgrade

What about removal? You can certainly fire any members of your board at your discretion. Every couple of years or so, I think that you should review your needs and evaluate how well your board has been meeting them. In the dynamic business environment we're in, you may need to replace individual board members to bring in different perspectives and backgrounds should you anticipate the need to make decisions in new areas. Always be on the lookout for people who can offer you advice for growth and development. Your board of directors should be a dynamic guidance system and one that you can modify to your needs over time.

ORGANIZATIONS OF THE FUTURE: SHOW ME SOME SUCCESS

> Where there is great doubt, there will be great awakening; small doubt, small awakening; no doubt, no awakening.
>
> *Zen saying*

THIS CHAPTER IS ABOUT WHAT I THINK will be the form of the organization of the future as all the forces and cycles that we have talked about so far alter how we work together.

As you will recall, one of the central theses of this book is that the future world of work will be one in which our identity is taken not so much from the organization that we work in as from the communities and social networks constructed by the new technology. In the future, maybe even today for some of us, it isn't the *organization that we work for so much as it is the people whom we work with.*

This chapter is organized into four basic sections. This first section serves as a link, or bridge, back to the first part of the book, which dealt with what's changing and how work is evolving. Next, I'll explore in detail an idea that I presented early on: namely, that we are dealing with a fundamentally different form of work organization called the *Hollywood model.*

After painting this picture of what I believe the future will look like, I'll turn to a more practical "how did we get there?" discussion centered around this emerging workplace design approach called Softwork™. This chapter concludes with an extensive case study of a firm that has actually adopted this new Hollywood model of working and transitioned itself to this new organizational form through application of the principles of Softwork. In short, I will close this chapter with the story of success of an organization that has actually made the transition.

When you are finally able to deal with all of these changes that are being created by cycles of history, rapid development of technology, and unraveling of the old social order, you finally get to answer the question, "How do we work together now?" If you stop and think for a minute, this is not a new question for humans. I'm sure that thousands of years ago in ancient Egypt, when the architects began designing pyramids, they first asked the question, "How are we going to get this done?"

The development of rudimentary technologies such as levers, wheels, and inclines was backed up by a change in thinking about the meaning of the universe and respect for ancestors. Great monuments were designed and planned. But the form of working together, which was based on an agrarian model, needed to give way to perhaps the first large-scale human work organization. Undoubtedly, this created much anxiety and uncertainty at the time. But we as humans usually prevail in the face of adversity, finding a way to solve social problems, as the early Egyptians did.

The same type of thing occurred during the Industrial Revolution when we began to move from a feudal form of social organization to what we now view as the industrial age. All these changes have followed a similar pattern, as we discussed in Chapter 1 of this book. This now brings us to the question, "What are our new forms of work organization going to look like?" I've been studying this issue intently for the last 10 years. After working in large organizations, small businesses, and start-ups, I've come to the conclusion that the old dinosaurs created by Alfred Sloan and Frederick Taylor are outmoded and, for the most part, no longer useful to our modern information-age society.

In Chapter 2, in our discussion of how work was evolving, I presented an initial model of the transition from "telework" to "virtuality" to a newly emerging form of work organization. I've labeled this new form of work organization "Hollywood" because in my direct experience we're seeing this new form emerge in the new media sector of our economy, where changes are the most rapid, technology is most intense, and innovation and creativity are the engines of commerce.

I'm not even sure of the proper terms to use for these new ways of working. I'm intrigued with biological and chemical models, as they may provide us with some of the first languages to talk about these things. Work organizations are growing up around us that are just now taking a visible form. I think that what we see growing here are really molecules—molecules of business that take on the characteristics of the combined atoms that come together to form them. They have relatively short lives, serve a single purpose, then disband, only to recombine in other forms for other purposes. They truly are the children of our rapidly changing and more connected planet.

HOLLYWOOD: A BUSINESS MODEL FOR THE FUTURE?

The advent of the Internet age has ushered in a period of significant development of new models of doing business and managing organizations. Various authors have talked about "the networked organization," "virtual corporations," "cellular firms," and "distributed firms." Futurist Alvin Toffler describes a "third wave" economy characterized by continual and continuous change, "demassified" manufacturing, mass customization, and intensive dependence on information and knowledge as sources of competitive advantage.

Developments in information technology (IT) are actually enabling, if not driving, enterprises to adopt new work practices, new organizational structures, and even new management styles in order to extend their businesses both domestically and abroad. As the pace of business activity increases and markets emerge and disappear almost overnight, different approaches are required to respond to these rapid changes. The traditional industrial model of hierarchical, formal, layered organizations may soon be antiquated and replaced by more flexible, dynamic structures. Mature organizations or industries with cultural barriers to such dramatic change risk falling behind and being unable to compete effectively.

A NEW APPROACH TO ORGANIZING WORK

We believe that successful models for work organization in the "new economy" will include small-scale networks of interlocked specialists coming together on a temporary basis to approach a focused market or project. This combination of relatively autonomous entities or "business atoms" will stay together just long enough to meet its members' specific goals and then disband, with individuals and teams moving on to other projects and other ventures. Formal work groups with member relationships that span long periods of time and numerous work efforts will be replaced with these focused, temporary, virtual organizations of organically formed business "molecules."

Yet our formal knowledge of how these new forms of organization and management actually operate is relatively limited. And while we sense that these new management approaches may be more appropriate for the new economy, there is little hard evidence that they actually produce higher-quality products and services for customers, a higher quality of life for employees, or higher levels of profitability for shareholders and other investors.

In my view, the most compelling present-day example of this new organizational model can be found in Hollywood. For large film ventures today, it is typical for literally hundreds of small firms and individual entities to coalesce around a project—usually a script. These projects are led by producers and directors who recruit talent for all key roles (including both on-screen and off-screen contributors). Often, the members of a film project participate in a shared equity model, and the final product is delivered through existing distribution channels. Combinations of talent from a particular film may work together on future endeavors, but in general, once a particular project is completed, the virtual organization that created it comes to an end.

The film industry offers a unique and rich example of how business and organizational structures have shifted over time from the large, vertically integrated production enterprises of the early studio era to the more loosely connected functional networks of independent actors, production companies, and distributors of today.

Similar organizational transformations have occurred in other traditional industries during the past half century as information technology has become increasingly pervasive in business and in our personal lives. Each stage in the evolution of computing has brought with it changes in how individuals within organizations interact with each other, with customers, and with information itself. No longer is IT merely an automation function. It has become the key business infrastructure of the Internet age, enabling businesses to be connected and related to partners, suppliers, customers, and communities around the world.

The most fundamental aspect of this continuing transformation has been the impact that IT has had on the basic costs of communication, information search, and conducting business across organizational boundaries. IT has reduced these costs so dramatically that the economic advantages of vertical integration have virtually disappeared in many industries. Today it can be more cost-effective to acquire needed goods and services from the marketplace (paying someone else a profit to provide them) than to own the production capabilities yourself.

APPLYING THE HOLLYWOOD MODEL OUTSIDE OF HOLLYWOOD

Could the Hollywood film production approach serve as an organizational model for the next century? I believe that more and more industries are taking on the characteristics of Hollywood—high fixed costs, low variable costs, a time-bounded need for highly specialized and scarce talent, and a powerful requirement for someone to manage or direct the creative process (the role in Hollywood played by individuals like James Cameron, Steven Spielberg, George Lucas, Penny Marshall, Rob Reiner, and others).

If, in fact, this model has applicability to other industries and product development processes, it will be important to understand how it actually works. That is, what are the key roles, management processes, working relationships, and shared values that characterize the Hollywood model, and what management skills and styles does it take to make the model work effectively? There are, after all, many well-known examples of Hollywood ventures that were well funded, staffed by stars, and directed by experienced professionals that nevertheless produced box-office disasters.

Figure 5-1 describes and summarizes two significant organizational trends that have emerged in the past decade (*telework* and *virtual teaming*) and compares these work patterns in form and symbol to our understanding of the Hollywood model for doing business. The team structures found in professional sports represent generic organizational models that exist in business today and provide useful metaphors for understanding distinctly different patterns of organizational behavior and their associated management implications.

As reflected in Figure 5-1, the organizational impact of telework in the late 1980s has very interesting similarities to the structure and behaviors of professional baseball. When telecommuting emerged as an alternative work option, the criteria for selecting candidates for this type of arrangement were highly individual in nature. Specific employees were selected on the basis of their roles, their contributions, and the degree to which their tasks were independent of others and thus could be seamlessly removed from and reintegrated into the day-to-day office work flow. Professional baseball has a parallel emphasis on individual contributions as well as patterns of independent activities. In baseball, team members' individual contributions are highly valued, but their activities occur in a more or less sequential order (e.g., pitcher throws ball, batter hits ball, fielder catches ball). In the business world, a useful parallel is that of a manufacturing assembly line where specific work is performed by one person and handed off to another to complete the next task. This type of organizational pattern requires a great degree of coordination among individuals, but each participant's primary focus is on his or her role and the execution of individual tasks.

By the mid-1990s, cooperative project teams had become the way to work. Technology was, and continues to be, a prime enabler of this distinctly different pattern of doing business. E-mail, networked computing,

FIGURE 5-1   New forms of work organization.

	Age of teleworkers	Age of virtuality	Age of Hollywood
Time	1989–1992	1993–1997	1998–2004
Emphasis placed on	People: *individual contributor*	Technology: *project team*	Organization: *teams of teams*
Sports metaphor*	Baseball	Football	Olympic basketball
Social metaphor†	Coordination	Cooperation	Collaboration
Commerce model	Manufacturing	Centralized computing	Internet
Exemplar firm(s)	GM	Sun, HP	DreamWorks, ISDW
Symbolic interaction	Work flow	Connectivity	Community
Time orientation	Past	Present	Future
Control style	Administration	Managing	Leadership
Focus of energy	Functional task completion	State of being (attitudes)	Purpose of enterprise

* Role relations differ. Baseball has unique roles defined by position, and action takes place in serial fashion. Football has unique roles also defined by position, but action occurs in unison. Basketball has varied roles played interchangeably and in unison.

† The underlying continuum of the "social metaphor" is one of increasing shared values. Coordination does not require shared values (or understanding of purpose/vision). Cooperation requires shared knowledge of what comes immediately before and after a particular social act. Collaboration requires a shared understanding of the entire interplay of all roles/positions and a common agreement on overall systematic strategy. Please refer to Chapter 2 for my discussion of the differences between these social psychological ideas.

and various business software capabilities all allow information to be shared and accessed by those who need it, when they need it, and wherever they are. Related efforts occur simultaneously and in parallel, and individuals on project teams work in tandem with other team members and other groups to meet overall project objectives. These patterns of interaction are more like those of a football team. In football, individuals are recognized, but generally there is much greater emphasis placed on the sum of a specialized unit's performance (e.g., offense, defense, special teams). Of course, the major contrast to baseball is the simultaneous flow of movement and activity (while the quarterback is dropping back to throw the ball, the line is blocking, the wide receiver is cutting downfield, and the tight end is faking in another direction). This concurrent activity requires everyone on the team to understand and follow a playbook strategy.

Finally, I believe the Hollywood organizational model can best be compared to an Olympic basketball team. Unlike professional sports teams, Olympic athletes join together for a unique, one-time event, and the "team" association among the individual athletes endures for only a short period of time. In contrast to baseball and football, where roles and positions are more specialized and rarely overlap, basketball players must be skilled in multiple areas of both offense and defense. They play these roles interchangeably and in unison. The interaction is highly collaborative, and movement seems at times to be almost instinctive between players who must execute, assess, correct, and respond very deliberately (and yet very quickly, too). There is little stoppage of play, and therefore only infrequent opportunities (halftime and time-outs) to reflect formally as a group on the team's performance and then to recalibrate. The critical success factor in basketball is a universally shared understanding of the entire interplay of roles and positions, as well as a common agreement on the team's overall strategy.

Baseball, football, and basketball sports models offer clues to effective management patterns that apply to business organizations as well. Just as roles, responsibilities, and shared values change as activities become more integrated, more real-time, and more collaborative, so do the roles of coaches/managers under different organizational structures. Management of a football team is the most hierarchical due to the strategy-intensive nature of the game and the need for a number of specialized teams within the overall structure. Baseball, on the other hand, requires only a general game plan, and therefore the scope of the manager's role is significantly diminished in terms of coordination at game time (with the exception of responsibility for periodic substitutions). Basketball team management demands both interpersonal skills and technical competence. Because player relationships are so critical to the team's success, a coach must be aware of the individual personalities in order to manage and develop both individual and collaborative skills and strategies. In this context, the scope of basketball management responsibilities is the broadest, ranging from microlevel player issues to macrolevel planning and strategizing—and much of the work of the coach must happen in real time.

Time

The time orientation that people have also changes as we move from the age of telework to the age of Hollywood. As you may recall from my discussion of the impact of time, or at least the perception of time, in Chapter 2, this is a very important aspect of how organizations function.

In the age of telework, we were really just emerging from the last stages of the industrial era. Emphasis was placed on history and on doing things today the same way that we did things yesterday. Our orientation to time was classic Taylorism. When we perfected a process, we wanted to continue that process in the same way. With the use of telephones and fax machines, we extended our work process from the central office into the home.

When we made a transition to the age of virtuality, things began to change. What I found in my research at that time was that after a period of about 18 months of being engaged in telework, people begin to actively reshape their day-to-day work process and become much more oriented to doing the right thing at the right time to support their electronic teammates. Conversations change to "Just how should we do this today?" That represents the shift in time orientation from the past to the present. On the downside of the shift comes an increasing use of voice mails, e-mails, and other forms of electronic communication to stay continuously in touch with everyone. Unfortunately, this quickly leads to communication overload, which is exactly what a present-time orientation does in the workplace.

As we make the transition from the age of virtuality to the age of Hollywood, we're beginning to see people's time orientation shift once more. This time the shift is from the present to a perception of time in the future. We now ask questions such as, "What impact is today's action going to have on our company tomorrow?" This forward-looking time orientation is one in which we're constantly examining what we think will be happening in the future. Coincidentally, this orientation toward the future also tends to shift people from looking at just today's business results to looking at longer-term issues and focusing more on the investment paybacks than on balance sheet bottom lines.

Control

Likewise, how organizations control the actual work process is changing. Telework was an age of administration. We accounted for things, we tracked things, and we inventoried things. This was very much a mechanical control discipline, which stemmed from a production view of the world in which objects were created as an output of the work process. Objects can be administered.

In virtuality, we began to see that the output of the work process was more knowledge-based and could not quite be controlled in the same way. Various resources needed to be connected, and their various interactions needed to be done in a cooperative fashion. So people became "managers." Their responsibility was to ensure that all members of the team were acting in a cooperative fashion to maximize the output of the team.

Now we are shifting again. This time the old paradigm of management no longer applies. Peter Drucker has expanded upon this detail at some length, and much more eloquently than I can possibly attempt. So I will just say that the control style that we see emerging in the future workplace is one of leadership. Leadership is about creating, communicating, and enlisting support for a vision of what's possible. Leadership is about clearly communicating ethical principles of behavior in the workplace and development of a spirit of community. That it is the task of people who are in charge of new business enterprises.

Focus

Focus of energy is a difficult concept to explain. However, I feel that this focus has shifted in tandem with our changing organizing metaphors about how we work. *Focus of energy* in a business enterprise may be defined as that thing that everybody can agree upon as being the most important thing going on.

Let me try to explain. In the age of telework, for example, there was an emphasis on measuring productivity. People responsible for developing and caring for these "alternative work programs" were always worried about measuring productivity. What was getting done, how much was getting done, and how quickly it was getting done. The energy in the work units focused on completing tasks. That's what everybody rallied around; that was the central focus of attention for the work groups.

People became a bit more concerned about the attitudes of people in virtual work groups. They were concerned about this because they knew that the "social glue" was what kept distributed work teams working together. The focus of energy was on job satisfaction, work, family life balance, and similar issues. The people responsible for these kinds of new work programs spent a lot of energy measuring people's attitudes and the attitudes of customers and collecting this information as a way to impact compensation plans and rework structures. What people felt and how they did their work became at least as important, if not more important, than how many things they managed to accomplish in a given period of time.

But energy is again refocusing. In the last few years we've begun to see open discussion of "spirituality in the workplace." We've seen organizations appointing individuals to be responsible for the ethical behavior of people in these organizations. It's OK today to ask the question, "Just what does this company do and why?" Organizations continuously reexamine their purpose. Some organizations make radical shifts and changes about the nature of what they do, the customers they serve, and the social impact they have on the communities within which they work.

Energy is now focused on purpose. As I have said many times earlier, people's sense of purpose no longer comes from the organizations in which they work, but it comes from something more internal to them and more connected to a larger community. This is a profound shift. Not that I believe it's any larger in magnitude than previous shifts in focus, but it's a shift that we are all much more conscious of, and it isn't occurring in the background—it's occurring in the open; it's explicit; and it's talked about by all members of future work organizations.

How does the Hollywood model apply to the new world of work? What I think is happening, even within our large organizations, is that the pressure of time to mount and complete projects has increased to the point where managers have to assemble new work teams almost instantaneously.

Over the past months, as I've been researching this book, I've seen numerous cases in which executives reported, "The way we are organized to do these projects simply doesn't work anymore." Almost in the same breath, they ask, "Just how can we learn to organize better at the same time we have to get the work done?" Unfortunately, I don't have an easy answer to this puzzling question. But I suspect it will require leadership that can motivate people to perform in uncertain environments and to let go of old habits and old ways of working so they have enough extra energy to learn new things.

The whole idea of looking to the movie industry for examples of new organizational structures came out of the discussion with two of my colleagues at Berkeley. As we were discussing some of the interesting things we were all finding in large information-technology organizations, it occurred to us that right in our midst was an industry that had moved from a group of loosely organized entrepreneurs to large organizations—"the studio system"—to a new form of getting their job done, characterized by extreme time sensitivity and placing a premium on creativity.

At that point, I began to delve more deeply into just how people in Hollywood move from the idea stage to finding and organizing resources and moving into production very quickly. While this work is still in progress, I believe that there's enough merit in this new organizing model to warrant application in other business areas. As you read this book, we are actually moving forward with this idea and trying it out in several different business sectors.

Another thing that we noticed in the Hollywood model was the impact of physical space on the performance of the actors. People familiar with facilities management are also aware of this factor, and many vendors such as Steel Case, Herman Miller, and HON have made entire businesses out of providing furniture and interior design services to increase the effectiveness of work spaces.

We also noticed that just as there is a lack of "producer roles" to integrate the social aspects of the new workplace of the future, there is lack of integration of the physical design aspects of work spaces of the future. Bringing teams together and getting them up to speed quickly requires that a minimum amount of time be spent on organizing the social and physical space in which they work. The analogy in the computer industry is "plug and play" which means machines are taken right out of the box, plugged in, and are ready to go. There's no setup time. There's no assembly time.

In order to address this need for a perspective that integrates the design in construction of both physical and social spaces, I've been working with a group of creative people to develop the new design approach. We're calling this new approach *Softwork:* not the opposite of hard work, but an approach to designing a work space that blends both social and physical comfort.

SOFTWORK™: BRIDGE TO THE NEW WORLD
OF WORK ORGANIZATIONS

Moving into a world of these new organizational forms requires that we step back and examine our basic cultural assumptions about work and how we are organized to do it. In the case of the Hollywood model, I do not believe that its creators consciously stepped back and went through this process of analysis; they simply were responding in very creative ways, as best they could, to the extreme pressures of competition and time.

In a recent article,[1] Peter Drucker points out seven basic assumptions about our organizations that he feels are no longer true and should be reexamined by business leaders. These assumptions are as follows:

---

[1] Peter Drucker, "Management's New Paradigms," *Forbes,* October 5, 1998, pp. 152–177.

1.   There is only one right way to organize a business.
2.   The principles of management apply only to business organizations.
3.   There is a single right way to manage people.
4.   Technology's markets and end users are fixed and rarely overlap.
5.   Management is legally defined as applying only to organizations' assets and employees.
6.   Management's job is to run the business rather than to concentrate on what is happening outside the business. That is, management is internally, not externally, focused.
7.   National boundaries define ecology of enterprise and management.

Drucker asserts that these assumptions no longer hold. That presents some profound implications to executives who are struggling to compete in a new environment. It means, for example, that there are many right ways to organize a business, and perhaps many different organizational forms need to exist within the same enterprise. That's a disconcerting statement, because it implies that there is not going to be the degree of uniformity and predictability that we're used to seeing in our workplaces. Drucker's other assumptions have similar implications: implications for how we manage people in the day-to-day environment and implications for how we manage our markets and the expectations of our customers. Also, it is quite clear that management's role is rapidly evolving and becoming one that is more focused externally and internationally.

None of this seems to come as a shock to those of you who are working in the midst of these new organizations. We take it for granted that we have to be fluid, mobile, and constantly changing, depending on what the project is, who the customer is, and who we have to work with at this point in time to be successful.

Peter Drucker's ideas serve to reinforce my contention that the trends we talked about in the first chapters of this book are more than something of academic interest. In fact, they are becoming real in our day-to-day work life.

Another interesting point to Drucker's analysis is that the entire formal approach to designing organizations—the workplace really—has been a phenomenon of the Industrial Revolution. As more and more knowledge builds up and people become smarter about understanding human behavior and the behavior of markets, the more formal we become in building our work organizations.

Now we're in the Internet age, and all of the things that worked quite well in the past no longer seem to work so well. So Drucker's call for examination and reformulation of our organizational design approach comes at a most appropriate time. If you look closely at several of Drucker's assumptions, you can read between the lines and see that he inherently realizes that our places of work and our places of living, learning, and leisure are no longer separate but are being pulled together through the power of our new technologies.

Inherent in Peter Drucker's myths is the underlying general assumption that a distinct and impenetrable boundary needs to be constructed between an organization, the external economy, and the lives of its workers. The old saying, "Leave your personal problems at the front door," really sums up the attitude of the managers who hold to Drucker's myths.

Technology is blurring these boundaries very rapidly. People have business phones at home; they carry beepers and cell phones; they constantly check their e-mail at night and on weekends. It takes a conscious effort for executives to go on vacation and resist the temptation of calling the office or checking their voice mail. Clearly, the boundaries that used to exist between work and leisure are disappearing with the power of the Internet. Concurrently, physical spaces for work and leisure are merging and overlapping with the intrusion of work into the home, car, and other areas of our life.

Drucker is making the case that the assumptions, or more properly the myths, that once governed how we manage the workplace no longer hold. This is a very insightful conclusion reached by a scholar who watched technology leap from the telegraph to the Internet. Part of the challenge we face, then, is to learn how to separate our lives into work, leisure, learning, and other human activities. In my experience with people engaged in Internet-based work, one of the most difficult things I have to teach them is when to stop working and when to start living. Not only do we need to reexamine our assumptions, but I would suggest that we also develop an entirely new discipline or approach to consciously constructing work environments.

The arrival of the digital workplace has been accelerated by several concerns of corporate managers. A recent article in the *Harvard Business Review*[2] signals a movement of alternative work ways into the mainstream of business. The article was written from the perspective of the facilities manager looking at the benefits that the corporation receives when it adopts telework options. The cost savings for adopting these alternative work styles can be tremendous.

But looming slightly over the horizon is yet another wave of innovation in the way people work. As our organizational structures move from coordinated ones to a collaborative model, so will the technology help us forge our

---

[2] Mahlon Apgar, "The Alternative Workplace: Changing Where and How People Work," *Harvard Business Review,* May–June 1998, pp. 121–136.

way into the future. This innovation, called Softwork, is a distillation of several design perspectives taken from facilities management, furniture manufacturing, mobile computing technologies, and organizational design.

The Softwork agenda is still being formed. The Softwork consortium, those who coined the term and are giving birth to this new design approach, define Softwork as follows:

> The informal work practices expressed through a range of activities and settings centered in physical and social comfort.

Few words adequately describe today's informal work activities with a broad enough meaning to encompass work behaviors and settings. We believe that our common language has not kept pace with the rapid change of work culture. As a result of the need for a simple, unifying word to talk about informal work, we have created a new term.

SOFTWORK: THE STORY
The Vision
Softwork is several things that are coevolving. It's a vision of design; it's a social movement expressing a philosophy; and it's a practice of helping others realize new work environments.

As a *vision,* Softwork is the design of social and physical environments in a way that fosters continuous learning and development of community spirit.

As a *movement,* we believe that Softwork is a physical expression of a need for a closer integration of people's need for balance in their work and other life spheres.

As a *practice,* Softwork is an evolving interactive business dynamic in which work is done in a range of informal settings, aided by distributed and mobile technologies.

The Business Proposition[3]
For executives of companies who are looking for ways to attract and retain key human resources, Softwork is an integrated suite of workspace design services that encourages continuous learning and creation of a sense of community and collaboration. Unlike product-oriented facilities management solutions, our service brings together space, tools, management practices, and human resource development techniques to form a total business solution.

[3] Geoffrey A. Moore, *Crossing the Chasm,* Harper Business Press, 1995.

How It's Done

A core belief of Software is that bringing work environments into closer alignment with basic human needs increases employee satisfaction and thus performance. We believe this because the basic social psychology of the workforce is changing to demand subjectively "better" environments, and our research demonstrates that employing Softwork principles correlates to positive shifts in people's attitudes toward work.

The practice of Softwork distinguishes itself from most workplace design processes in the following ways:

- *It operates from principles:* We work from a visible, comprehensive set of assumptions that are lived out in our practice.

- *It's participative:* We work with our clients to develop unique solutions to their business problems, solutions that are in tune with their work culture.

- *It's interactive:* We do initial designs, prototype them, evaluate them, and constantly refine them as we recognize changes in business environments, technology, and human resource requirements.

Softwork Principles
Develops and Fosters Community

People desire to live in communities. It gives them a sense of identity, belonging, and unity with others. As people have become mobile, they have begun to sense a loss of community. The personal relationships that you forge in the workplace have begun to substitute for those that we once had in our neighborhoods and villages.

One of the catch phrases of the new workforce is, "It's not who I work for but who I work with that's important to me." Softwork has developed a principle of practice that seeks to consciously develop a sense of community among people in the workplace. Promoting close, informal, and frequent interaction among people is one way to do this. Providing visual and physical cues to the entity and status within the work group is another way we practice this principle.

Sustains Learning

The only competitive advantage that people have today is to continuously improve their current skills and develop new ones. The resurgence of adult education, the demand for on-the-job training, and a desire for people to seek out new work environments are all evidence of this. Learning is an activity that is fundamental to today's work world.

Learning is an activity that spans a range of specific tasks. In Softwork environments, these activities include research, knowledge creation and management, and dissemination. As a key component of a Softwork environment, learning activities need to be supported by the tools provided to people, the physical environment in which they use them, and a management system that clearly compensates people for collaborative learning activities.

Provides a Means to Negotiate the Demands of Work Life

The pace of today's work life is increasing very rapidly. The demands placed on most people to balance a productive and satisfying work life with a satisfying and nurturing family life are becoming untenable. This leads to burnout, which in turn leads to disaffected workers and loss to the organization.

While there are no simple solutions for balancing these demands, we believe that work environments that more closely integrate the needs for child care (or elder care) in flexible work hours and other work alternatives can provide the means to help people more closely balance these competing demands.

Acknowledges and Encourages Different Work Types and Styles

Much is said about having management more easily accept different types of work, such as flextime, telecommuting, and job sharing. There is also a trend toward more openness in different styles of work, which today we see manifested in terms of "casual work."

It is certain that the types and styles of work will grow with the development of more sophisticated technologies and the integration of varied cultures into the workforce. This provides us with the constant challenge to come up with unique design solutions and the necessity of integrating these new types and styles of work into a coherent structure.

Provides Accessibility to Key Resources

These new work styles are being driven by the increasing demand among employees that they be given access to the latest technology and most up-to-date tools. These tools may take the form of ergonomically designed furniture and other artifacts or they may take the form of access to information such as the Internet.

The workplace needs to incorporate wider and easier access to these key resources. We foresee more open access to other people (through collaboration), tools (such as computers), space (multiple environments), and information (company information as well as external data resources).

Promotes an Egalitarian Workplace
Without doubt, we're seeing a flattening of work organizations and a decrease in status and power differentials among people in these workplaces. That is not to say that we will find a workplace emerging that is leaderless and managed in a totally ad hoc style. I don't believe that is the case. However, I do believe that the workplace is becoming more egalitarian and team-oriented and that it is being driven toward collaboration as a way to get work done. The spatial, technological, and management practice manifestations of this "egalitarianism" are blended into our design solutions.

Participatory Design
Designing the workplace is an activity that requires the integration of several design perspectives: ergonomics, graphics, interior arts, technology, and organizational form. Existing bodies of literature exist for ergonomics, graphic design, and interiors. But because of technology, workplaces have always been the result of information architecture. Work is being separated in time and space with the advent of the distributed organization. Softwork assumes that information environments are the basic unit of organizational design. These environments are coming into increasing use as a design tool.

Designing the workplace means, in essence, putting data into context so that it can be used as a basic ingredient of the productive process. There is a fundamental shift in the quality of information in today's economy.[4] The basic laws of economics have been upset—no longer does scarcity operate as a central principle of determining value. Information can be made ubiquitous instantaneously. As a result, fixing value becomes complicated. It is within this context that workplaces and information environments, must be designed.

Information is different from data. Data becomes information when it is placed in a social context. Information technologies are coevolving with human organizational forms. Entirely new forms of human networks are growing around us, spurred on by the increasing pervasiveness of accessible information. For example, these information environments are sometimes called *distributed business enterprises.* But the real trend is to reverse the separation of home and workplace that began with the advent of Industrial Revolution. Designing information environments for work today is really engaging in *community reconstruction.*

---

[4] Carl Shapiro and Hal Varian, *Information Rules,* Harvard Business School Press, 1999.

The workplace is no longer an element distinct from other human habitations. The workplace, school, home, and community center are moving closer together. Now, when we embark on a workplace design process, it becomes a much larger enterprise. We must consider the social factor in the design process. These new values—the new paradigm—become a driving force. In order to include these subtle social factors in the design process, we recommend using the participatory design process.[5]

The participatory process can take several forms. The most common is the use of focus groups—a rather naive approach. Many more techniques exist that involve users in the design process itself—not as observers or bystanders but as full participants, equal with designers and developers. Ideally, users begin working with technology creators at the conceptual stage of development. Usually, they form into teams of 7 to 15 people, and the team itself goes through a "team-building process" to clarify goals and vision. As much attention is paid to team development as to product development, and a by-product of the design team process is that communication patterns among members are clarified and strengthened. The users on the design team become advocates for the use of the technology and assist in the reverse translation of product capabilities into the workplace.

Figure 5-2 is a diagram of the stages of the participatory process. Each point in the loop actually contains another series of loops so that the

[5] The subtle point is that participatory design is essentially a political process which proceeds from a set of assumptions about human nature. Pelle Ehn, the best-known Scandinavian practitioner of participatory design, states: "Participatory design concerns questions of democracy, power and control at the workplace. In this sense, it is a deeply controversial issue from a management point of view."

FIGURE 5-2   Stages of the participatory design process.

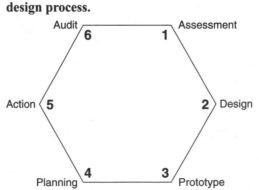

process can iterate around any issue. The value of the process is that it is complete. That is, no critical factors are left out of the design process if the pattern is followed. For example, you cannot jump from design to action or full-scale implementation without prototyping and planning.

The participatory process should extend beyond more traditional concerns for workplace appearance, positioning of entrances, hallways, placement of furniture, and so forth. Softwork is as much form as substance. As with architecture, there is a certain aesthetic to Softwork. Elegance and simplicity are guiding design principles when users are involved in the process. As capability grows, so does complexity. This places a design premium on constructing a good, extensible foundation. If you have to go back and redesign core modules in order to add a person, team, or environment, you don't have elegance.

Users can inform this process by recounting how they actually could and would use the space. Live testing helps considerably. Part of the process is to bring a genuine business problem to the design group. This ensures that the design is grounded in practicality. You can't design skyscrapers without considering gravity, nor can you design good software without considering practical utility. Because users are the experts in this domain, the participatory process is gaining credence among advanced space planners.

Interactive Design
The participatory process needs to be followed in order (1-2-3-4-5-6-1). As it is iterating, it is repeated as many times as necessary to achieve the desired results with increasingly fine-tuned design and increased granularity. The key to success in using this design team model is not to omit any steps. As we have said, people often want to jump from point 2 (design) to point 5 (action) without going through the necessary intermediate steps. This leads to disaster and failure of design. On the other hand, some people, groups, and companies never get past step 1.

The heart of the participatory process is that each step is interactive, jointly involving the designers and end users. It is far more intrusive than bringing in end-user groups, showing them an existing product, and asking for input. Participatory design means just that: users of technology have roles as equal partners in the design process. Myriad techniques to facilitate group interaction can be used in the process, depending upon group characteristics, history of interaction, and time constraints.

Participatory design is necessary in its application to *organizational design*. The idea of consciously designing a work organization is considered radical in some circles of managerial thought. However, recent experiments in Scandinavia have shown that organizational design can be practiced as a discipline with positive results. In fact, given the economic drivers of business enterprises discussed in this book, organizational design is a necessary component of contemporary management practice.

Pelle Ehn has stated that "democratization of the workplace is mandatory for a successful enterprise." Further, he says that technology changes the way we work. We must understand and appreciate the politics of this in design. What designers often miss is the human interaction of the *process of work.*" In addition, Kari Thorsen feels that preparing people for organizational change is part of the process of using new technologies. There are social barriers to doing so in most organizations. Softwork is a root behavior of progressive organizations that stems from work culture. The term's value lies in its simplicity and imagery, as it proves useful for discussions about the qualities and conditions people seek in their work lives.

These Softwork environments are only now beginning to appear in traditional workplaces. They're seen as avant-garde ways of organizing the workplace. I believe that as these new environments spread throughout organizations we will begin to see them emerge as islands within larger structures that eventually will be bridged together to become connected to our home workplace. The distributed workplace will have truly emerged and become a normal way of working. This is the physical manifestation of the future of work. The practice of Softwork doesn't have a manual yet. We are quite literally creating an interdisciplinary design process on the fly. However, we've already learned a few things:

- Each of the team members needs to understand and appreciate the relative contribution of the others and the discipline they represent.
- There has to be a high level of trust and professional respect among all team members.
- At each stage in the design process, different people will alternately take leadership and follower roles.
- Display of creative thinking needs to be done graphically through a set of symbols.
- A certain amount of education is needed to convey the design alternatives to the clients.
- Alternative processes of divergent and convergent thinking are required.
- Social processes of the workplace cannot be designed in a vacuum; they require an understanding of cultural context.

In the process of developing this new perspective, I was lucky enough to find a company that actually has been putting into practice the principles of Softwork. I'm going to present this company to you as a case study showing how a group of businesspeople with a good idea can design an organization to support that business proposition. Further, they do it in a way that realizes the power of these new work forms and tests the design approach of Softwork in the real-world environment.

CASE STUDY: VIA INTERNATIONAL

VIA International is a channel strategy consultancy formed by three friends in 1992. Sharing a work history at a large consulting firm, the founders began with two very simple goals in mind. First, they wanted to make a difference. Second, they wanted to be worldwide. Coming from a pre-telework age, the founders somehow intuitively sensed that a different kind of work organization needed to be built.

VIA has grown from these three original founders to a company of 60 people, with annual revenues of $10 million. Company offices are in Chicago, London, and Singapore. Though still small, VIA is a successful company by any measure of business performance.

WHAT IS UNIQUE ABOUT VIA?

Three qualities of VIA that exemplify its status as a Hollywood-model company are its structure, compensation process, and business planning model. Not surprisingly, each of these is expressed in the physical design of the company's work space, too. One of the reviewers of this case study posed a very pointed question, "What is it about the new technology revolution that makes this seemingly unlikely model of work organizations so successful?" That is the key question!

It's not the technology itself. It's the way in which people consciously choose to use the technology that makes it unique, especially in the case of VIA. The people who head VIA are continuously seeking new ways to use developing technology to improve the quality of their work lives. They are on a journey that they know will never end. It is this constant quest, this openness to change, both social and technical, that makes this unlikely model of work organization possible.

Structure

VIA is structured around a nonhierarchical system of management. The company groups and regroups around client engagements, where teams of people with the right mix of skills come together for each project, and a team leader emerges who organizes the work of the team. It is truly an archetype of the Hollywood model I've defined.

Internally, each office of VIA is run by a three-person management team that is selected with heavy input from the people in that office. This is especially true of the larger offices in Chicago and London. This management team is composed of one individual who takes an internal, or operational, focus on the office; another individual takes an external focus; and a third serves to balance both perspectives in the day-to-day decisions that need to be made. These positions rotate on an irregular basis as the demands of the business dictate. Even the founders of the organization may have to account for their activities to this management team.

The smaller offices with only a few people are developing in this direction, but don't need the sophisticated management procedures that the larger offices have. This structure is serving VIA quite well. It has evolved over time as the company has realized that putting people in positions that they are most suited for, both intellectually and temperamentally, is really the best business practice. VIA recruits new members through a process of intense, interactive interviews with a number of people in the firm.

A unique feature of VIA's structure is how it makes internal decisions. It uses a three-step process: *consult, decide, and communicate.* Any member of the team is free to propose an idea and consult with people in the firm about its viability. Feedback is solicited from VIA team members. The business proposal is then either approved or disapproved by the designated decision maker. If his or her ideas are not approved, the originator is free to resubmit a modification of the idea to the members.

Once an idea is approved, it is the responsibility of its originator to communicate the new procedure or process to the entire company. The originator then takes on the responsibility of shepherding the idea into existence. If funding is required for implementation, the office management team gives approval for such funding, and a person then becomes accountable to this management team for implementation progress and completion.

Pay for Performance

VIA has developed a very intricate process for establishing the compensation levels of its members. First, VIA is an open-book firm. That means that all financials, current performance figures, and future projections are available for inspection to all the members of the firm. Yes, that means that everybody knows how much money everybody else earns. This was a very significant development in the growth of VIA. If you've ever worked for an open-book company, you know that the potential for jealousy, petty argu-ments, and competition is tremendous. There have been times in VIA's his-tory where this process did not appear to be working. However, what I discovered was that the tension surrounding this pay-for-performance process is not caused by jealousy regarding absolute rates of compensation; it is more an issue of internal equity of compensation. That is to say, the focus people have is not one of a power relationship—"I made more money than you did"—but rather whether a team member's compensation ade-quately or unfairly reflects his or her contribution and potential.

In Chapter 2, I said that people make decisions based on need and requirements in an intimate fashion when they are truly collaborating. I interpret VIA's concern for equity as an expression of this type of behavior. What I heard during my interviews on this topic was that people would look at the organization, the team, and the perception of what was needed to be successful and use that as a basis to make judgments about whether their workers were being adequately compensated.

Every person at VIA works according to a yearly cycle of submitting a compensation request and work plan for the following year. This is submitted to a panel composed of the management team, a representative from business services support, consultants, and an outside director from another office. This proposal is discussed with the panel to set performance expectations for the coming year and to blend each individual proposal into a larger work plan. These plans are then published for everyone to see. The individual and the panel agree on what the compensation plan will look like. People are also free to meet with the panel to comment on others' compensation plans.

Throughout the course of the year, each individual meets with the panel three times to review progress, readjust goals, and receive feedback. At the end of the year, there is a 360-degree feedback process, which generates even more information about performance.

Each individual typically selects a mentor within the organization—someone he or she can use throughout the year to receive guidance, direc-tion, and feedback. At the end of the year, there's a final meeting between each member and compensation panel to review individual progress against plan and to agree on where the compensation process begins for the following cycle.

As I write this, VIA is improving this process to include development plans and career path ideas in everyone's annual work and compensation plan. This may seem like a very cumbersome, bureaucratic, process. But it's not. The entire submission, review, feedback, and meeting process takes approximately three days per year for each member of the company. Three days a year is a small amount of time to devote to your work planning, compensation, and feedback process.

Another key element of VIA's pay-for-performance process is that it's conducted in a community spirit. People generally want to help others prosper so that everyone can contribute to the overall performance of the team. The basic organizational structural unit of VIA, the work team, is self-organizing and fits within a larger structure that makes it easy to reward extraordinary performance and to note performance that adversely impacts the entire team.

Compensation also includes base salaries, expected business performance bonuses, and extraordinary personal contribution bonuses. Those three factors contribute to the total cash compensation. In addition, VIA also has a stock-sharing program that allows everyone in the company to participate in ownership. This ownership program is heavily encouraged and promoted as a way of influencing behaviors in the direction of overall company performance.

Business Planning

As you would expect, the business planning process at VIA is also very democratic. It's conducted on an annual cycle and includes everyone in the company. Each of the company's offices is a profit and loss unit. There is a feed-forward process that allows all of the members in the various offices to share their views, goals, and desires with the directors. There are numerous discussions throughout the company about its purpose, its mission, feedback from customers, and ideas for continuous improvement. Overall corporate goals are established by the six-person board of directors and then communicated downward to each of the offices. The planning process starts with revenue and profitability goals for each office. Then the meetings take place, which are facilitated by the person on the office management team responsible for financial review. Once broad figures are established, the team then engages in a process of looking at what resources will be needed to generate that level of revenue. It's at this point that the compensation planning process links up with the overall business planning process. People quickly get to realize from each of their perspectives how much revenue needs to be created to support their compensation plans. This also leads to the discussion about the resources required in terms of information systems, additional personnel, physical space, marketing budgets, and other supporting activities to generate this revenue.

At this time, subgoals to meet these resource requirements are established. These subgoals, or "buckets," are each allocated financial resources. People step forward to take ownership of the buckets. They're accountable to the management team throughout the year to track their expenditures and deliver goals as they relate to the overall business performance parameters established in the planning process.

Planning is a unifying, community-based process at VIA. Consensus is formed during this process as commitments are made to specific goals. All of these commitments are available for review by everyone throughout the year, which means that at any point in time, any individual in the company can instantaneously review where the firm stands in terms of meeting that year's business plan.

In the new work world, the ability of every member of the work team to have instantaneous, visible, and reliable feedback on the overall performance of the firm is absolutely critical. With constantly shifting work groups, it's the only way for people to discover, over time, just what their individual efforts are contributing to the good of the whole.

Openness provides a psychological connection between the individual and the larger work unit. Openness allows each person to plan their activities with a future orientation that seeks to serve a higher purpose than merely fulfilling their own individual needs. Openness builds community!

Space

VIA also manifests its core cultural values in the way its physical work space is designed. The company's work space is designed to reflect living patterns of residential spaces. In fact, when their work space was designed, they engaged a residential architect to help them make decisions and understand the impact of physical space on work behavior. This was done, again within the teams setting, after several attempts and failures to get more traditional corporate real estate/facilities management professionals to help them build a workplace of the future.

The work space at VIA is very open, combining elements of comfort and function. What VIA has is a very dressed-down, informal, and "soft" workplace. Because it is very homey, people actually enjoy being in the space. During my interviews for this case study, I was able to observe numerous instances of people interacting in ways that would not have been possible in the more traditional "cube farm" environment. The environment at VIA has been a major determining factor in people choosing to work for VIA.

CONCLUSION

VIA is what the workplace of the future can be. It is collaborative; it's about community; it's very respectful of all of its people; and it is led by people with a clear vision of the future, a sincere desire to serve their customers, and a wish to foster the development of all people in the company.

6

TECHNOLOGY: TELL ME HOW TO DO IT

> You've got a fundamental transformation under way in about five industries that are going to all embrace this technology (the Internet and the Web). There's the telecommunications industry, which is a couple of trillion dollars worldwide. The media industry, starting with publishing and going on to broadcast media. Third is general services—travel services, information services, financial services. Fourth is software—desktop software itself is going to get a hell of a lot cheaper. And, finally, consumer electronics is going to embrace this technology. Televisions are going to have built-in Internet interfaces.
>
> *Jim Clark*[1]

THIS CHAPTER IS ABOUT TECHNOLOGY, but not the technology that you normally think of in terms of computers, wires, and hard, tangible things. Of course, these typical things are included in my discussion of technology—but I have a much broader vision that I would like to explain.

I started out this book by saying that one of the most profound changes occurring as we move to the new world of work is a change in technology that parallels changes in organizations and people. I also stated that as we move

---

[1] Jim Clark, chairman of Netscape Communications Corp., quoted by Don Tennant, "Netscape's Jim Clark Takes Bill Gates to Task," *Infoworld Electric,* February 9, 1996.

forward, technologies are going to become less of a tool to do a specific job and more of a matrix that helps us connect to one another in a more social sense. It's my prediction that technology is going to move us, as people, from being isolated individuals to being members of new communities.

This prediction sounds very counterintuitive to some of my colleagues. They have pictures of people sitting in front of computers connected to the Internet talking to one another but never really relating with one another. I don't share that vision. The purpose of this chapter is to present you with a different picture and to explain what impacts we can expect that technology (in my definition) will have on us all in the workplace.

I will begin this chapter with a rather extended definition of what technology is, trace its history, and outline for you some things that we know for sure, some things that we don't know yet, and briefly, some things that we don't know we don't know. Next I will talk about the effects technology has—the effects it has on large corporations and, finally, the effects it has on groups.

The last part of this chapter will be devoted to a view of the future looking out over the horizon of about 10 years and trying to bring some clarity to the emergent new work world we will be living in. In conclusion, I'm going to offer some very general guidelines about technology and how to select it so that we use technology and are not used by it.

The overarching change taking place as we enter the twenty-first century is that the personal technologies that came to us with the computer revolution of the 1960s and 1970s are dying. Just when we thought that we understood the world of personal computers and networks, it's all going away. At least it's going to a place where we don't see it all the time and is becoming somewhat invisible. The shift, the death of the PC, is occurring as the technology capability of the computer is being embedded in a variety of consumer electronic products.

We have cellular telephones now that can check our e-mail and our voice mail. We have palm-size electronic devices to do calendaring, scheduling, simple calculations, graphics, and even some rudimentary word processing. We have paging devices that can transmit and receive textual information and graphics. The list goes on and on, and every day brings us a new consumer electronic product that mimics some of the functionality we are used to using and seeing in the personal computer.

The rapid development of the Internet of the early 1990s has radically changed the world of computing. It's a fairly safe bet today that the Internet browser will become our window into the electronic world and that what we think of as televisions and computers will merge and become one.

These changes have some very significant implications for how we will be working together in the next century.

THE EMERGENCE OF A SOFTER WAY OF WORKING

I have a different view of what technology really is. Different from what most people think. Technology to me is not only the normal hardware and software, but it includes a component I talked about in Chapter 1 called *wetware*. Wetware is your brain. It's the intellectual capital we all carry around inside of us—a technology that receives expression when we use hardware and software. It is something intangible, but really the essence of technology. Technology as a tool is really the physical manifestation of human thoughts and desires—that's what I mean what I talk about technology.

Definition of Technology

Defining technology is a difficult task. A review of the research easily produces half a dozen definitions. Your choice of definition often influences the conclusions you reach in examining the effect technology has on organizations. I choose to use a rather expansive definition of *technology*. Technology is much more than hardware, software, and supporting peripheral equipment. In my view, technology also includes ways of thinking about organizational processes. In a sense, these are *mental technologies.*

Richard Scott gives the best overview of the expansive vision of technology. He points out that a great deal of clarity is required to understand how technology impacts organizational structures. He argues that "technology, technical systems, task environment, and environment" are ideas which overlap and often lead to confusion in discussions about technology. He shares my view that technologies impact organizational processes in several ways, including how we get information, what we do with it, and how we present conclusions to others.[2] I'm sure you all have experienced organizational cultures in which overheads or slide shows are the norm for giving presentations. These technical ways of communication are a direct reflection of the dominant view of technology in that organization. We have to understand what these norms are to effectively communicate within that culture. That the Internet allows us to cross these boundaries, in almost invisible fashion, can create difficulties if we don't know what technical language the natives speak when we land on their cybershores.

This definition of technology, extended to include operations and knowledge, is critical. Operations are processes—"how we get things

---

[2] See Scott (1992), Table 9-1.

done around here." Knowledge is how we think about operations. This difference in how we see operational activities and how we see planning is important. Technology is often seen as a tool that helps us do things. But technology can also be a mental tool that helps us plan how to do things. For example, something that helps with what-if analysis would, in my definition, be considered a technology. Spreadsheets are a technology, as is the PC that runs them.

As another example of this, consider a centralized word processing operation in a large corporation. When I examine technology, I go beyond the visible computers and software to include the ways in which they are used and the manner in which that part of the business process is integrated into the whole of the operation. Given this broad definition we know the following:

1. The greater the technical complexity, the greater the structural complexity. The structural response to technical diversity is organizational differentiation. That means the more complicated our technology, the more complex our organization. More technologies mean more departments to control and maintain them. A company with three database platforms will have three IS organizations to take care of them.

2. The greater the technical uncertainty, the less the formalization and centralization. The less we can predict, the more flexible we will be. When we can't predict which way a technology will go, we won't set up a standard operation.

3. The greater the technical interdependence, the more resources must be devoted to coordination. The more different technologies we have, the more people we will devote to keeping track of it.

What are the practical implications of these things we know about how technology impacts organizations? Let's step back a minute and think about what this means in terms of the Internet. One of the impacts of the Internet has been to simplify and standardize technology. This means that technology used in the everyday workplace is actually getting simpler and easier to understand. It follows from our first assumption that organizations using Internet technology should actually become simpler and less differentiated. Put another way, our organizations are going to be smaller and less compartmentalized. For you as a manager, the implication is, "Don't build large, complex organizations based on Internet technology." Keep it simple; keep it small; and keep it standardized.

Along with simplification, the Internet brings us a higher degree of uncertainty. At first this seems to be a contradiction, but actually it's not. The Internet does bring with it simplification and standards of communication rules, or protocols. But what also happens is that, because the basic technology can be so easily extended, we don't actually know what kinds of things people are going to be putting into it in the future. That means we're more uncertain about what capabilities we will have six months or year from now than we were back in the old days of the mainframe technology. Looking at assumption number 2, I would predict that organizations of the future, based on Internet technologies, will be less formal and less centralized. This fits exactly with our observations regarding the Softwork concept and the demand of new companies to remain informal and somewhat dispersed.

The Internet promotes interdependence across organizations. That means that your company and its operations depend more and more on how your suppliers and your customers' business operations are performed. As supply-chain systems become more closely linked, for example, it becomes more important for you to know and understand the operations of your suppliers. Looking at assumption number 3, then, we would predict that as companies move to Internet-based business models, more and more of their resources are going to be devoted to coordinating activities *across* organizations than *within* organizations. One thing I like to look for in organizations is whether they have formal jobs with the title of "expediter" (or something similar) to denote someone responsible for getting things done more quickly.

I think that a job title of the future is going to be something like "liaison" or "customer interface engineer." The idea is that we're going to have to move people from being responsible for organizing things inside a company to organizing the flow of information and goods from one company to another and from outside the company to inside the company. An inward focus on coordination is a dying need in the Internet age.

History

Here is a most revealing comment found in the published research: "Yet after decades of research relating organizational technology to organizational structure, the evidence for technology's influence on structure is, at best, confusing and contradictory."[3] This means that all that research and all those experts really don't know what's going on now and cannot predict with certainty what will happen in the future.

---

[3] M. Burkhardt and D. Brass, "Changing Patterns or Patterns of Change: The Effects of a Change in Technology on Social Network Structure and Power," *Administrative Science Quarterly* 35, 1990, pp. 104–127.

This theme has been evident for almost a decade. In 1984, as personal computers were making significant headway into large organizations, it was reported that "advancements in management information technologies in the past half decade are bringing to organizations forms and functions unanticipated even a few years ago."[4] A few years later, the same cry: "Results of studies of the organizational impact of computer-based information systems (CBIS) are contradictory and uncertain."[5] Finally, in 1988, academic researchers began to ask for explicit statements of assumptions and the use of cogent theories in organizational research, noting that 30 years had passed since the seminal publication of Leavitt and Whisler's article in the *Harvard Business Review* (1958) speculating on technology's impact on management—with little agreement being reached in the interim.[6]

To the nonacademic person, this may lead to the conclusion that researchers really don't understand what they are doing. While I would not argue that point here, there is an explanation for why research literature offers no clear-cut explanations of technology's effects. The major reason is the lack of a unified underlying theoretical perspective. Every researcher comes at the question from a different set of assumptions and gets different results. Perhaps a better way to approach this question, from the viewpoint of managers and lowly users of the technology, is to look at what we know, what we don't know, and what we can speculate that we don't know we don't know.

What We Know

With the introduction of a new technology, certain employees seem to increase their social power and become more central to the decision-making network—that is, employees who master the technology, which becomes a new way of communicating in the organization, rise in value. Therefore, early adopters of new technologies emerge over time as the more powerful; late adopters become relatively less empowered. Those who first understand how to use the technology control the organization. Also, it appears that those who are at the center of learning about the technology later emerge as the controlling influences.

[4] Foster and Flynn (1984).

[5] Richard Leifer, "Matching Computer-Based Information Systems with Organizational Structures," *MIS Quarterly,* March 1988, pp. 63–73.

[6] M. L. Markus and D. Robey, "Information Technology and Organizational Change: Causal Structure in Theory and Research," *Management Science* 34(5), May 1988, pp. 583–598.

With the Internet, this means that people who begin to understand how electronic commerce technologies are going to impact their organizations will be the ones to move into leadership positions of the organization in the near future. The implication for you, then, is to move yourself as quickly as you can into the center of the department in your organization that is on the leading edge of integrating Internet technologies into your company.

In the Communities of Commerce project, we observed that integration of the Internet into existing businesses is actually coming through the marketing function, not the information technology function. This is easy to understand when you realize what's really happening is that the Internet is improving the communication between the company and its customers. Buzzwords and acronyms aside, what we really see going on is improvement in how companies communicate with customers, which is clearly a marketing function.

Technology has different impacts in different segments of our society. Individuals, work groups, organizations, and societies are all subject to different impacts in terms of power and status relations and decision making. For example, a technology that promotes empowerment and group cohesion at a company level can at the same time begin to exclude other groups from the mainstream. The pervasiveness of personal computer technology can arguably be seen as improving the quality of work life for thousands of Americans. At the same time, computer-illiterate populations are becoming increasingly isolated from the rest of society because of their lack of access to, and knowledge of, these newer technologies. Within 15 years, if you don't know how to use the Internet, e-mail, and databases, you won't be able to find a job that pays more than minimum wage. How are our education systems responding to this technology challenge? How are our competitors around the world responding? These are questions I think you need to ponder as we move forward into a new world of work.

What We Don't Know
What we don't know can be summed up in three broad questions:[7]

- How do we think about technology and organizations?
- How do we pick a level of organization to analyze this?
- How do we measure change?

How we think about technology and structure must be explicit and commonly understood for people to engage in a discussion of the topic. We

[7] Fry (1982).

must all use the same words, terms, and mental models or we talk past one another. Ever been in a briefing by a technology vendor who assumes you understand all the acronyms they use?

Where do we draw the lines around what we are looking at? Technically, this is the issue of specifying the level of analysis. It makes a whole world of difference whether we're trying to look at how technology impacts a small work team or trying to look at how it impacts the entire firm. It is essential for everyone involved, no matter what the process is, to clearly define the boundaries up front. For example, if we're going to integrate the Internet into an organization, perhaps it would be better to specify that we're going to do a pilot study to examine how the Internet impacts one particular product or one particular geographic region before we try to generalize its impact on the entire organization. This complex issue needs to be put on the table up front in any process that seeks to bring technology into an organization. Don't confuse how PCs will impact people working in the same building with how the Internet is going to impact coordination with your customers. These are two entirely different levels of analysis, and you need to be clear about which one you want to focus on. How do you measure change? Do you focus on the individual, on the group, or on society? Do you look at attitudes, behaviors, intentions—or at something entirely different? My favorite example of this conundrum is productivity. How do you measure productivity? The promised increases in productivity have not been documented with the introduction of computing technologies in large organizations—at least not at the organizational level. However, if you ask individuals if they are more productive after learning how to use computers, most will reply yes and then go on to give several specific examples. You should specify up front just what it is you're trying to change. Are you bringing Internet technologies into your organization to increase productivity? If so, then just how are you going to measure that? Do you want to increase the level of customer satisfaction? If so, how are you going to measure customer satisfaction? These are all open issues, and you need to clearly define your terms and focus at the outset.

What you need to define is the overall relationship between technology and your organization, just what level of relationship you want to look at, and then how you will measure the results. My advice is to be clear, consistent, and concise.

What We Don't Know We Don't Know
It is difficult, if not impossible, to talk about what we don't know we don't know. We would like to suggest that a way to start thinking about this issue

is to turn the question around. How can individuals, work groups, business enterprises, and societies organize themselves to take advantage of capabilities offered by communication technologies, specifically the Internet? I have seen consistently that the effects of technology, when observed in hindsight, are explained away as "unintended consequences." In other words, "We didn't expect that to happen."

We still approach the question from a cause-and-effect perspective. This way of thinking is empty-headed in today's world, with its ever increasing rates of change. As we move into the next millennium, it is becoming evident that how people organize to work, play, and police themselves can be influenced by the use of developing technologies. But what thought is being given to questions of social equity, enhancements of the quality of community life, and cross-cultural communication? These, perhaps, are the areas in which we don't know what we don't know, and they deserve tremendous effort. There is no crystal ball; we can't anticipate everything; but we can put intelligent systems in place to carefully monitor what is going on and to give us some early warnings of things going awry. I am a proponent of using such things as organizational modeling technologies and forecasting software to help you continuously monitor the impact of technology on organizations. This is really critical with the Internet because changes tend to happen so fast that our more traditional look-behind accounting models don't pick up on significant changes until it's already too late or they've passed us by. People at MIT have developed very powerful tools in this respect, which are now available in commercial form as I Think software. I believe that more and more of these tools will become available to us in the near future, and I encourage you to consider using them as part of your normal way of doing business. A simple search of the Web using the keywords "systems dynamics" will connect you to a number of resources that can help.

Technology Effects
I view organizations as intelligent systems capable of learning new behaviors. Organizations interact with their external environment in complex ways based, in part, on how they analyze and synthesize information about the environment.[8] In this sense we can see organizations as communities. The use of communication technologies helps people experience each other, share perspectives, and develop social bonds. You cannot assess the

---

[8] See R. Westrum and K. Samaha, *Complex Organizations: Growth, Struggle and Change,* Prentice-Hall: Englewood Cliffs, NJ, 1984.

effectiveness of a communication system without a clear understanding of its purpose. Technologies can be used to inhibit interaction as well as to promote it. Experience with a technology also has an effect. That is to say, simply linking people together electronically does not automatically yield increases in performance or radical shifts in ways of organizing.

One of the underlying themes I am developing here is that the use of a sociotechnical design approach is very promising. This theoretical idea lies at the heart of the Softwork design process discussed earlier. Nowhere is this more evident than when we are examining communication technologies.[9] A sociotechnical approach to organizational design presumes a certain type of culture. Cultures that are open and participatory in nature make most effective use of this approach. Cultures shape and define the use of communication technologies according to how well they match the dominant values. Therefore, an examination of technology's effects needs to proceed from an understanding of the dominant values expressed (or not expressed) by enterprise leaders and members. Go back for a moment to Chapter 5 and review the design assumptions we used in the Softwork approach. Relate the descriptive statements to the culture of your own organization. If you take each of those design principles and rate them on a scale of 1 to 5 (5 being "very descriptive of my organization" and 1 being "not descriptive at all"), you will get a quick idea of your organization's preparedness to accept changes that the Internet is going to bring about.

Effects on the Large Corporation

Quite obviously, any change in the way we communicate with one another creates a possibility of changing how we interact in the work unit. However, as we have seen, there are no consistent findings about how this has worked in the past—let alone predictions for the future. However, when I asked noted historians of technology diffusion to give me a bottom-line answer, they outlined five consistent long-term trends of the impact of technologies on large organizations.[10]

[9] See, for example, E. Trist, "The Evolution of Sociotechnical Systems as a Conceptual Framework and as an Action Research Program," in A. H. Van de Ven and W. F. Joyce (eds.), *Perspectives on Organizational Design and Behavior,* Wiley: New York, 1981.

[10] We would like to thank Professor Ronald Westrum, Eastern Michigan State University, for comments and insights into this process—specifically, his views as outlined in "The Historical Impact of Communications Technology on Organizations," Working Paper Number 56, *Institute for the Study of Social Change,* Purdue University, 1972. Although this analysis may seem somewhat dated, we are aware of nothing in the current literature that contradicts Westrum's conclusions.

1. *Improvements in communication technology lead to increased information flow.*   Improvements come in two ways. First, the increase in simple bandwidth allows more data to flow. This is similar to increasing the number of lanes on a freeway. More lanes allow more cars to travel on the road. Second, improvements can also be in the form of connectivity. Technologies can increase the number of possible members in a network, and network density increases. Therefore, the absolute volume as well as the density of the connections may increase. That is exactly what is happening with the Internet. The high-flying tech stocks of today are those that represent technologies which increase communication bandwidth (witness Cisco and Lucent Technologies).

2. *Improvements in communication technology tend to centralize power and control.*[11]   Historically, this is true. Whether this trend will continue remains to be seen. It appears that the Internet is increasing the centralization of power, but in smaller units of organization. More smaller businesses growing up based around the Internet, though highly centralized in themselves, are increasingly interconnected in networks. The large monolithic bureaucracy of the past is going away.

3. *Improvements in communication tend to increase geographic decentralization.*   The ubiquity of modern telecommunication networks speeds up this process. We are rapidly reaching the point where, for voice and data communication, cooperating work groups can be located anywhere on the planet. Moreover, such spatial separation is largely invisible to group members. As anecdotal evidence of this trend, we note the typical first question in a conversation over a cellular phone link: "Where are you?"

4. *Improvements in communication technology tend to increase the rationality with which an organization's goals are pursued.*   The underlying assumption here is that increased volume and connectivity reduce the amount of uncertainty in the business environment. Leaders are better positioned to understand the competitive forces that are operating and, as a result, become more sensitive to changes in customer behavior, thus presenting the *possibility* of making more rational, calculative decisions based on goals of efficiency.

5. *Improvements in communication technology tend to increase the pace of organizational life.*   Being connected to more and more commu-

---

[11] We note this trend here because, in our experience, many large organizations have a relative paucity of communication technologies compared with competitors in their sector. Therefore, as communication technologies enter the workplace, they may first serve to centralize control and later begin to permit decentralization.

nication channels usually increases the pace of interaction. Now, we have voice mail systems, e-mail systems (perhaps more than one), and telephones—all of which can create interruptions in the flow of work. It should be noted that this is not in itself necessarily a positive effect. I have found in my research with teleworkers that lack of interruptions is associated with increases in productivity. It appears that there is an optimum pace of work dependent upon task and individual characteristics.

Integrating the Science of Technology with the Art of Management

Introducing technologies into large, complex organizations creates a change in the communicating process among people; a change in the routinized work-support systems; and, finally, a change in the persistent patterns of worker interaction, especially in information-intensive industries. The driving technology of such change is software—software that controls and shapes communication among workers, software that paints a picture of organizational functioning, and finally, software that molds how information is presented to worker and customer alike.

My work with business managers consistently points to a lack of constructive ways of thinking about technology introduction and guidelines for managing that process as the major limiting factor in the effective use of computers and telecommunications. I have found that there is a direct relationship between the introduction of specific technology platforms and major organizational change issues.

Work organizations can be seen as being composed of different levels of aggregation. Figure 6-1 shows our view of these levels of organization. Work activity truly starts at the level of the individual worker. Individuals come together to form teams, which call for coordinated action and a pattern of work flow. Note that all groups of workers are not necessarily *teams*. The failure to recognize this basic distinction is often the first task I face in helping managers develop more effective organizations.

"Teams of teams" can be seen as the next level of complexity in this framework. These work groups are cross-functional and begin to move the work process across different task groups, such as marketing, engineering, or operations. Groups then combine into enterprise-level entities that we call businesses. Finally, we see increasing awareness that businesses are linked in whole economies functioning interdependently. However, a realization of cross-industry impact is often difficult to see except at the CEO and board level. This may be changing with the advent of electronic commerce and the Internet, which make every business an international operation.

FIGURE 6-1   Technology's impact in the workplace diffusion of technology over time.

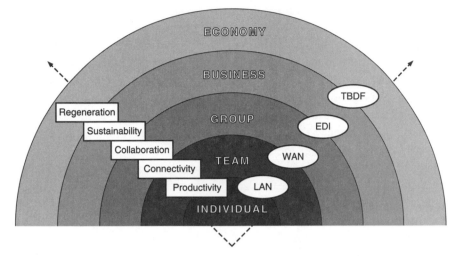

Technologies enter the workplace at all these levels. However, I believe a progression of technology diffusion can be seen evolving from the interface between individual and team to linkages across business units and the economy in general. Figure 6-1 displays these core communication technologies on the right side (inside the arches). Technology bridging these boundaries entered the American workplace in the last few years and now is being diffused at the rate of several thousand connections a month, with the implication that individual workers are being electronically connected into work teams at a maddening rate through the use of local area networks (LANs).

At the next level of organization, wide area networks (WANs) begin to bridge the space and time gaps between teams. Linking buildings and floors within buildings is the current manifestation of WANs. However, technically there is no reason why a specific business could not have functional units scattered over a large geographical area by means of dedicated electronic connections. Groups are linked together as business units through the technology of Electronic Data Interchange (EDI), a protocol for information exchange among different technology platforms (e.g., Apple and IBM or Digital Equipment and Unisys). EDI is deployed over even greater time and geographic distances—sometimes spanning several time zones and states or provinces. Now we have the emergence of Extensible Markup Language (XML) which will become the EDI of the Internet.

Finally, businesses merge into economies, and Trans Border Data Flow (TBDF) technologies link them. At this level of work organization, technology transcends geopolitical boundaries and we see globalization of work activity. For example, in my practice, we see software specifications being developed in the United States; these specifications are transmitted electronically to Asia, where the software is written; and the software product is then transmitted electronically to the customer in Europe or North America. This is what the Internet is really all about: breaking down existing political and economic boundaries because they become transparent!

It is my experience that identifiable and specific organization development issues emerge with the introduction of technologies into the workplace. I have begun to map the pattern that connects technology introduction to change issues. Figure 6-1 is a graphic depiction of those relationships. When LANs are installed and individual workers become connected to one another, management begins to focus on a concern for productivity. Concerns are voiced about cost-benefit ratios of computers and the speed of the work flow. Productivity concerns, initially phrased in terms of individuals, move toward a concern for team productivity. Coordination of work tasks becomes the aim of management interventions.

Wide area networks bring forth an emphasis on connectivity: How do we connect people? Who gets connected? How do we maintain security? These questions move to the foreground and shift the scope of problem deliberation to a higher level. Connectivity, in this sense, is more than just the technical dimension—it is social connectivity as well. Management attention begins to work on balancing the social and tasking needs of the work team. The issue of collaboration also emerges. Collaboration, in my experience, is much more than simply coordination or cooperation. Collaboration means working on developing a unifying vision of the purpose of the team, its tasks, and the larger group to which it is linked.

Now, individuals and teams can begin to harness the energy of working toward a common purpose. In itself, electronic connection brings a more diverse view of work and the work environment to workers, and that diverse view leads to collaboration. As WANs evolve into Electronic Data Interchange (i.e., e-commerce) networks, an even wider worldview is made available. Worldview issues subsume collaboration among teams about how the organization can fit in, sustain, and grow. The enterprise is now seen as part of a larger system. The organizational question becomes, "To what end are we working?" Management has the opportunity to shift its awareness to long-term growth and questions of purpose.

The organizational impact that technology has when it begins to connect people across political boundaries is exactly what is happening to the organization that we used in the case study in Chapter 5. VIA international is now going through a gut-wrenching, soul-searching process to regenerate and reconceive itself from a global viewpoint. The offices of 20 or so people that function quite well in the world of Softwork must now learn how to work together in a global environment. I believe a large part of this change is occurring quite simply because the conductivity that the technology has provided has raised old levels of organizational issues.

As the enterprise connects itself to the global economic structure and as data flows across political boundaries, it becomes possible to consider an ultimate large system and to take an end-to-end view of the whole system, while deriving sensitivity toward renewing the forces that brought the organization into being in the first place. "How can we build a learning organization?" is the question currently asked as a manifestation of the concern for generation-regeneration of individual motivation, team spirit, group loyalty, business purpose, and service to larger society.

As I said in the beginning of this chapter, the introduction of advanced information technologies into large organizations creates change in the way people interact, the processes they use to do business, and—ultimately—the structure of the organization. It is my experience that an attempt to take advantage of technology without systematic thinking and systematic planning leads to inadequacies in the development of control systems, in employee acceptance, and in strategic benefit, often resulting in a tremendous waste of financial resources.

I recommend creating awareness of the personal and business impacts of the change being contemplated. Where possible (not merely where necessary), incorporate users and users' customers into the design process. Demand breakthrough performance of your managers based on the desires of your users. Demand that the technology serve not only the job being done, but the long-term view of what that job should be doing. Throughout the process, develop everyone's ability to think systematically and tackle tough, emotional issues with order and skill.

FUTURE WORLD

What is the future world going to look like in terms of technology? That's a pretty big question to answer within the confines of this book. But I would like to touch on three main points. First I think technology is going to continue on its path of being smaller, faster, cheaper, and less visible in our everyday world. I also think that the intersection of computing and telecommunications, which we now see as the Internet, will bring about a fundamental shift in perception of distance, just as it will change our perception of time.

Wearable computing is about to enter the new world of work. The traditional interface that has existed between humans and technology is disappearing very rapidly. We first saw wearable computing in the form of space suits worn by astronauts. These suits connected astronauts to their spacecraft, to their communications links, and finally, to the planet Earth. Wearable computers briefly appeared within the virtual-reality context of the late 1980s. It's becoming much more serious now, and there are even international symposiums on wearable computers. Remote sensing, data collection systems, military applications, cameras, and adjuncts to sensing abilities are among the major new applications in this field.

As it becomes possible to directly link human sensing systems such as eyes and ears into computing platforms, this trend will grow even faster. Other functions such as embedded defibrillators and computer-enhanced neural communication patterns are probably within three to five years of being a reality.

Many exciting potential applications exist that could help us harness the power of technology and do away with a physical separation between humans and technology. *In the long term, I believe that the interface between technology and human biology will become so blurred that it will be difficult to separate a discussion of technology impacts from human evolution.*

Death of Distance

The second major shift in technology as we enter the new age of work is going to be the death of distance. The emergence of the distributed work world was the signal that the physical distance between people was no longer a barrier to collaboration. Here's what one journalist has to say about the death of distance:

> Relentless technological change is driving down many of the elements in the cost of a telephone call. Already, the cost of carrying an additional call is often so tiny that it might as well be free. More significantly, carrying a call from London to New York costs virtually the same as carrying it from one house to the next. The death of distance as a determinant of the cost of communications will probably be the single most important economic force shaping society in the first half of the next century. It will alter, in ways that are only dimly imaginable, decisions about where people live and work; concepts of national borders; patterns of international trade. Its effects will be as pervasive as those of the discovery of electricity.[12]

---

[12] Frances Cairncross, "The Death of Distance," *The Economist,* September 30, 1995, Telecommunications Survey, p. 5.

If technology begins to fundamentally shift our perceptions of space and time, elusive questions arise about how we come together to work. If it no longer matters where we are or what time it is where we are, a whole new set of interaction possibilities opens up for us. Organizing work teams goes from asking "Where can we get a conference room?" to "Do you know anyone out there who can help us?"

Because time and distance are intricately linked, the death of distance begins to impact the perception of time. It means that we need to learn how to work when time never stops and the work continues elsewhere on the planet while we decide to take a break and sleep, play, or engage in some other activity. Our sense of natural rhythms will be fundamentally altered. Our natural link to the cycles of the moon and the sun will be changed. I cannot predict the impact of these changes, only that they will be far-reaching.

What about the changes in technology? Joseph Coates, one of the most respected futurists, has this to say about long-term technology effects.

> Another effect, particularly in the advanced nations, will be the move to distributed work. Information technology makes it practical to reverse the 200-year trend of going to work by bringing the work to the worker. In the USA, for example, 60% of the workforce are information workers. It is now practical to bring the work to perhaps 90% of those workers anywhere. The consequence is not merely a new place to do work, such as the home. Distributed work will alter the structure and organization of communities, the use of transportation, the location of businesses, the activities and organization within the home and even the very structure of housing. For many people, it will effectively fill the locational gap between work and family life.[13]

In a recent article, Coates has traced the likely outcomes of nine specific information technologies. Take a look at what he sees happening with these key information technologies in Table 6-1. The technologies we see today as being separate will become more highly integrated and more pervasive in our lives. The social/psychological impact of that is, in my opinion, that we will no longer see technology as something separate from people, but as just another aspect of our environment that more closely connects us with each other and with other systems on this planet.

It is my belief that the long-term impact of technology upon the future will be for us to see ourselves as part of something much larger than ourselves. I predict that we'll be more in tune with the effect of our actions on each other and on the environment.

[13] Joseph Coates, "Long Term Technological Trends and Their Implications for Management," *International Journal of Technological Management,* vol. 14, no. 6/7/8, 1997, p. 582.

TABLE 6-1 Long-term technological trends and their implications for management.

Technology	Likely outcomes
Information Technology	
• Fiber optics	Redistribution of work and work patterns; growth of polycentric cities; less daily commuting; less stress on mass transit and roads; all structures wired for high-information activities
• Networks	All infrastructure will be smart
• Mechatronics	All physical devices will sense their internal and external environment and be linked into networks for better monitoring, control, and management
• High-speed computers	Every aspect of urban management will be embraced by scientific models employing highly reliable, large databases
• Digitized data	Facilitates the massive database required for managing urban complexes
• Image technology	Widely used as an adjunct to design, to redesign, to planning; walk-through will be routine for all structures well before they are built
• Geographical information systems	Careful monitoring of all logistics, traffic, goods movement; monitoring for excessive release of heat, chemicals, and other undesirables from buildings and structures
• Robotics	Extensive use in all kinds of physical tasks: housing, construction, site preparation, building, demolition, fires, earthquakes, riots
• Artificial intelligence	Broadly applied to all systems and devices which previously have either depended on human judgment for their effective operation or which have been basically unintelligent, that is, responding to arbitrary routines

Joseph F. Coates, Int. J. Technology Management, *vol. 14, no. 6/7/8, 1997.*

A GUIDE FOR USING TECHNOLOGY IN THE WORKPLACE OF THE FUTURE

I promised to give you some specific guidelines on how to select technology to be used in the workplace in the future. The idea behind this approach is to arm you with the questions you need to ask yourself, your colleagues, and particularly the vendors of technology before you make a purchase decision.

Of course, you should still consider the standard issues of price, quality, service, and how effective the technology is in meeting its design goals. But I'm going to give you six additional specific things to think about when you're in the process of selecting a technology to help you do your job better. However, first I have to start with some background, because if you don't really understand why you're asking these questions and what these questions have to do with promoting a greater sense of connectivity and relatedness between people, then the answers will have little meaning.

Philosophy of Technology Design

"The future of software design is philosophy." This headline appeared in a nationally syndicated column on innovation by Michael Schrage in November of 1991. This small article clearly focused on the dominant technology design issue for the 1990s. Design of technology systems, and hence working organizational structures, proceeds from a set of philosophical assumptions. Sometimes these assumptions are explicit, sometimes not. Schrage's point is that not only should they be made more explicit, but they should also be examined in the context of their relevance to the collective social good. Let's look at my assumptions about human behavior and technology.

Charlie's Assumptions About Technology

1. People strive to develop in a positive fashion toward greater self-actualization. They are always trying to be better and realize their full potential.

2. The meaning of work is derived from the phenomenon of interaction with others and with the environment. Work gives meaning to our lives that derives from how we interact with one another.

3. Symbiotic evolution of people and social groups is facilitated by open communication. We can all learn and grow together if there is open communication.

4. Purposeful communication provides a material benefit to human action. Being clear and honest in our communications leads to fewer misunderstandings and more satisfaction in our relationships.

5. A person or group has meaning only within the identity of a larger social context. That is, our identity derives only within the context of being a part of a bigger group or community.

6. Development of technology tends to increase the scope and rate of human interaction. We get more connected every day, and there is always more information coming at us.

7.   Clear, concise conversations, based on mutual nonjudgmental respect, provide a clear pathway for people to transcend narrow, self-serving behavior.

8.   The creative aspect of people arises from the act of serving beyond self. We can realize our creative potential when we put self aside and strive for a greater good.

These guidelines were developed from a new social psychology that assumes reality is a result of our interactions with one another. We construct our realities in the process of communicating, working, and living with one another. Further, a large part of this process is symbolic in nature, includes nonverbal communication, and is rich with symbols.

Design as Opposed to Engineering

A distinction can be drawn between *engineering* and *design*. These are not mutually exclusive concepts, but I believe that managers must find a way to make a conceptual shift in decision making—away from the perspective of engineering and toward the design perspective. *In short, in the world of the future you must adopt a design perspective on technology instead of an engineering perspective.*

A good way to understand this distinction is by analogy. My analogy uses architects and builders. *Designing* is to *engineering* as *architecting* is to *building*. Each of these processes of creation is correlated with a social role, world outlook, and set of values. In other words, design and architecture move concepts from idea to reality.

A paradigm shift in how we think about design is occurring. Similar shifts in thinking also appear to be occurring in many other areas. This represents a general direction of change in mind-set from a mostly linear pattern to a more systematic mind-set. What we find is a difference in how we "think things up" and the kind of thinking it takes to actually "make them happen." Both designing and engineering perspectives have merit when applied in the proper context.

Although the roles of technology architecture and engineering may be linked and overlap, where you start the process of creating a technology can yield a vast difference.[14] Drawing on my analogy, beginning construction of a house by a builder yields a vastly different outcome from one that starts with an architect. A builder usually begins by looking at what constrains

---

[14] K. Krippendorf, "Imaging, Computing and Designing Minds," *Design Management Journal,* winter 1991, p. 29–36.

the process: cost, time, and material availability. On the other hand, an architect usually begins with looking at the potential.

These perspectives need to be eventually reconciled, but the processes are different. Beginning with constraints means that you then move toward opening up—a divergent thinking process. The other way around leads to moving toward the center—a thinking process of convergence.

We certainly know that attitudes and behavior are linked together. Your attitudes toward your job, toward the task at hand, and toward a customer impact your behavior—and consequently affect your business performance. Your attitudes toward a technology, its possible uses, and your ultimate goal are all related to your behavior in developing or creating the product. But, these attitudes are based on a relatively stable set of personal *values*.

Therefore, the contrast between roles (e.g., engineer and designer) is markedly seen in the difference in value sets held by these two groups of people. The shift in values has been toward the inclusion of technology users in the design and development process. *This value is focused around the principle of building technology in the service of the user.* Systems are never goals in themselves. The purpose of the system is to serve users and control the business process embedded in a group of larger systems. As a corollary, software is increasingly designed and built by *virtual groups* of people for use by *virtual groups* of people. The dynamics of distributed group interaction clearly affect the design process as well as the acceptance of the resulting product.

History of Technology Design: "We're Not in Kansas Anymore!"
Humans can trace the history of technology design back as far as the creation of fire; the details of the process are, of course, lost in antiquity. Technological development of steam power, transportation, clock mechanisms, and architecture began with a goal of economic gain. The criterion for gain was based on goals of *efficiency, speed,* and *cost.* These design forces came directly from the intended application value of the technology.

Technology was created for purposes of profit and control of the means of production—not from an aesthetic motivation. The underlying philosophical bent was seemingly the control of nature by man. Concerns about despoiling the environment or any impact upon the human condition were remote from the minds of most people engaged in creating these early technologies.

The United States developed international telecommunications networks, created nuclear power, and had the rudiments of present-day computer technology by 1949, and the beginnings of a new design paradigm were born. The Tavistock Institute was working in the coalfields of south-western England using sociotechnical design to improve both productive efficiency and the quality of work life.

Design was still something that engineers did. Scientists in white lab coats created wonders, and they were greatly admired (Edison, Bell, Einstein, Fermi). Their legacy passed to the engineers who applied their concepts and made them usable. Telephones, automobiles, and household appliances flowed into the marketplace. Whole economies shifted, and the world balance of power hinged on who controlled technological production. Technology design was based on technology capability.

During the late 1960s, a fundamental shift happened. We went from a mechanistic, controlling paradigm to a more holistic, symbiotic approach to the use of technology. In 1979, P. Schwartz and J. Olgivy, detailing a shift in cognition of design, published a landmark paper at Stanford University. There was an increasing awareness that the design of technology systems and human work organizations could no longer be logically separated from one another. Organizational design began to emerge as a distinct practice allied with, but separate from, management science. Power in organizations began to move down and out. The seeds of the virtual organization had been planted.

Software Development as an Example

Where did this leave technology in general and software development in particular? The change can be tracked with the movement of software development from the mainframe to smaller, decentralized environments. As with the Industrial Revolution, software development went through evolutionary changes in the way it was done. We moved from the 1950s era of users talking to programmers and mysterious coding languages through the 1960s when we derived second-generation languages and made the distinction between operating and application levels; the 1970s saw the introduction of new specialties and the advent of systems analysts and, later, systems engineers.

All this was very logical, linear in form, and fundamentally bureaucratic. If the bureaucratic model of economic activity led to increased efficiency and decreased variance, then why not apply it to the building of software? The simple answer is that these models don't work very well for software development. While they are excellent at hashing out the syntax (the language) of it all, they are ineffective at dealing with different semantic (values) views.

As software development projects became ever larger and more complex, people began to think of concurrent engineering, database modeling, and other ways of viewing the process as a whole system. Finally—after incubating in human awareness for 30-odd years—came *participatory design,* built upon the seminal ideas of those folks back in the English coal mines.

Virtual Design: Design as "Minding"

Recently, a trend of thinking has developed within the field of product design that parallels the sociotechnical perspective in organizational design. This approach has been called *product semantics,* or, "What will this product mean to the user?"

> Product semantics is developing notions of sense, meanings, cognitive models, types, signs, perceptions and motivation as tools that facilitate communication among designers that help pose user-enabling research questions. I contend that design is more than the subjective component of engineering, the artistic aspect of marketing, and the unspeakable part of management. Design can develop a coherent discourse of its own.[15]

Krippendorf goes on to outline five characteristics of the design process as a minding process. Design becomes a creative, conscious process of "creating meaningful interfaces in the social practice of living." The minding-as-designing metaphor assumes the following:

1. Different people have various cognitive models of the same thing—including the workplace. Different generations in the workplace is an example of this in practice.
2. This perspective provides people with the capability to construct their own realities of the workplace. Users can manipulate it (the product of design).
3. It is based upon user-centered research, which seeks to understand the shared meaning people take from function, experience, and purpose.
4. Design is a recursive process. It feeds upon itself.
5. Design embodies an idea of social organizations. That is, the concept of product semantics implies that things take on meaning from within a social context. The useful meaning of a tool emerges when we use it. A spreadsheet becomes something that helps us track investments—not an abstract mathematical model.

These distinguishing characteristics of the contemporary design perspective fit quite well with my own assumptions because Krippendorf's per-

---

[15] K. Krippendorf, "Imaging, Computing and Designing Minds," *Design Management Journal,* winter 1991, p. 29–36.

spective is, at its base, interactive, social, and experiential. These three qualities function at the heart of any human organization. Perhaps you are wondering, "So just what does all this mean for me in the everyday world?" This somewhat long-winded background explanation is cogent to my six rules of technology design.

Here's where I hope you are heading with your thinking at this point:

1.   You realize that anyone's view of technology is based on a set of assumptions about how people behave.
2.   You know that different sets of assumptions lead to different expectations about what technology can do.
3.   The interaction of any technology into a work organization will have a corresponding impact on how work gets done and what questions emerge as being the most important for managers to answer.
4.   Designing and implementing technology in organizations is a creative, interactive process characterized by a design perspective, *not* an engineering perspective.

With that in mind, here are my six principles of technology design. Write these down somewhere in your own words and with your own examples and carry them with you when you're in a situation to help people make decisions about technology and how it can be used. I actually incorporate these six principles into technology overview documents for Internet business plans. When the business planners go to the technology vendors seeking quotes for the production of Web sites and related software, they share these six principles that vendors must use in developing the technology. These principles are of practical use. They will reduce miscommunication and cut through the technological mumbo jumbo that seems to surround the Internet these days.

Six Principles of Technology Design

Many disciplines of design (e.g., architecture, graphics) have developed principles of design that guide the activities of people working in the field. Creativity in design uses these principles in new and innovative ways. I use six principles of design to guide my activities in helping people create communications technologies to serve the purposes of organizations. These principles are borrowed from the field of architecture and modified by my own experience. The underlying philosophy, of course, is to design technologies to support the healthy functioning of an organization over time. These six design principles are as follows:

1. *The requirements must embody the essential principle of arrangement. Design must connect the elements of your social world.*   Technol-

ogy systems must open your social world, not restrict it. The analogy here is an open-systems approach in both networking and operating systems for computer platforms. A technology must become a conduit for communication among people within the work group. A technology that restricts, inhibits, or disconnects people from each other would be a violation of this principle. We need open systems on the Internet, not proprietary ones. Witness what happened to Apple.

2. *Connections in space are essential. Parts of the environment must relate in time and space, which reflects your requirements of use.*   It is necessary for the system to preserve a history of its operation and provide an avenue to project itself into the future. This relates parts of the enterprise in time. The most common manifestations of this principle would be business simulation applications based on historical data. Often, systems are designed that do not permit use of historical data for analysis, and such designs violate this principle. You need to be able to trace customers' usage pattern of your Web site, for example.

Connections in space means a system that operates across large networks and on a global scale. Small systems that cannot connect to other entities would violate this principle. Connections in space also implies a uniformity across several parts of the enterprise process. Therefore, well-designed systems connect parts of the business enterprise smoothly. For example, having disparate electronic mail systems to support engineering, marketing, and accounting would violate this principle at the enterprise level of analysis.

Relationship in time and space must reflect your requirements for use. What do you need to do with this system, and where are the people who will use it? Technological elegance does not always translate into good design if it fails to meet the end users' requirements for use (as defined by them).

3. *Design against entropy. Components must be designed in ways that work against the strong tendency toward entropy.*   All systems tend toward entropy, or decay into randomness. Components of the technology system must be constructed to guard against this tendency. For example, systems that encourage the cloning of information and automatic dispatch will overload the communication structure with uselessly replicated information.

An additional design against entropy could be a method that seeks out relevant information and presents it in an easily understood form. We are seeking systems designs that promote the "essentialization" of information flowing in the system, not those that overwhelm us with data.

4. *Open access must be provided.*   Just as handicapped access is mandated in public buildings, we suggest that access to information networks (both public and private) be an essential design principle. The spread of metropolitan area networks (MANs) and Electronic Data Interchange (EDI) are making this access principle a critical feature of all system designs.

The proliferation of networks is making the idea of interoperability a key concern of designers in the late 1990s. Questions about who has access to what become designer concerns. With application of an open-access principle, inherent social values are embedded into system design. Designers should try to make these social decisions conscious ones.

5. *Cost of use must be acceptable.* People won't use systems they can't afford. Overpriced systems fail in the marketplace, no matter how well they function. However, the issue is more complicated than price. True business value is as much a phenomenon of perception as it is a fact. People often pay premiums for real estate locations or for designer labels that imbue them with status. I suggest that the same psychology operates with technology and must be considered in the design of the system that carries an acceptable cost of use. The cost of a system has an added social psychology component based on how effective it is found to be in actual use.

6. *Technology systems must be aesthetically pleasing.* *Aesthetics* is the study of art and beauty, and *beauty* is often defined as the "quality of being pleasing in form." This is the most subjective design principle and is therefore the most difficult to articulate. *Simplicity, elegance,* and *grace* are words that come to mind. Good aesthetic design creates a desire for use. You are drawn to it and find it pleasurable to use.

Elegant designs are often the signature of the designer. You see the design and you know who designed it—or at least the company that produced it. The essence of design is uniqueness with purpose. Apple's recent resurgence with the iMac and the new Volkswagen Beetle are examples of design elegance.

So, you have six guiding principles. The next time you are thinking about buying a personal computer, an Internet browser, or perhaps even a ballpoint pen, get out your list and see if the technology decision you are about to make completely satisfies these six conditions. If not, keep looking!

WORKPLACE DESIGN

Selecting technologies cannot occur in a vacuum. I talked earlier about the Softwork design process in which technology plays a key part. Designing the workplace is an activity that requires the integration of several perspectives:

- Ergonomics
- Technology
- Organizational form
- Graphics
- Interior design

We know a lot about how these different professions approach design. I would like to focus on the latter two, *graphic design* and *interior design,* in order to integrate the design of technology platforms and organizations—the marriage of two otherwise unlinked practices. Workplace arrangements have traditionally been the result of information architecture. Work is now being separated in time and space with the advent of the (virtual) distributed organization brought on by the spread of the Internet.

Designing the workplace means putting raw data into some social context so that it can be used as a basic ingredient of the productive process. There is a fundamental shift in the quality of information in today's economy. The basic laws of economics have been upset. No longer does scarcity operate as a central principle of determining value. Information can be made instantaneously ubiquitous. As a result, fixing value becomes complicated. It is within this context that virtual workplaces, or information environments, must be designed.

Information is different from data. Data becomes information when it is placed in a social context. Information technologies are coevolving with human organizational forms. Entirely new forms of human networks are growing around us, spurred on by the increasing persuasiveness of accessible information. For example, these information environments are sometimes called *distributed business enterprises,* or *virtual workplaces.* But the real trend is to reverse the separation of home and workplace that began with the advent of the Industrial Revolution. *Designing information environments for work today is really engaging in community reconstruction. That's why we need to understand what communities are and why they have persisted in human history.*

The workplace is no longer an element distinct from other human habitations. The workplace, school, home, and community center are moving closer together. Now when we embark on a workplace design process it becomes a much larger enterprise. We must consider many social factors in the design process. This new value system—the new paradigm—becomes a driving force.

There could be no better end to this discussion on technology than a quote from Pelle Ehn, who stated, "Democratization of the workplace is mandatory for a successful enterprise." Further, he stated, "Technology changes the way we work. We must understand and appreciate the politics of this in design. What designers often miss is the human interaction of the process of work."

7

RESOURCES

RESOURCES FOR CHAPTER 1—BACKGROUND

Glossary

Consultant   Same as **Independent contractor.**

Distributed workers   Those who work with others, including supervisors, at a time and place different from their teammates or coworkers.

Extranet   Private network that connects a company's telecommunication network to its customers and suppliers.

Freelance workers   Same as **Independent Contractor.**

Home-based workers   Those who own and operate a business entity physically colocated with their primary residence.

Independent contractor   A person who does not have employee status.

Independent knowledge worker   A person employed by several companies who engages in provision of intellectual services.

Internet   Connection among a group of smaller telecommunication networks. Global in scope.

Intranet   Private network within a company that connects employees to central and remote offices. Restricted in scope.

Remote worker   A person who works for one company as an employee and works regularly from his or her home or satellite office all of the time.

Telecommuter   A person who works for one company as an employee and who works regularly from his or her residence two to four days a week.

Teleworker   Same as **Telecommuter.**

URLs

http://www.iser.essex.ac.uk/

http://www.kubrussel.ac.be/psw/csc.html

http://www.1-888.com/longwave/

http://www.abacon.com/sociology/soclinks/schange.html

Books and Magazines to Read

DeKerckhove, D., *Connected Intelligence,* Sommerville House, 1997.

Heflin, J. S., *Generations Apart: Xers vs. Boomers vs. the Elderly,* Prometheus Books, 1997.

Strauss, W., and N. Howe, *The Fourth Turning: An American Prophecy,* Broadway Books, 1988.

Business Week

The Economist

Professional Organizations

American Sociological Association

American Historical Association

RESOURCES FOR CHAPTER 2—CYCLES OF CHANGE
Electronically Distributed Work Communities: Telework to Virtuality, the Last Transition
The History of Telework

Some segment of the population has always been involved in work away from a central location. These people have typically been home-based entrepreneurs, site-independent professionals, individuals with disabilities, or those who work at home to save on child-care costs. Many white-collar workers have used the home to supplement their office work, either to finish work started at the office or to earn additional income.

During the energy crisis of the mid-1970s, commuters were confronted with the prohibitive costs of traveling by car to and from work over long distances. In response, some high-technology organizations began allowing their employees to access their computers from home via remote terminals over telephone lines. This practice led to a particular brand of home work termed *telecommuting.* The early promise of telecommuting led some to propose a vision of the future in which large numbers of employees routinely elected to remain at home full time, conducting the affairs of their work remotely from their own "electronic cottages."

During the 1980s, several companies experimented with the concept of telecommuting in the form of pilot programs, informal endorsements, and formal policy changes. IBM, for example, initiated a program to supply its employees with computer hardware for use in supplementing their office work with work at home. Early evaluations of the programs indicated that people felt generally positive toward the notion of using computers at home, and many expressed a desire to use the technology more than they had.

Not all programs met with employee approval, however. Some were initiated to cut company costs by offering home workers lower pay in exchange for the "privilege" of working at home. In an atmosphere of exploitation, unions soon became involved in fighting the concept of tele-commuting and were instrumental in limiting its practice among low-skilled clerical staff. Other sociotechnical obstacles were also encountered in the widespread acceptance of telecommuting. Managers balked at not being able to see their supervisees directly and reported a loss of control over employees' productivity. Teleworkers themselves complained that staying at home for extensive periods of time deprived them of desired social contact and informal communication with their colleagues.

In spite of these obstacles, telework has continued to evolve as an attrac-tive alternative to office work, at least for some people, and the concept is expanding to entail more than just calling the office from home on occasion. In part, this evolution has been facilitated by the development of cost-effective computer communications that, in concert with rising transporta-tion costs, have encouraged people to substitute movement of electronic information for movement of themselves. In fact, among the high-tech com-panies of California's Silicon Valley, where traffic congestion is endemic, informal approval of telecommuting is necessary to attract and retain many talented employees. As an added incentive, companies in many regions (especially in California) are receiving pressure from air-quality manage-ment legislation to permit telecommuting as a viable option for improving air quality.

What appears to be emerging in the diffusion of telecommuting tech-nology, then, is not a wholesale acceptance of full-time home work but an evolution toward more flexible organizational structures to permit tele-work, along with other work options, when needed to meet organizational and employee needs. This trend is leading to what Gil Gordon described as the emergence of "hybrid" organizations designed to support changes in lifestyle and to meet multiple member needs. There is some evidence that this trend toward new organizational forms is already occurring. Handy describes several alternative forms of working being adopted in the United

Kingdom that allow workers and managers to be increasingly separated in time and space.

The flexibility inherent in the structure of hybrid organizations allows companies to adapt to changing environmental and social demands. It was the use of flexible work strategies and telecommuting in the San Francisco Bay Area, for example, that minimized the impact of massive traffic congestion following the collapse of the Bay Bridge and Oakland Cypress Structure during the Loma Prieta earthquake of 1989. Computer industry experts predict that telework would provide an opportunity "for entirely new kinds of companies to emerge, with distributed business structures uniquely suited to the opportunities presented by telecommuting infrastructures." We believe that this confluence of forces provides a special research opportunity to examine empirically an organizational form in its development.

What We Know About Telework

A significant portion of research in the area of telework has taken the form of descriptive research concerning the demographics of the telecommuting workforce or development of telecommuting managerial policies. Bob Kraut at Carnegie Mellon University reports that motives for telecommuting varied widely and that the individual effects of working away from the traditional office varied as a function of job classification and perceived economic trade-offs. From this research, we know that, overall, more men than women work at home, principally because they use the home for part-time work or overtime work related to a primary job, while more women work at home to the exclusion of all other employment. (See the information button on my home page at www.isdw.com for an up-to-date survey report on telecommuters.) In terms of job engineering, we know that high-skill, high-status professional telecommuting jobs have been designed to enhance employee satisfaction, while low-skill, low-status clerical jobs are offered to cut overhead and labor costs and often disregard issues of employee morale.

Empirical research on the social-psychological aspects of telecommuting, however, is more suggestive than conclusive. Most studies claim that teleworkers are generally satisfied with working away from the office, and a few have made claims that telecommuting boosts productivity. It must be remembered, though, that most of this research was conducted on volunteers in telecommuting pilot programs for whom satisfaction would be expected, given the self-selected nature of the sample and the novelty of the program. At least one study suggested that full-time telecommuters are at risk of feeling socially isolated and experiencing job burnout. Although another study reported similar feelings of isolation among participants in informal telecommuting programs, it also reported that on some occasions telework actually *improved* employees' coworker relationships. This latter study did not reach conclusions on why the effect would occur and for what kinds of employees, however, and typifies the incompleteness of the early literature.

There is evidence that telecommuters are selective in the type of work they do at home versus the type of work they do at the office, with work in the office made up of social, interpersonal tasks (meetings, interviews, etc.) and work at home reserved for purely cognitive functions. Data supporting that notion suggest that employees communicate face-to-face and by telephone more in the office than at home. This is not to say that employees who work at home do not communicate with their colleagues, however. The same data indicate that employees who work at home communicate more by electronic mail than by other channels. Employees are still fulfilling communication needs but are doing so in another, more controlled and asynchronous, channel.

Little is understood about the social-psychological impacts of telecommuting as a substitute for work conducted in a typical business setting. Most survey samples have been taken from employees already in telecommuting programs, and these samples suffer from self-selection biases. Important questions need to be answered concerning selection of appropriate employees for distributed work, work-task selection, and management controls. Of particular concern to managers is the effect of telework on employee morale and the change in informal interaction patterns in the work environment. Closely coupled with these concerns are questions about power/status relationship changes between employers and supervisors and among the social network of employees themselves. Managers' fears of losing control have the paradoxical effect of limiting telecommuting options for clerical staff while increasing telework options for professionals.

The emergence of telework, I believe, is the first evidence of a changing work environment that has profound social implications. It is the manifestation of the "atomization of the economy" and the emergence of new structures of working social networks. I suspect that a balance between task orientation and the socioemotional aspects of workplace interaction are being significantly shifted by adoption of telework technologies in American government and business.

Is Your Business Ready for the Future of Work?

One of the questions I get quite frequently from people is, "How can I know if my company is ready for this new way of working?" Of course, there's no simple answer to that question because companies all differ in their culture, their business environment, and the work that they do.

However, over the years I've compiled a list of issues and concerns that seem to be the important ones for companies who are asking the basic question. I've assembled these questions and issues in the form of a checklist for you to use if you find that your work group or your boss is asking you this key question.

Obviously, the more urgent the changing needs of your business and the better the planning process that you currently have in place, the greater the need—and the greater your chance of success—for quickly moving your company into the new way of working. Again, this is just a checklist designed to get your thinking headed in the right direction so that you can plan a transition to the new world of work and not simply react to current forest fires in your organization.

Telework Checklist

What are the three most significant business issues facing your company in the next 5 to 10 years?

1.
2.
3.

How would you rank the following topics in terms of importance to industry in the next 5 to 10 years?

_____ Changing demographics of workforce
_____ Capability level of entry-level workers
_____ Need for creativity and flexibility of management
_____ Flexible pension plans
_____ Increased use of advanced technology
_____ Customer service
_____ Other

How optimistic/pessimistic are you concerning your business's chances for increased competitiveness in the next 5 to 10 years?

```
     1    2    3    4    5    6    7    8    9    10
    |___|___|___|___|___|___|___|___|___|___|
  Optimistic                                  Pessimistic
```

How urgently do you think your company needs to respond to changing conditions in the workplace?

_____ Very urgent

_____ Somewhat urgent

_____ Not urgent at all

_____ No opinion/don't know

Who in your company has the responsibility for developing strategic plans to respond to changing business conditions?

Many people talk about significant changes in organizational structure to make companies more responsive to customer demands and make the workplace more meaningful to employees. Do you see any structural changes occurring in your business in the 5- to 10-year time frame? If so, what types of changes?

_____

_____

What time frame does your company use for long-range planning?

_____ 60–90 days

_____ 6 months

_____ 1 year

_____ 5 years

_____ Longer (please specify: _____)

What is the most significant driver in your business planning process?

_____ Profitability

_____ Market share

_____ Strategic position

_____ Other (please specify: _____)

_____

Please comment on the following topic areas as they are reflected in the long-term management direction of your company.

Organizations as learning entities:

Self-educating workforce:

Business intelligence as a core function:

Investment in human capital:

Does your company regularly assess employee attitudes concerning conditions of work? Motivation? Changing beliefs?

URLs

http://www.telecommute.org/
http://www.tjobs.com/
http://www.ectf.org.uk
http://www.gilgordon.com/

Books and Magazines to Read

Tapscott, Don, *Blueprint to the Digital Economy,* McGraw-Hill, 1998.
Fast Company
Business 2.0

Professional Organizations

American Telework Association
International Telework Association

RESOURCES FOR CHAPTER 3—COMMUNITY

Simply defining communities isn't good enough. What do people want from their community? If, as I contend, community structures are the engine of transformation in this transition period, just what is it about them that people value? What is it about communities that people are attracted to that can be harnessed to help promote social and commercial development? For an answer to that, I turned to John Gardner, former secretary of education, who identified the following 10 key characteristics of community:

- A forward view
- Reasonable base of shared values
- Wholeness incorporating diversity
- Caring, trust, and teamwork
- Effective internal communication
- Participation
- Affirmation
- Links beyond the community
- Development of young people
- Institutional arrangements for community maintenance

I used these community characteristics in a study of the attitudes of the "emerging workforce" to determine which community aspects were most valued by our new Internet-enabled workers. Here's what I found out about distributed workers and community. The following case study was conducted in the mid-1990s under the sponsorship of AT&T. We selected 94 respondents to represent various categories of professionals who were teleworkers. Half of the sample came from large companies and the other half came from independent workers.

The interview questionnaire that follows was the basic data collection instrument used. I've included the case study here to demonstrate just what it is about communities that alternative workers desire. The questionnaire is included for your own use as a way of helping you analyze if you, your job, and your organization seem to lend themselves to adopting an alternative work style.

This basic questionnaire is part of an ongoing study that ISDW is conducting. If you care to, you can copy it and send it to me. The questionnaire is also available at our Web site (www.isdw.com) for download and completion, in which case you can mail it back electronically.

Case Study

About Your Community

I am very interested in the characteristics of your community, because distance workers appear to be relocating to live in areas they find more enjoyable. By your *community*, we mean the town, village, or city where you live and do distance working.

Communities can be described in many terms. Some of these characteristics are listed in the form of statements. Please indicate how descriptive these statements are of the community you live in.

1 = Very descriptive (everyone in the community would agree)
2 = Descriptive (most people in the community would agree)
3 = Somewhat descriptive (half of the people in the community would agree)
4 = Not very descriptive (only a few people in the community would agree)
5 = Not at all descriptive (no one I know in the community would agree)
6 = I don't know

RESULTS
(Average scores)

_____3__ People in our community share the same purpose for living here.

_____3__ My community is very diverse in cultural and ethnic makeup.

_____4__ Teamwork of community members is very important and valued.

_____4__ People in our community are recognized publicly for their contributions.

_____4__ Everyone in our community communicates well with each other.

_____3__ My community has a distinct and unique identity.

_____2__ My community is connected economically and politically to other communities.

_____3__ New members are welcomed to our community.

_____4__ My community can easily resolve conflicts among its members.

_____3__ The members of my community invest time and energy to developing the community.

_____3__ There are adequate resources in my community to help it thrive.

I believe it is clear from this case study example that workers of the "Third Turning" generation are attracted to communities where an emphasis is placed on teamwork, recognition, communication, and conflict resolution. Those very qualities of social life which work against alienation help form a sense of identity through civil interaction. Not quite the picture one gets of isolated gated communities of suburbia or anonymous walk-ups in the old central cities.

ISDW INTERVIEW QUESTIONNAIRE ON DISTANCE WORKING BEHAVIORS
Coordinates: ISDW@AOL.COM or www.isdw.com

Description
The purpose of this questionnaire is to collect information regarding people's attitudes and behaviors related to working at a distance from your employer. For purposes of this research project, *distance working* is defined as:

The conduct of work activity at a time and place different from a centrally located office. This work may be done in a residence (e.g., telecommuting), a remote location (e.g., telework center), or in other public places such as libraries or restaurants (e.g., nomadic work). In this questionnaire, *telework* **and** *distance working* **are synonymous terms.**

Instruction
This questionnaire is designed to be a self-assessment instrument to help you clarify your values and needs as a distance worker (i.e., a worker in the future). There are no right or wrong answers. After you have completed the questionnaire, go back and review it to see if your current work situation really suits you or if something needs to be done to bring the work environment more in line with your desires.

Section 1. ABOUT YOUR WORK
01.   What is your official job title?

02.   In a few words, describe what kind of work you do:

_____

_____

03.   Most distance work has been described as "knowledge work." We would like to get a better idea of just what types of work activity are done by distance workers. During your distance work time, what percentage of time do you spend?

____ Reading	____ Writing
____ Communicating with coworkers	____ Communicating with customers
____ Performing mathematical calculations	____ Analyzing data
____ Electronic publishing	____ Computer programming
____ Drawing	____ Filing
____ Other _____	

04.   What is the name of the firm you are employed by?

04a. What is this firm's major line of business?

05.   How many people does this firm employ?

06.   What percentage of these employees engage in distance work?

07.   For the next section of questions, please answer based on your average workweek experience.

_____ How many hours do you work?
_____ How many hours do you work in your residence?
_____ How many hours do you work in a telework center?
_____ How many hours do you work in other physical locations?

08.   How important is rapid access to data in your job? (Check response.)

_____ Very important _____ Important _____ Somewhat important
_____ Not important

09.   Do you access remote databases as a normal part of your job?
_____ Yes _____ No

10.   Do you utilize any commercial electronic information delivery systems such as a wire service or stock quotation service?
_____ Yes _____ No

10a. If yes, which ones?

_____

_____

_____

_____

11.   Different jobs require different sets of skills. Thinking about your work at a distance, please tell us how important these different skills are in getting your job done.

1 = Very important 2 = Important 3 = Somewhat important 4 = Not important

_____ Analytical skills   _____ Communication skills
_____ Interpersonal skills   _____ Systems thinking skills
_____ Research skills

12.   How many people do you coordinate your work with?_____

13.   How frequently do you communicate with your coworkers?
_____ Two or more times per day   _____ Once a day
_____ Three or four times a week   _____ Once a week
_____ Once every two weeks   _____ Once a month
_____ Other _____

14.   How often do you meet face-to-face with your supervisor and/or coworkers?
_____ Two or more times per day   _____ Once a day
_____ Three or four times a week   _____ Once a week

____ Once every two weeks   ____ Once a month
____ Other_____

15.   How does work direction from you supervisor come to you? Please complete in percentages. Percentages should total to 100%.
____ Face-to-face   ____ Postal service
____ Express post   ____ Courier
____ Telephonically   ____ Fax
____ Electronic mail   ____ Web-based communication
____ Other_____

16.   How do you transmit your work product to your coworkers?
____ Face-to-face   ____ Postal service
____ Express post   ____ Courier
____ Telephonically   ____ Fax
____ Electronic mail   ____ Web-based communication
____ Other _____

17.   How do you transmit your work product to your supervisor?
____ Face-to-face   ____ Postal service
____ Express post   ____ Courier
____ Telephonically   ____ Fax
____ Electronic mail   ____ Web-based communication
____ Other_____

18.   How do you transmit your work product to your customers?
____ Face-to-face   ____ Postal service
____ Express post   ____ Courier
____ Telephonically   ____ Fax
____ Electronic mail   ____ Web-based communication
____ Other_____   ____ N/A

19.   How do you measure your productivity? If numerous measures are used, please rank them in order of importance to your employer (1 being most important).
____ Time spent working
____ Number of products produced
____ Quality of work product
____ Level of customer satisfaction
____ Other _____

20. In your own words, briefly describe how you add value to your work. For example, computer programmers translate calculation requirements into a language a computer can use. Another example may be a researcher who finds many facts in different places and integrates them into a report. How do you, as a distance worker, add value to your company?

_____
_____
_____
_____

21. What technology do you require to do your job at a distance? Please indicate level of importance.

1 = Very important 2 = Important 3 = Somewhat important 4 = Not important

_____ Usual office supplies   _____ Single telephone line
_____ Multiple telephone lines   _____ High-speed telephone
                                                     (e.g., 56 Kps or ISDN)
_____ Cellular telephone   _____ Fax machine
_____ Personal computer (desk-based)   _____ Personal computer
                                                     (laptop)
_____ Personal digital assistant   _____ Palmtop computer
_____ Pager   _____ Computer workstation
_____ Modem   _____ Wireless access to the
                                                     Internet
_____ Video teleconferencing   _____ Access to the Internet
_____ World Wide Web   _____ Online computer
                                                     services (e.g.,
                                                     CompuServe, America
                                                     Online)

22. How many international time zones separate you and your employer's primary location? _____ (for example, Los Angeles and New York are 3 times zones apart; New York and London are 6 time zones apart)

22a. What is the direct distance in miles between your residence and your employer's primary location? _____

22b. How long does it take you to travel from your home to your employer's office? _____ hours _____ days

23. How important are the social relationships (not work-task-related) you have with coworkers?

____ Very important ____ Important ____ Somewhat important
____ Not important

24.   How quickly do you usually become aware of changes in work proce-
dures when they occur in your central office?
____ Immediately   ____ Same day
____ Same week   ____ Same month

Section 2. ABOUT YOU
The purpose of this section is to collect background information on distance workers. This information will be used in comparing results of this
research program to the general population. Please answer all questions.

Your responses will be completely confidential.

01.   What is your age? (Please check appropriate box.)
____ Under 25   ____ 25 to 34   ____ 35 to 44
____ 45 to 54   ____ 55 to 64   ____ Over 65

02.   What is your gender and civil status? Are you:
____ 1. Male (married)   ____ 2. Male (unmarried)
____ 3. Female (married)   ____ 4. Female (unmarried)

03.   What is your yearly income derived from distance working activities?
____ Under $15,000   ____ $15,000–30,000   ____ $30,000–45,000
____ $45,000–60,000   ____ $60,000–75,000   ____ $75,000–90,000
____ 90,000–100,000   ____ $100,000–125,000 ____ $125,000 and over

04a. Do other members of your household engage in distance work?
____ Yes   ____ No

04b. If yes, how many? ____

05.   Since you have been teleworking, would you say your personal stress
level has:
____ Decreased quite a bit   ____ Decreased somewhat
____ Stayed the same   ____ Increased somewhat
____ Increased quite a bit

05a. If your stress level has decreased, do you have any medical evidence
of this, such as lowered blood pressure? Please specify: _____
_____

06.   Below are pairs of words that describe opposite emotions. Please
place a number that most accurately reflects how you feel when working at
a distance (happy = 1 and sad = 7).

1—2—3—4—5—6—7
_____ happy ---------------------------sad
_____ productive ---------------------stifled
_____ satisfied ----------------------dissatisfied
_____ listless ------------------------energized
_____ distracted ---------------------focused
_____ isolated -----------------------involved
_____ angry--------------------------calm
_____ anxious -----------------------worry free
_____ stressed -----------------------peaceful
_____ confident ---------------------unsure
_____ secure -------------------------insecure
_____ introspective ------------------gregarious
_____ unconcerned ------------------vehement
_____ active--------------------------passive
_____ organized ---------------------cluttered

07.   There are many personal reasons for working at a distance from your employer. Below are some reasons people give for teleworking. Using the following scale, please indicate how often you anticipate telecommuting for each of the reasons listed.

Not at all   Occasionally   Frequently
   1-------------2-------------3-------------4-------------5

_____ To accommodate child care   _____ Because of personal emergencies
_____ To work without disruptions   _____ For financial reasons
_____ For ecological reasons   _____ In order to live where I want
_____ Because of company   _____ To cut down on personal stress
      incentives   _____ To accommodate a disability
_____ To find privacy when
      working
_____ Other _____

08.   People are motivated to work by different things. We would like to know what job-related factors you find personally important and rewarding.

1 = Very important 2 = Important 3 = Somewhat important 4 = Not important

_____ Financial compensation   _____ Social relations with coworkers
_____ Opportunities for   _____ A sense of personal
      advancement   accomplishment
_____ Quality of work   _____ Ability to contribute to team efforts
      environment

____ Technical difficulty   ____ Benefits (e.g., medical insurance)
of job   ____ Geographic location
____ Retirement plans
____ Other _____

09.   How many children under 5 years of age live with you? ____

10.   What is your educational background?

____ High school graduate   ____ Some college or technical school
____ College or technical   ____ Some graduate school
school graduate
____ Completed graduate degree(s)
____ Other _____

11.   Are you currently enrolled in a continuing education program?
____ Yes ____ No

12.   Are you currently engaged in a structured learning program?
____ Yes ____ No

13.   Are you currently engaged in an online learning program?
____ Yes ____ No

14.   How do you acquire new work-related skills? (Check all that apply.)

____ Formal educational programs in accredited institutions
____ Company-sponsored training programs
____ Online learning communities
____ On-the-job experience
____ Informal contact with peers
____ Other _____

15.   How long have you been at your current position (rounded up to nearest year)?

____ 1 year ____ 1–3 years ____ 4–5 years ____ 6–10 years
____ 11–20 years ____ Over 20 years

16.   How long have you been employed at your current company/organization (rounded up to nearest year)?

____ 1 year ____ 1–3 years ____ 4–5 years ____ 6–10 years
____ 11–20 years ____ Over 20 years

17.   Do you have a physical disability which impedes your mobility?
____ Yes ____ No

18.   Do you provide elder care to a member of your family or community?
_____ Yes _____ No

19.   Is there anything else that we have not asked about that you feel is important to your ability to be a successful telecommuter? If so, please list it below.

Section 3. ABOUT YOUR GOALS

People differ in what is important to them in a job. In this section, we have listed a number of factors which people might want in their work. We are asking you to indicate how important each of these is to you.

In completing the following section, try to think of those factors which would be important to you in an ideal job; disregard the extent to which they are contained in your present job.

Please note: Although you may consider many of the factors listed as important, you should use the rating "of utmost importance" only for those items which are of the most importance to you. With regard to each item, you will be answering the general question: "How important is it to you to. . . ." (Choose one answer for each line across.)

1 = Of utmost importance to me 2 = Very important 3 = Of moderate importance 4 = Of little importance 5 = Of no importance

How important is it to you to:

01. Have challenging work from which you can get a personal sense of accomplishment?	1	2	3	4	5
02. Live in an area desirable to you and your family?	1	2	3	4	5
03. Have an opportunity for high earnings?	1	2	3	4	5
04. Work with people who cooperate well with one another?	1	2	3	4	5
05. Have training opportunities (to improve your skills or to learn new skills)?	1	2	3	4	5
06. Have good fringe benefits?	1	2	3	4	5
07. Get the recognition you deserve when you do a good job?	1	2	3	4	5
08. Have good physical working conditions (good ventilation and lighting, adequate work space, etc.)?	1	2	3	4	5

09.   Have considerable freedom to adopt your own
approach to the job?   1   2   3   4   5

10.   Have the security of knowing you will be able to
work for your company as long as you want to?   1   2   3   4   5

11.   Have an opportunity for advancement to higher-
level jobs?   1   2   3   4   5

12.   Have a good working relationship with your
manager?   1   2   3   4   5

13.   Fully use your skills and abilities on the job?   1   2   3   4   5

14.   Have a job which leaves you sufficient time for
your personal or family life?   1   2   3   4   5

Section 4. ABOUT THE SATISFACTION OF YOUR GOALS
1 = Very satisfied 2 = Satisfied 3 = Neither satisfied nor dissatisfied
4 = Dissatisfied 5 = Very dissatisfied

In the preceding questions, we asked you what you want in a job. Compared
to what you want, *how satisfied are you at present* with:

01.   The challenge of the work you do to the extent to
which you can get a personal sense of accomplishment
from it?   1   2   3   4   5

02.   The extent to which you live in an area desirable
to you and your family?   1   2   3   4   5

03.   Your opportunity for high earnings in this
company?   1   2   3   4   5

04.   The extent to which people you work with
cooperate with one another?   1   2   3   4   5

05.   Your training opportunities (to improve your
skills or learn new skills)?   1   2   3   4   5

06.   Your fringe benefits?   1   2   3   4   5

07.   The recognition you get when you do a good job?   1   2   3   4   5

08.   Your physical working conditions (ventilation,
lighting, work space, etc.)?   1   2   3   4   5

09.   The freedom you have to adopt your own
approach to the job?   1   2   3   4   5

10.   Assurance that you will be able to work for this
company as long as you want to?   1   2   3   4   5

11.   Your opportunity for advancement to higher-
level jobs?   1   2   3   4   5

12.   Your working relationship with your immediate
manager?   1   2   3   4   5

13.   The extent to which you use your skills and
abilities on your job?   1   2   3   4   5

14.   The extent to which your job leaves you sufficient
time for your personal or family life?   1   2   3   4   5

15.   How often do you feel nervous or tense at work?

_____ 1. Always
_____ 2. Usually
_____ 3. Sometimes
_____ 4. Seldom
_____ 5. Never

16.   How long do you think you will continue working for this company?
_____ . Two years at most _____ 2. From two to five years _____ 3. More than
five years (but I probably will leave before I retire) _____ 4. Until I retire

17.   If an employee did take a complaint to higher management, do you
think he/she would suffer later on for doing this (getting a smaller salary
increase, getting less desirable jobs in the department, etc.)?

_____ 1. Yes, the employee would definitely suffer later on for taking a complaint to higher management.
_____ 2. Yes, probably.
_____ 3. No, probably not.
_____ 4. No, the employee would definitely not suffer later on for taking a
complaint to higher management.

18.   How often would you say that your immediate manager is concerned
about helping you get ahead?

_____ 1. Always _____ 2. Usually _____ 3. Sometimes _____ 4. Seldom
_____ 5. Never

Section 5. ABOUT YOUR MANAGER AND WORKPLACE
The descriptions below apply to four different types of managers. First,
please read through these descriptions:

Manager 1   Usually makes his/her decisions promptly and communicates them to his/her subordinates clearly and firmly. Expects them to carry out the decisions loyally and without raising difficulties.

Manager 2   Usually makes his/her decisions promptly, but before going ahead tries to explain them fully to his/her subordinates. Gives them the reasons for the decisions and answers whatever questions they may have.

Manager 3   Usually consults with his/her subordinates before he/she reaches his/her decisions. Listens to their advice, considers it, and then announces his/her decision. He/she then expects all to work loyally to implement it whether or not it is in accordance with the advice they gave.

Manager 4   Usually calls a meeting of his/her subordinates when there is an important decision to be made. Puts the problem before the group and invites discussion. Accepts the majority viewpoint as the decision.

Manager 5   Usually calls a meeting of his/her subordinates when there is an important decision to be made. Puts the problem before the group and tries to obtain consensus. If he/she obtains consensus, he/she accepts this as the decision. If consensus is impossible, he/she usually makes the decision him/herself.

01.   For the above types of managers, please mark the one which you would prefer to work under.

_____ 1. Manager 1 _____ 2. Manager 2 _____ 3. Manager 3 _____ 4. Manager 4
_____ 5. Manager 5

02.   To which of the above four types of managers would you say your own manager most closely corresponds?

_____ 1. Manager 1 _____ 2. Manager 2 _____ 3. Manager 3 _____ 4. Manager 4
_____ 5. Manager 5 _____ 6. He/she does not correspond closely to any of them.

03.   Considering everything, how would you rate your overall satisfaction in this company at the present time?

_____ 1. Completely satisfied _____ 2. Very satisfied _____ 3. Satisfied
_____ 4. Neither satisfied nor dissatisfied _____ 5. Dissatisfied _____ 6. Very dissatisfied _____ 7. Completely dissatisfied

04.   How often would you say your immediate manager insists that rules and procedures be followed?
_____ 1. Always _____ 2. Usually _____ 3. Sometimes _____ 4. Seldom
_____ 5. Never

Use the following table as a basis for your answers to questions 5 and 6. How frequently, in your experience, do the following problems occur?

1 = Very frequently 2 = Frequently 3 = Sometimes 4 = Seldom 5 = Very seldom

05.   Being unclear on what your duties
and responsibilities are   1   2   3   4   5

06.   People above you getting involved in details
of your job which should be left to you   1   2   3   4   5

Section 6. ABOUT GENERAL BELIEFS
We are interested in whether the personal opinions of employees differ from country to country. Listed below are a number of statements. These statements are not about the company as such, but rather about general issues in industry.

Please indicate the extent to which you personally agree or disagree with each of these statements (mark one for each line across). Remember, we want your own opinion (even though it may be different from that of others in your country).

1 = Strongly agree 2 = Agree 3 = Undecided 4 = Disagree 5 = Strongly disagree

01.   A corporation should have a major
responsibility for the health and welfare of its
employees and their immediate families.   1   2   3   4   5

02.   Having interesting work to do is just as important
to most people as having high earnings.   1   2   3   4   5

03.   A corporation should do as much as it can
to help solve society's problems (poverty, discrimination,
pollution, etc.).   1   2   3   4   5

04.   Staying with one company for a long time is
usually the best way to get ahead in business.   1   2   3   4   5

05.   Company rules should not be broken even when
the employee thinks it is in the company's best interests. 1   2   3   4   5

06.   The private life of an employee is properly a
matter of direct concern to his/her company.   1   2   3   4   5

URLs

http://www.fas.harvard.edu/~libcse10/

http://www.well.com/user/hlr/texts/VCcivil.html

http://monolith.yawc.net/vc/

http://www.virtual-village.co.uk/

Books and Magazines to Read

Work and Rewards in the Virtual Workplace, Crandall, N., and Wallace, M. (1998), AMACOM

Rheingold, Howard, *The Virtual Community: Homesteading on the Electronic Frontier,* HarperPerennial Paperback, 1993.

Professional Organizations

American Management Association

National Community Development Association

RESOURCES FOR CHAPTER 4—PEOPLE
The Attentional and Interpersonal Style (TAIS) Inventory

I like the TAIS as an assessment system. However, I am quite biased because I also use it in some of my research. I would encourage those of you who are interested in exploring this in more detail to consult the TAIS Web site and go from there (reference at end of this section).

The Enneagram

The Enneagram has a long history. It comes to us from ancient times where it was developed as a guide to helping people understand how they saw the world that they considered their life's mission to be. Many authors have used the Enneagram to provide a visual way of showing people how they interact with one another. For me, however, the real strength of the Enneagram approach is that it also identifies the negative tendencies we have. Under times of stress, we tend to "revert to type"—in Enneagram terminology, our behavioral addiction is intensified. This is the dark side of us. This is the way we start to behave when times are trying. When we behaved this way as children, we were sent to our rooms. When we behave this way at work, we find ourselves isolated and shunned from the rest of the group.

The Enneagram is an increasingly popular tool for interpreting how personality affects relationships, the workplace, and one's inner life of thoughts and feelings because it answers the question, "Why do people do what they do?" This knowledge moves beyond other personality systems in which you can easily be overwhelmed by the details of people's many characteristics and preferences, for the Enneagram presents nine personality types (see Figure 7-1) by investigating our unconscious motivations as human beings. In the process, human behavior becomes understandable (http://www.hurley-dobson.com).

The nine types are as follows:

1. The Achiever—an intense, hardworking, focused perfectionist.
2. The Helper—an empathetic, service-oriented, flattering rescuer.
3. The Succeeder—an image-oriented, accomplished, efficient performer.
4. The Individualist—a self-absorbed, sensitive, creative overanalyzer.
5. The Observer—a noncommittal, deliberate, reflective loner.
6. The Guardian—a responsible, opinionated, community-oriented moralist.
7. The Dreamer—an analytical, entertaining, self-indulgent fantasizer.
8. The Confronter—a competitive, blunt, passionate maneuverer.
9. The Preservationist—a secretive, unemotional, affable problem solver for others.

FIGURE 7-1   Enneagram nine personality types.

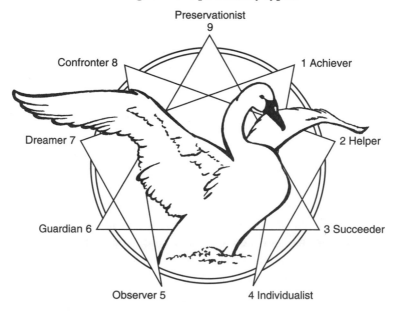

Think of the Enneagram as another way of looking at ourselves and also as a way to make visible the darker side—the side we try to work on as we make the transition to the new world of work.

The Observer

I have included a complete description of one of the nine Enneagram types. I picked type 5, the Observer, because this type of person is most typically found in management and executive positions in corporate America. This, in my experience, is the kind of person that we keep running into in the work world of old. But if you are not an Observer yourself, you may find it difficult to get along with these people and understand or appreciate them. I have also included a fairly lengthy description of the prime addiction for Observers. When under stress, they tend to be selfish, uncompromising, and controlling. We include this extended analysis of one particular type of person characterized by the Enneagram to enable you to deal with this kind of person. In my experience, most traditional managers and executives are a type 5—Observers.

These people resist change and a rapid transition to the future world of work. If you're interested in promoting the transition to the future of work and find yourself in a large organization, you're going to have to deal with Observers and convince them that there is something to be gained from making this transition.

Please pay particular attention to the behaviors associated with the Observers' prime addiction. These are behaviors that emerge in staff meetings and in most interpersonal interactions when they are under stress. When Observers exhibit these are behaviors, you should back off, retreat, rethink your strategy, and use a different approach.

> Our greatest pretenses are built up not to
> hide the evil and the ugly in us, but our
> emptiness. The hardest thing to hide is
> something that is not there.[1]

---

[1] This excerpt by Eric Hoffer is reprinted with permission from Hurley and Dobson, *What's My Type? The Nine Prime Addictions,* HarperCollins, San Francisco, 1992.

Here are some questions to help you determine whether you fit into the Observer category:

1.   Do you relish, even require, extended periods of time alone to ponder and sort out the important issues of life?

2.   Do you have an unquenchable thirst for new experiences, new adventures, or new knowledge, and are you quickly bored by repetition?

3.   Do you usually have a point of view different from everyone else's
and find yourself amazed at the lack of rational thinking behind
others' conclusions?

4.   Do you enjoy talking about and planning a project for months, even
years, but find your enthusiasm slipping away at the prospect of
begining the hard work of actually doing it?

5.   In personal relationships, do you often feel frustrated and pull back
because others misread your intentions?

6.   Are you generally impatient with group decisions, becoming rest-
less and irritated as others ramble on and on about unrelated and
unimportant issues?

7.   Do you tend to see the absurdity of life and enjoy throwing people
off guard by pointing out the ridiculous with wit and humor?

8.   Do you place great value on individualism, personal freedom, and
space and become quickly interested in anything new, unexpected,
or unexplored?

9.   Are the social interactions of your life initiated primarily by others,
even when you want to be included or want some form of communication?

Personal perspective.   Observers are factually oriented people who focus
their thinking and calculating on the world outside themselves. Their goal
is objectivity; their method is to live in the world of ideas as if it were the
outer world.

Peering out from their sacred ivory towers, Observers sit back and
watch the world in a cool, dispassionate manner. They think distance creates an objectivity that allows them to discover the real meaning of any
issue, person, or situation. This separation from the world disconnects them
from their true inner strengths of communication, sensitivity, and versatility. After gathering data, they withdraw to an interior cloister to consider,
calculate, and finally reconstruct all they have observed according to a pattern that is logical to them.

Observers feel caught in, and so they want to avoid, a feeling of personal emptiness. Their dysfunctional motivation results in a striving to feel full of knowledge. Their basic life issue is knowing, and their prime psychological addiction is greed.

Orientation to the world.   Observers experience the world as intricate and interesting, so they are inclined to observe reality without becoming involved in it. They want to observe, know, and comprehend everything and to see how it all fits together. Their identity lies in knowing and assimilating, thus making confusion and vagueness their enemies.

Need for privacy.   From the perspective of Observers, their time is best used in observing, thinking, calculating, and in finding patterns of meaning. Other people may see them as stingy with their time and energy because they are slow to make commitments and they need what seems to others an inordinate amount of time to weigh all the possible consequences before they commit themselves. Observers fear that commitments will draw them away from their passion for being alone to think or to focus on projects that not only interest them but also release their creativity. Treasuring their time and energy, they find it important to conserve them and not foolishly fritter them away. They may also find that, unless they spend a good deal of time alone, they become confused and quickly drained of energy.

Separation from the world.   Observers are loners, detached from the world. They have little respect for ways of understanding that are not logical and analytical and therefore rarely use them. They tend to isolate one moment from another, compartmentalizing all reality. Their chief way of relating to the world is not directly but through an elaborate perceptual system that they themselves create. This system is a grid of categories that they place over reality to understand it. No two Observers will develop the same system, and each one is confident that his or her system is the best.

Need for clarity.   Observers are competent, careful planners who have a penchant for redefining the issues, always trying to achieve greater clarity and simplicity. In their continual mental search for precision, Observers tap their own wellspring of resourcefulness, which allows them to circumvent creatively any obstacle that might arise. This persistent search for lucidity makes Observers inventors and original thinkers.

Desire for knowledge.   Observers take great pleasure in being known as wise. They hoard their knowledge and do not share it until someone asks the right questions. To offer information prematurely would be similar to wasting expensive perfume on the desert air. They value perceptions and knowledge for their own sake and have no need to put them to any immediate, practical use. Observers are plagued by a sense of inner personal emptiness. Knowledge is the commodity that fills their hollow spaces. In their quest for knowledge, they often collect huge libraries of books and other learning materials. Often they are driven to become experts in a particular area and amass a complete library in this chosen field. They are lovers of realism and collectors of facts on many subjects of interest.

Decision-making style.   Although Observers make decisions all the time, they do not necessarily see themselves as decision makers. Instead, they think that all they are doing is stating the only logical solution to the puzzle at hand. Observers will tend to avoid decisions in the realm of relationships, leaving those to people they deem more qualified. Their approach is impersonal, and they can tend to overlook others' feelings as they examine the pertinent facts. Facts will override feelings in the decision-making process when an Observer is in charge.

They research the facts thoroughly, methodically categorize the information, and reach logical conclusions. Because they complete this process quickly, they are generally impatient with the process of group decision making. In committees, for example, they think that others have not done their homework and are wasting valuable time by rehashing old material and focusing on inconsequential details. One of the most difficult things for Observers is to learn to be open to examining and valuing alternative points of view.

When they are responsible for decisions, they plan ahead for any possible obstacle that might arise. Thus, many people think they spend far too much time in the planning phase. Yet, once the project begins, it moves quickly, and there are seldom corrective measures that need to be addressed later. All the details are taken care of with a precision that is amazing to others.

Leadership style.   Observers are headstrong people who would prefer to be leaders in an organization or on a project. They are confident that they either possess or can acquire the information, knowledge, and inventiveness to direct and lead or that they can hire someone who has the qualifications needed to do an excellent job. If they are not careful to avoid it, they can communicate this confidence in their abilities to others in a distasteful, patronizing manner.

A key element in Observers' ability to lead lies in their openness to doing new things. Although far from being rebels, they are thoroughly aware of the consequences of clinging to the past. They promote progress with logic and humor by inspiring others to have the courage to discard outmoded ideas or practices. The most difficult and frustrating problems that

Observers encounter in leadership stem from their undeveloped interpersonal skills. In general, they communicate too seldom. When they do, they often use a condescending and directive tone that can intimidate others and breed resentment.

Observers are confident that their system of gaining knowledge is superior to all others. Because they seclude themselves to process the information, their perceptions tend to be contrary to those of everyone else, and they usually find fault with any plan or idea presented to them. This characteristic can prove to be frustrating to those who work with or for Observers.

For example, coworkers or subordinates who submit a proposal, believing that the issues at hand have been clarified, may receive it back in short order marked with notes and deletions that indicate an expectation for sweeping changes. Repeated experiences of this kind can cause coworkers to lose enthusiasm and pride in their work as well as diminish their capacity to use their initiative and creativity. Observers' full potential to lead is realized only to the extent that they develop their ability to relate interpersonally.

Living with family and friends.   Observers maintain an inner distance from everyday family life. Although physically present, for the most part they preserve their status as objective third parties to any confusion or dissent that might be taking place. Baffled by the energy expended over unruly feelings, they find themselves incapable of bringing logic to the situation, and remaining aloof appears to them to be the only sensible solution.

Family learning experiences.   Observers plan and create interesting educational occasions for spending time with either individual family members or with the family as a whole. These activities frequently involve travel and/or the outdoors. Bonding with their families and the love that Observers have for them is most poignantly experienced and recalled through these shared adventures.

Impersonal interactions.   Because Observers overemphasize factual information, in personal relationships they can seem remote, lost in thought, not present to others, or antisocial. It is difficult for them to express feelings; therefore, they seek revenge in superficial interactions in which they inquire into subjects that interest them. Though they can become excited about these interactions, their enthusiasm is not for the personal contact but for the knowledge they are gaining through it.

Disregard for feelings.   If asked how they feel, Observers tend to report what they think about what they feel. They consider their feelings unimportant, leaving others confused about how to respond to them. When Observers see other people's hesitant or negative reactions toward them, they retreat inward, convinced that they do not have the social graces necessary to communicate with people.

Observers live in a world governed by ideas, reflection, and inspiration that keeps them from realizing the value of sharing their inner selves. They often compensate for feelings of emotional inadequacy by sporadically overindulging in physical pleasures. These binges may then be followed by short-lived bursts of strict self-discipline.

Initiating communication. In relationships, Observers do not make their needs known or their desires felt. Unsure of themselves and reluctant to entangle themselves in personal relationships, Observers avoid the possibility of becoming vulnerable by leaving all social overtures to others. Many Observers would not think to call a friend, ask someone out, or initiate a social gathering. They may even give the impression that it is not important to them to be included—when, in fact, it is.

Cryptic communication. Observers are slow to speak, but when they do, they say something only once; they regard repetition as boring and unnecessary. Appearing to be assertive and pushy in speech, they exacerbate their problems with others both by their ability to think out exactly what their position on the topic is and by the terse manner in which they communicate it. There is a finality to their logic, like a treatise complete with conclusion; if others do not appreciate this wisdom, Observers may simply consider them to be shallow.

Discomfort in social situations. Because Observers feel inept and awkward in social situations, they often conclude that they are unlikable and so avoid experiences that would force them or others into situations in which they feel uncomfortable. Their pattern of long periods of silence followed by assertive statements can annoy others, as can their emotional reserve and noncommittal attitude. When they are silent, others may become uncomfortable because Observers intentionally give the impression that they know more than they are saying.

Self-reliance. Observers think that with enough careful planning and proper follow-through a person can always be in charge of his or her own life. Therefore, when things do not go as planned or when the unexpected happens, they quickly determine that someone else's incompetence has mucked up the works. Feeling let down by others, Observers become more self-directed and look squarely to themselves for stability.

Because it is difficult for Observers to admit that they do not know something, it is almost unthinkable for them to ask for help. To avoid becoming indebted to others, they are determined to get beyond the obstacle of the moment by themselves; thus they become resourceful people. Although they will not risk intruding on an outsider's life for fear of rejection, those who are included within their close circle of friends or family will feel their strong, loving protection and will feel free to ask anything of them.

Positive qualities.   Observers, as they mature and move into the process of transformation, develop many attractive qualities. They have an irrepressible curiosity and interest in people, the world, and the universe, which makes them perceptive listeners. Not threatened by new concepts or new ideas, they are the ideal candidates to promote growth and change because they can present progress in logical, acceptable terms with cleverness and humor. Loving adventure and freedom and having great courage, Observers are excited and stimulated by experimenting with new possibilities. Yet they rarely are rebellious, for they have a deep respect for the past. These spiritual people accept others with a nonjudgmental attitude that becomes a channel through which they foster independence, delegate responsibility, and enable others to discover and act on their own inner wisdom.

Observers, who see the absurdity in life, either charm people with dry, intellectual wit or delight them with raw, bawdy humor. As they develop, they find themselves much sought-after companions and, to their great surprise and delight, highly attractive to the opposite sex.

Remember, all the negative qualities of Observers are but distortions of this pattern's strengths and positive qualities.

Intensifying the prime addiction.   Observers intensify their prime addiction by moving with the arrow and taking on the worst qualities of the Dreamers (see Figure 7-2). When demands for involvement threaten to compromise their freedom, when outside circumstances begin to devour their thinking time, or when they feel prematurely coerced into sharing their prized resources, Observers quickly retreat and become more firmly entrenched in their preferred theoretical center.

With the focus on their mental constructs, they move further and further from reality, until their point of view becomes so eccentric as to be almost completely removed from reality. Others reject their vision because it is more of a self-indulgent intellectual fantasy than a helpful or practical reality. But even when their idiosyncratic way of thinking isolates them from others and the world, Observers deny their feelings of loneliness, rejection, and pain. They remain unaware that the only locks on the door of their solitary cell are their own lack of feeling and refusal to become involved in life.

Neutralizing the prime addiction.   Observers neutralize their prime addiction by moving against the arrow and developing the positive qualities

FIGURE 7-2   Intensifying prime addictions: moving with the arrows.

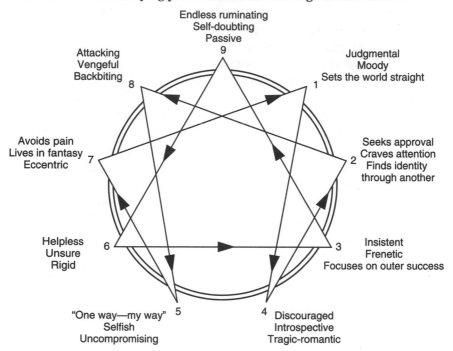

of the Confronters. Confronters are known for their ability to accomplish. They spontaneously splash their abundant energy in every direction in an attempt to make things happen.

Healthy Observers become involved in the world around them. By imparting their knowledge and wisdom freely to others, they often become highly valued teachers. In using their knowledge in ways others can appreciate, they find the fulfillment of having an effect on the world and making their mark in it. In activating the energy of their repressed centers, they find that spontaneous relationships soon yield a life of fulfillment. Their enduring gratitude reveals a deep sensitivity to the people and issues important to them.

Resistance.   Becoming involved with others and with the world may threaten Observers, for they do not easily risk giving up their independence or freedom. Instead, they convince themselves and others that they have nothing of distinctive value to contribute. Nothing could be further from the truth. As theory-centered people who have a natural curiosity about and love of life, Observers are always insightful. Their wealth of wisdom and ideas benefit those who cherish the beauty of truth as they integrate it into their daily lives.

Reward.   The gift of becoming involved in life will lead to true freedom. In no longer isolating themselves to protect a freedom they do not
possess, Observers can direct their energies toward transforming objective knowledge into the wisdom of experience. Formerly superficial
social interactions become relationships of choice, respect, freedom, and
unity.

Life Colors[2]

The *Life Colors* assessment perspective has been developed by Pamela
Oslie, who lives in Santa Barbara, California. Pamela has used this approach numerous times with hundreds of clients, has published two books
on the topic, and gives frequent workshops throughout the United States.
Her approach comes from a belief that we all radiate energy and that this
energy can be perceived by some as colors. You are probably thinking,
"This guy really *is* from Northern California." But hang on a second; take
some time to read through this last assessment approach that I'm suggesting you use.

Accept for a moment the hypothesis that we all have certain predispositions for how we behave. Also accept that some people are extremely sensitive to these ways of behaving. Oftentimes we see certain people as being
highly intuitive, with the ability to just "sense" the qualities of people
almost as soon as they meet them. We certainly know that skilled psy-
chotherapists can very quickly perform an assessment of people's behavioral patterns after interacting with them for only a short amount of time.
So it is with Life Colors. Try it on and see if it fits.

I'll share with you a little bit about myself. While there are many types
and combinations of colors that lead to different preferences and behavior
patterns, some are quite striking. I am, for example, a "Violet/Green" person, and I've included a description of a Violet/Green person for you to take
a look at. Everyone who knows me well and has read this description says
that it closely matches their perception of me. When I'm hiring a person or
trying to develop a work relationship with a colleague, I will often take a
copy of this description (of who I am) and share it with them. This helps
them get a quick, clear picture of my tendencies, foibles, and generally how
they can expect me to behave. In this way, I have found the Life Colors
approach to be a marvelous adjunct to the other two approaches that I use
quite frequently in my practice: TAIS and the Enneagram.

---

[2] This excerpt is reprinted with permission from Pamala Oslie's *Life Colors,* New World
Library, Novato, CA, 1991.

I start my description of the Life Colors approach with two of Pamela's short checklists, which identify typical attitudes associated with different life colors. Next is a brief description of major color types, followed by a complete description of the Violet/Green person, which concludes with an outline of some of the careers that would appeal to this kind of person. Enjoy.

Blue

Blues are some of the most loving, nurturing, and supportive personalities of the aura colors. They live from their hearts and emotions. Their purpose for being on the planet is to give love, to teach love, and to learn that they are loved.

Blues are constantly mothering and taking care of everyone. They want to make sure that everyone feels loved and accepted. Consequently, they remember everyone's birthday, take care of them when they're sick, and consistently provide a shoulder for everyone to cry on. People are always turning to Blues for comfort and counsel because Blues will always be there for them. They are the natural counselors, teachers, and nurses.

Yellow

Yellows are the most childlike personalities in the aura spectrum. These playful characters have a great sense of humor. They love to laugh and to make others laugh. Their life purpose is to bring joy to the planet and to help heal it.

Yellows believe life is meant to be enjoyed. They do not like to take life seriously, nor do they like to work. Their work must be "play" for them. Yellows advocate relaxing, keeping life light, and having fun. They like to keep life spontaneous.

Violet

Violets are here to "save the planet" and change it for the better. Violets have an inner sense that they are here to do something important, that their destinies are greater than that of the average person. Because this is a Violet age, any Violets who are not accomplishing what they came here to do are, at this time, experiencing an inner push—even an inner "earthquake." Some inner force seems to be shaking them up and pushing them to move into action to fulfill their purpose for being here.

Violets have very charismatic and magnetic energy, so people are drawn to them. Violets also love to be the center of attention. They are natural performers. Violets are developing their skills and taking on their roles as leaders on the planet. While some are showing up as leaders, others are joining together in groups to work for common causes, such as Greenpeace, Comic Relief for the Homeless, Farm-Aid, International Wildlife Coalition, and "We Are the World" 's Band-Aid.

Green

Greens are extremely bright and intelligent. They process quickly, jumping from one to ten. They do not like dealing with all the steps and details in between. A project which is too detailed is slow, tedious, and boring for Greens. Instead, they prefer to deal with ideas and concepts. They prefer to develop the idea, organize the plan to accomplish the end product, and then delegate or hire someone else to take care of the details.

These quick-thinkers are very organized and efficient. They write lists and efficiently check off the items on the list as they are completed. Greens recognize patterns and discover solutions very quickly. These ambitious personalities are driven to accomplish, becoming very intense and serious when working toward their goals. They push themselves, always appearing to be in a hurry. A Green is the prime example of a workaholic and a perfectionist.

Violet/Green (What Charlie Grantham Is Really Like)

This color combination is one of the most powerful in the spectrum. With the Violet's vision and the Green's ability to accomplish projects, there is little these two aspects cannot achieve when they work together. When this combination is balanced and in power, the Violet/Green can write, produce, and direct an entire movie almost single-handedly. He or she can build a financial empire that surpasses most others. This combination, when in power, is virtually unconquerable.

But because Green and Violet are two of the most dynamic and powerful Life Colors, they also create some of the fiercest battles when out of power. A Green is one of the only Life Colors who can successfully sabotage or hold back the charismatic Violet. The Green aspect doesn't usually trust, and therefore judges, the Violet's vision. The Green aspect wants to know *how* the Violet aspect plans on accomplishing his or her project. If the Violet is out of power, he or she can't see the steps or describe the plan, only the final picture. The Green challenges the dream, declaring it to be impractical, unrealistic, and full of pitfalls, listing all of the reasons why it *can't* work: the timing isn't right; there isn't enough money, training, or education; people won't respond to it; they'll think it's foolish; it's far too grandiose.

If the Green aspect is allowed to talk the Violet aspect out of his or her dream, the person will become discouraged, depressed, and ultimatcly lose respect for him- or herself, discarding "foolish" visions. When the Violet aspect has a vision, he or she can't allow the Green to reduce it to rubble and must therefore inspire the Green to come up with the plan to achieve the dream. A scattered Violet often sees too many potential visions, which can drive the Green crazy. The Green aspect wants order, discipline, and control. The Violet/Green would be wise to make a list of priorities, so that the Green feels that things are under control.

Violet/Greens are frequently afraid of their own power. They are afraid of their Green aspects becoming insensitive and controlling and their Violet aspects becoming arrogant. These two aspects can have a deep mistrust of each other's negative capacities, and therefore usually end up suppressing the positive qualities as well. The Violet distrusts the Green's aggressive, powerful nature, fearing it will scare away other people. The Green distrusts the Violet's vision, fearing that failure to manifest the vision will cause loss of respect among peers.

In power, these two lead by example. They earn the respect of those around them by accomplishing and fulfilling their dreams. In power they have no need or desire to abuse or hurt other people. Werner Erhard, Bruce Springsteen, and Tony Robbins are some examples of Violet/Greens in power who have accomplished great projects that have inspired and empowered the world. Violet/Greens are multitalented individuals.

There are other Violet/Green personality traits that can cause inner conflict. Violets love to travel, for example, and Greens don't want to be bothered by the inconvenience of traveling. If Violet/Greens do travel, they travel first-class. They prefer nice hotels, fine restaurants, and efficient travel arrangements.

There are also conflicts regarding relationships. The charismatic Violets attract people to them like magnets, while the Greens' protective shield usually pushes people away. Greens have high standards when choosing friends. Violets enjoy socializing with people, while Greens prefer to spend time alone. A balance is necessary for this combination; otherwise, they will never be in agreement or in harmony.

A Violet prefers the companionship of a loving, supportive, and inspiring mate. However, the Green has such high standards and is such an intense workaholic that few mates are able to keep up with this strong combination. The passion, energy, and desire to accomplish are so strong with Violet/Greens that it can be a challenge to satisfy their hunger. This desire to expand, to explore new territories, and to reach new heights can affect every area of their lives—career, relationships, finances, and even sex. While Violet/Greens are driven to fulfill their visions and high ideals, they may also be unable to find special mates to match their power and energy.

Money can create an interesting dilemma for this combination. While both of these Life Colors want money, Greens desire it for the power and possessions it can buy, and Violets want it for the freedom it gives. Violets can only work on projects that they believe in. If the Green aspect wants to take on a job or project merely for financial gain, this combination will experience conflict. Violet/Greens may sabotage projects or punish themselves for becoming involved in things that they really didn't want to do. Both these colors are able to generate money easily. Greens and Violets are often among the wealthiest individuals on the planet. Violet/Greens should never experience financial difficulties, unless they hold back on their powerful capabilities or overspend because the Violet aspect feels unfulfilled. Occasionally, the Violet/Green will create a lot of money and use it to benefit others.

Family situations can also be challenging for Violet/Greens. Violets love their families and want to spend quality time with them. They see the value in being emotionally available to their children and spouse. However, they also feel that they have valuable work to accomplish on the planet. Greens are usually workaholics and rarely at home, which can cause problems for the Violet/Green personality.

Violets are usually affectionate and compassionate parents. Greens, who want discipline and control in the home, have a hard time showing their emotions. If the Green aspect—who is never at home because of work—snaps at his or her children, then the Violet aspect feels guilt-ridden and torn. Parenting can be quite a challenge for Violet/Greens. However, if they can create a schedule that includes time for business as well as family, they will lead a happier and more fulfilling life.

Deciding upon a life purpose and goals is one of the strongest conflicts for Violet/Greens. Violets have a strong desire to help save the planet, to inspire humanity, or to benefit people somehow. Greens are more concerned with learning, accomplishing, and financially providing for themselves and their families. Greens feel that trying to change the world is not only impractical, but improbable as well. If Violet/Greens successfully create huge financial empires but do nothing to help improve conditions on the planet, they will feel empty and unfulfilled. The Violet's dreams and desires cannot be ignored. Both the Green and Violet aspects need to be fulfilled.

The Green aspect often bargains with the Violet by promising to pursue the Violet's vision "as soon as I am financially established and successful." However, no matter how much money the Green acquires, it is never enough. The Violet/Green becomes more and more frustrated, caught between the desire to make more and more money and the urge to live his or her Violet vision.

This combination should definitely be self-employed. Violet/Greens have too much vision and power to be limited by anyone. They must either create a profession that allows for financial success while accomplishing the vision of helping people, or they must allow the two aspects to take turns. For example, the Green can run a bank or sell real estate, but the Violet must be able to get involved in causes and "Violet activities" after business hours.

People who have Violet/Green auras often impact the planet in a powerful way. Violet visionaries who want to make sure they have enough intelligence, ambition, and drive to accomplish their goals often strive to add Green abilities and characteristics. The following careers appeal to Violet/Greens:

Producer, director, manager

Television station owner, performer, writer

Seminar coordinator, speaker, publisher

Financial broker, stock market investor or adviser

Corporation owner, entrepreneur, political backer

Politician, business owner, business consultant

Real estate agent, advertising and marketing agent

Bank owner or manager

Now that you had a taste of what some of these assessment techniques can do, I invite you to check out the references that follow so you can obtain a more in-depth understanding of each of them—their power, their limitations, and potential uses. These resources will not make you a master of any one of these techniques, but will show you, in some detail, what they are and how they can be used.

URLs

http://www.enhanced-performance.com

http://www.hurleydobson.com/

http://www.auracolors.com/

Books and Magazines to Read

Frager, Robert (ed.), *Who Am I?*, Putnam and Sons, 1994.

Levine, R., *A Geography of Time*, Basic Books, 1997.

Palmer, Helen, *The Enneagram*, HarperCollins, 1991.

Psychology Today

RESOURCES FOR CHAPTER 5—ORGANIZATIONS
Is Your Organization Ready to Move into the Future of Work?

1. Mission
   What business are we in?
   How are we unique in the eyes of the customer?
   What is our future development direction?

2. Structure
   In what form should we be organized to support our mission?
   How will management control be exercised?

3. Systems
   What technology platforms and architecture are needed?
   How do we ensure reliable connectivity with customers and suppliers?

4. People
   What are the critical capabilities needed by our employees?
   How do we continuously build their capacity to develop?

5. Process
   How do we bring orderliness to our internal processes?
   How do we concentrate our efforts to minimize waste?

6. Product
   What qualities will our products have with respect to the following:
   > Price/cost?
   > Quality?
   > Effectiveness in use?

7. Customers
   Who are they?
   How do we best communicate with them?
   How do we get continuous feedback from them?

8. Product (2)
   What are our customers (current and desired) using to meet their needs?

9. Competition
   Who is seeking to establish relationships with our customers?

URLs

http://www.odnet.org/

http://members.aol.com/odinst/index.htm

http://www.s-d-g.com/

http://www.idrc.org/

http://www.ifma.org/

Books to Read

Horgen, Turid, et al., *Excellence by Design,* John Wiley & Sons, 1999.
Robertson, Ken, *Work Transformation,* HNB Publishing, 1999.

Professional Organizations

Organizational Development Network
International Development Research Council
International Facilities Management Association

RESOURCES FOR CHAPTER 6—TECHNOLOGY
URLs

http://www.thestandard.net/
http://www.zdnet.com/
http://www.commerce.net/
http://home.cnet.com/
http://www.itaa.org/
http://www.ieee.org/
http://www.acm.org/

Magazines and Books to Read

It's all on the Web!

Professional Organizations

Association of Computing Machinery
Institute of Electrical and Electronic Engineers

Bibliography

Altman, I., *The Environment and Social Behavior.* Monterey, CA: Brooks/
Cole Publishing Company, 1975.

Altman, I., and B. Rogoff, "World Views in Psychology: Trait, Interaction-
ist, Organismic, and Transactionalist Approaches," in *Handbook of
Environmental Psychology,* D. Stokols and I. Altman (eds.), New York:
Wiley, 1987, pp. 7–40.

Ambrosio, J., "Software in 90 Days," *Software Magazine,* Jan. 8, 1988, pp.
34–35.

Applegate, L. M., J. I. Cash, and D. Q. Mills, "Information Technology and
Tomorrow's Manager," *Harvard Business Review* 66 (Nov.–Dec.
1988): 128–36.

Attewell, P., and J. Rule, "Computing and Organizations: What We Know and
What We Don't Know," *Communications of the ACM* 27 (1984): 1184–92.

Bandura, A., "Self-Efficacy: Toward a Unifying Theory of Behavioral
Change," *Psychological Review* 84 (1977): 191–215.

Barnett, Christopher. *Cyber Business: Mindsets for a Wired Age.* New York:
Wiley, 1995.

Beer, S., *Diagnosing the System for Organizations.* New York: John Wiley,
1985.

Becker, F., and Steele, F., *Workplace by Design: Mapping the High-
Performance Workscape.* San Francisco: Jossey Bass, 1995.

Benedikt, Michael, *Cyberspace: Essays from MIT.* Cambridge, MA: MIT
Press, 1995.

Bennett, John, *The Sevenfold Work.* Daglingworth: Coombe Springs Press,
Coombe Springs, WV, 1979.

———, *The Dramatic Universe.* 2d ed., Charles Town, WV: Claymont
Communications, 1987.

Birch, D. L., "The Atomization of America," *Inc.* (March 1987): 21–22.

Bordwell, D., J. Staiger, and K. Thompson, *The Classical Hollywood Cinema: Film Style and Mode of Production to 1960,* New York: Columbia University Press, 1985.

Brass, D. J., "Technology and the Structuring of Jobs: Employee Satisfaction, Performance, and Influence," *Organizational Behavior and Human Decision Processes* 35 (1985): 216–240.

Bredin, Alice, *The Virtual Office Survival Handbook: What Telecommuters and Entrepreneurs Need to Succeed in Today's Nontraditional Workplace.* New York: John Wiley, 1996.

Bridges, W., *Organizations in Transition.* W. Bridges and Associates 1(1), 1988.

Burkhardt, M., and D. Brass, "Changing Patterns or Patterns of Change: The Effects of a Change in Technology on Social Network Structure and Power," *Administrative Science Quarterly* 35 (1990): 104–127.

Cairncross, Frances, *The Death of Distance.* Boston, MA: Harvard Business School Press, 1997.

Coase, R. H., *The Firm, the Market, and the Law.* Chicago: University of Chicago Press, 1994.

Coleman, David, and Raman Khanna (eds.), *Groupware: Technologies and Applications.* San Francisco, CA: Prentice Hall, 1995.

Conrath, D. W., "Communications Environment and Its Relationship to Organizational Structure," *Management Science* 20(4) (December 1973): Part 2, 586–603.

Crandall, N. F., and M. J. Wallace, *Work and Rewards in the Virtual Workplace.* New York: American Management Association, 1998.

Daft, R. L., and Lengel, R. H., "Organizational information requirements: Media richness and structural design," *Management Science* 32(5) (1986): 554–571.

Dale, Robert, and Barbara Opyt, *Lotus Notes for Web Workgroups.* Santa Fe, NM: OnWord Press, 1996.

Davidow, William H., and Michael S. Malone, *The Virtual Corporation: Structuring and Revitalizing the Corporation for the 21st Century.* New York: Harper Business, 1992.

Davidson, Let, *Wisdom at Work.* Burdett, NY: Larson Publications, 1998.

Davis, S., and C. Meyer, *Blur: The Speed of Change in the Connected Economy.* Reading, MA: Addison-Wesley, 1998.

DeForest, Ann, "Wasserman," *International Design* (March/April 1990): 68–71.

DeKerckhove, Derrick, *Connected Intelligence: The Arrival of the Web Society.* Toronto, Canada: Somerville House Press, 1997.

Di Martino, V., and Wirth, L., "Telework: A New Way of Working and Living," *International Labour Review* 129(5) (1990): 529–554.

Drucker, P., "The Coming of the New Organization," *Harvard Business Review* (January–February, 1998): 45–53.

——— "The Age of Social Transformation," *Atlantic Monthly* (November 1994): 53–80.

Ehn, Pelle, Comments from a panel discussion at the *Participatory Design Conference* in Seattle, Washington, 1990.

Emery, F., and E. Trist, "The Causal Texture of Organizations," *Human Relations* 18 (1965): 21–32.

Er, M. C., "A Critical Review of the Literature on the Organizational Impact of Information Technology," *IEEE Technology and Society Magazine* (June 1989): 17–23.

Finholt, Tom, and Lee S. Sproull, "Electronic Groups at Work," *Organizational Science* 1(1) (1990): 41–64.

Fischer, C., R. Jackson, C. Stueve, K. Gerson, L. Jones, and M. Baldassare, *Networks and Places.* New York: Free Press, 1977.

Foster, L. W., and D. M. Flynn, "Management Information Technology: Its Effects on Organizational Form and Function," *MIS Quarterly* (December 1984): 229–236.

Fry, Louis, "Technology-Structure Research: Three Critical Issues," *Academy of Management Journal* 25(2) (1982): 532–552.

Furger, R., "Quake Effects May Alter Work Patterns: Firms Seek Alternate Work Arrangements to Ease Traffic Problems, *InfoWorld* (October 30, 1989).

Gardner, John, *Ingredients of Community, Leadership Studies for the Independent Sector.* Washington, DC: Department of Education, 1991.

Goldman, Steven, et al., *Agile Competitors and Virtual Organizations: Strategies for Enriching the Customer.* New York: Van Nostrand Reinhold, 1995.

Goodman, P., and L. Sproull, *Technology and Organizations.* San Francisco, CA: Jossey-Bass, 1990.

Gordon, G., "Corporate hiring practices for home workers: Who, Why, How Many and What Does It Mean?" *Proceedings of Conference on the New Era of Home Work: Directions and Responsibilities,* 1987.

Grantham, C. E., *Social Networks and Marital Interaction.* Palo Alto, CA: 21st Century, 1982.

———, "Visualization of Information Flows: Virtual Reality as an Organizational Modeling Technique," in *SoftWhere: Applications of Virtual Reality,* A. Wexelblat (ed.), New York: Academic Press, 1993a.

———, *The Digital Workplace: Designing Groupware Platforms,* with L. D. Nichols. New York: Van Nostrand-Reinhold, 1993b.

————, "Design Principles for the Virtual Workplace," *Proceedings of the ACM SIG on Computer Personnel Research,* Denver, CO, 1996a: 21–38.

————, "Working in a Virtual Place: A Case Study of Distributed Work," *Proceedings of the ACM SIG on Computer Personnel Research,* Denver, CO, 1996b: 38–52.

Grantham, C. E., and J. J. Vaske, "Predicting the Usage of an Advanced Communications Technology," *Behavior and Information Technology* 4(4) (1985): 327–335.

Greenbaum, J., and M. Kyng, *Design at Work: Cooperative Design of Computer Systems.* Hillsdale, NJ: Erlbaum, 1991.

Grenier, Raymond, and George Meter, *Going Virtual: Moving Your Organization into the 21st Century.* Prentice Hall, 1995.

Grudin, J., "Groupware and Social Dynamics: Eight Challenges for Developers," *Communications of the ACM* 37 (1994): 93–105.

Hagel, John, and Arthur Armstrong, *Net.gain: Expanding Markets through Virtual Communities.* Boston: Harvard Business School Press, 1996.

Hall, Edward T., *The Hidden Dimension.* New York: Anchor-Doubleday, 1966.

Handy, C., *The Age of Unreason.* Cambridge, MA: Harvard Business School Press, 1989.

Hills, Melanie, *Intranet as Groupware.* New York: John Wiley, 1997.

Hinds, P., and S. Kiesler, "Communication Across Boundaries: Work, Structure, and Use of Communication Technologies in a Large Organization," *Organizational Science* 6(4) (1995): 373–93.

Hurley, K. V., and T. E. Dobson, *What's My Type? Use the Enneagram.* San Francisco, CA: Harper, 1991.

Imparto, N., and O. Harari, *Jumping the Curve: Innovation and Strategic Choice in the Age of Transition.* San Francisco, CA: Jossey-Bass, 1996.

Jacobson, Robert, "Designing Information Environments," *BYTE* 16 (11) (October 1991).

Jacoby, W. E., "Strategic Information Systems Planning and Implementation in the U.S. Financial Services Industry," Ph.D. thesis, University of London, 1995.

Johansen, Robert, and R. Swigart, *Upsizing the Individual in the Downsized Organization.* Menlo Park, CA: Addison-Wesley, 1994.

Kaufmann, W., *Nietzsche: Philosopher, Psychologist, Antichrist,* 4th ed. Princeton, NJ: Princeton University Press, 1974.

Keidel, R., "Baseball, Football, and Basketball: Models for Business," *Organizational Dynamics* (spring 1984): 5–18.

Kling, Rob, "Social Analysis of Computing: Theoretical Perspectives in Recent Empirical Research," *ACM Computing Surveys* 12(1) (1980): 61–110.

Kotter, John P., *Organizational Dynamics: Diagnosis and Intervention.* New York: Addison-Wesley, 1978.

Krippendorf, K., "Imaging, Computing and Designing Minds," *Design Management Journal* (winter 1991): 29–36.

Kugelmass, Joel, *Telecommuting: A Manager's Guide to Flexible Work Arrangements.* Lexington, KY: Lexington Books, 1995.

Langhoff, June, *The Telecommuter's Advisor: Working in the Fast Lane.* Newport, RI: Aegis Publishing, 1996.

Laumbacher, R., Malone, T., and the MIT Scenario Working Group, "Two Scenarios for 21st Century Organizations: Shifting Networks of Small Firms or All-Encompassing 'Virtual Countries'?" working paper, MIT, 1997.

Leonhard, Woody, *The Underground Guide to Telecommuting: Slightly Askew Advice on Leaving the Rat Race Behind.* New York: Addison-Wesley, 1995.

Lewis, J., *Whom God Wishes to Destroy—Francis Coppola and the New Hollywood.* Durham, NC: Duke University Press, 1985.

Lloyd, Peter, and Roger Whitehead, eds., *Transforming Organizations through Groupware: Lotus Notes in Action.* GB: Springer Verlag, 1996.

Lucas, H. C., *The T-form Organization. Using Technology to Design Organizations for the 21st Century.* San Francisco, CA: Jossey Bass, 1995.

Mahfood, Phillip, *HomeWork: How to Hire, Manage and Monitor Employees Who Work at Home.* Chicago: Probus Publishing, 1992.

Mantovani, Giuseppi, *New Communication Environments: From Everyday to Virtual.* Bristol, PA: Taylor and Francis, 1996.

Martin, James, *Cybercorp: The New Business Revolution.* New York: American Management Association, 1996.

Michalski, J., "The Economics of Connectivity," *Release 1.0* (December 1995): 1–9.

Miles, R. E., C. S. Snow, J. A. Mathews, G. Miles, and H. J. Coleman, "Organizing in the Knowledge Age: Anticipating the Cellular Form," *Academy of Management Executive* 11(4) (1997): 7–24.

Minoli, Daniel, *Distance Learning and Application.* Boston: Artech House, 1996.

Mohrman, S., S. Cohen, and A. Mohrman, *Designing Team-Based Organizations.* San Francisco: Jossey-Bass, 1995.

Morgan, Gareth, *Images of Organizations.* Beverly Hills, CA: Sage Publications, 1986.

Morley, Eileen, and A. Silver, "A Film Director's Approach to Managing Creativity," *Harvard Business Review* (March-April 1997): 59–70.

Nadler, D., "The Effective Management of Organizational Change," in *Handbook of Organizational Behavior,* J. W. Lorsch, (ed.) Englewood Cliffs, NJ: Prentice-Hall, 1987.

Nilles, Jack, *Making Telecommuting Happen: A Guide for Telemanagers and Telecommuters.* Van Nostrand Reinhold, 1996.

Nonaka, I., and H. Takeuchi, *The Knowledge Creating Company.* New York: Oxford University Press, 1995.

O'Connor, R. J., "Quake Gave Us Needed Jolt to Get Serious about Telecommuting," *San Jose Mercury News,* October 29, 1989, F1.

Olson, M. H., "Telework: Practical Experience and Future Prospects," in R. E. Kraut (ed.), *Technology and the Transformation of White-Collar Work.* Hillsdale, NJ: Lawrence Earlbaum, 1987.

O'Malley, C., *Computer Supported Collaborative Learning.* New York: Springler-Verlag, 1995.

Oravec, Jo An, *Virtual Industry, Virtual Groups: Human Dimensions of Groupware and Computer Networking.* New York: Cambridge University Press, 1996.

Oslie, Pamela, *Life Colors.* Novato, CA: New World Library, 1991.

Passmore, William, *Designing Effective Organizations.* New York: John Wiley, 1988.

Prahalad, C. K., and G. Hamel, "Core Competence of the Corporation," *Harvard Business Review* 68 (3): 79–3.

Pratt, J. H., "Home Teleworking: A Study of Its Pioneers," *Technological Forecasting and Social Change* 25 (1984): 1–14.

———, "Socio-Issues Related to Home Based Work," in M. Helander (ed.), *Handbook of Human-Computer Interaction.* North-Holland: Elsevier, 1988.

Pye, David, *The Nature of Aesthetics of Design.* New York, Van Nostrand-Rhienhold, 1978.

Rheingold, H., *The Virtual Community: Homesteading on the Electronic Frontier.* New York: Harper Perennial, 1994

Rogers, Y., "Exploring Obstacles: Integrating CSCW in Evolving Organizations," *Proceedings of the Conference on Computer Supported Cooperative Work,* October 1994, Chapel Hill, NC.

Roskies, E., J. K. Liker, and D. B. Roitman, "Winners and Losers: Employee Perceptions of Their Company's Technological Transformation," *Journal of Organizational Behavior* 9 (1988): 123–137.

Rice, R., *The New Media: Communication, Research and Technology.* Beverly Hills, CA: Sage, 1984.

Ritzer, George, *Sociology: A Multiple Paradigm Science.* Boston: Allyn and Bacon, 1975.

Rubin, D., "Research on the Long Term Effects of Home Terminal Use," AIR Technical Report #24901-FR-12/82, Palo Alto, CA: American Institutes for Research, 1982.

Saffo, P., "Future Tense," *InfoWorld* (January 7, 1991): 49.

Sakaiya, Taichi, The *Knowledge-Value Revolution*. New York: Kodansha International, 1991.

Savage, Charles, *Fifth Generation Management: Co-creating Through Virtual Enterprising, Dynamic Teaming, and Knowledge Networking*. Boston: Butterworth-Heinemann, 1996.

Schrage, Michael, "Innovations," *San Francisco Chronicle,* November 10, 1991, E-14.

Schwartz, P., and J. Olgivy, *The Emergent Paradigm: Changing Patterns of Thought and Belief,* Analytic Report No. 7 Values and Lifestyles Program, Menlo Park, CA: SRI, 1979.

Scott, W. Richard, *Organizations: Rational, Natural and Open Systems,* 3d ed. Englewood Cliffs, NJ: Prentice-Hall, 1992.

Scott-Morton, M. S., ed., *The Corporation of the 1990's.* New York: Oxford University Press, 1991.

Shaffer, C. R., and K. Anundsen, *Creating Community Anywhere*, New York: Putnam Publishing, 1993.

Shepp, Debra, and Brad Shepp, *The Telecommuter's Handbook.* McGraw-Hill, 1995.

Siegel, J., V. Dubrovsky, S. Kiesler, and T. McGuire, Group Processes in Computer-Mediated Communication: Organizational Behavior and Decision Processes, in press.

Siegel, L., "More Workers Able to Avoid Traffic as Telecommuting Becomes More Popular," *The New York Times,* January 22, 1990, B1.

Sproull, L., and S. Kiesler, "Reducing Social Context cues: Electronic Mail in Organizational Communication," *Management Science* 32 (1986): 1492–1512.

Stewart, Thomas A., *Intellectual Capital.* New York: Currency/Doubleday, 1997.

Storey, J., "The Management of New Office Technology: Choice, Control and Social Structure in the Insurance Industry," *Journal of Management Science* 24(1) (1987): 43–62.

Strate, Lance, ed., *Communication and Cyberspace: Social Interaction in an Electronic Environment.* Crosskill, NJ: Hampton Press, 1996.

Tapscott, Don, *The Digital Economy: Promise and Peril in the Age of Networked Intelligence.* New York: McGraw-Hill, 1996.

Tart, Charles T., *Waking Up.* Boston: Shambala, 1987.

Taylor, J. R., and J. M. Katambwe, "Are New Technologies Really Reshaping Our Organizations?" *Computer Communications* 11(5) (1988): 245–252.

Toffler, Alvin, *The Third Wave.* New York: Morrow, 1980.

———, *Power Shift,* New York: Bantam, 1990.

Tomaskovic-Devey, D., and B. J. Risman, "Organizational, Managerial, and Employee Constraints on the Technological Reorganization of Work: The Case of Telecommuting," paper presented at the 1988 American Sociological Association Annual Meeting.

Vaske, J. J., and C. E. Grantham, *Socializing the Human-Computer Environment.* Norwood, NJ: Ablex, 1990.

Verity, J. W., "Rethinking the Computer," *Business Week* (November 26, 1990): 116–124.

Williams, F., R. E. Rice, and E. M. Rogers, *Research Methods and the New Media.* New York: The Free Press, 1988.

Index

221

About the Author

Dr. Charles Grantham manages an extensive applied research program at the Institute for the Study of Distributed Work. Currently a Visiting Research Fellow at the Hass School of Business, UC Berkeley, he has previously held faculty positions at several universities. Formerly the Executive Director of Research and Development at a regional Bell operating company. Dr. Grantham has coauthored several textbooks and appears regularly on national news broadcasts to discuss the social ramifications of new workplace trends.